Second Edition

AQA French

Foundation

GCSE

Marie-Thérèse Bougard

Lol Briggs

Séverine Chevrier-Clarke

Jean-Claude Gilles

Oliver Gray

Steve Harrison

Ginny March

Nelson Thornes

First edition published in 2009 by Nelson Thornes Ltd

This edition published in 2013 by:
Nelson Thornes Ltd
Delta Place
27 Bath Road
CHELTENHAM
GL53 7TH
United Kingdom

13 14 15 16 17 / 10 9 8 7 6 5 4 3 2 1

A catalogue record for this book is available from the British Library

ISBN 978 1 4085 2169 4

Cover photograph: Chase Jarvis/Getty
Illustrations by Kathy Baxendale, Mark Draisey, Robin Edmunds, Tony Forbes, Dylan Gibson,
Celia Hart, Abel Ippolito, Andy Keylock, Dave Russell and Martin Sanders
Page make-up by Hart McLeod, Cambridge
Printed and bound in Spain by GraphyCems

Contents

Context – Leisure, Topic 3 – Free time and the media
3.1 Free time activities (at home and away)   3.2 Shopping, money, fashion, trends
3.3 Advantages and disadvantages of new technology

Context – Leisure, Topic 4 – Holidays
4.1 Holiday possibilities and preferences   4.2 Where you've been and where you're going
4.3 What to see on holiday and getting around

Context – Home and environment, Topic 5 – Home and local area
5.1 Home   5.2 My local area   5.3 Routine and celebrations

Context – Home and environment, Topic 6 – Environment
6.1 Current problems facing the planet   6.2 Local issues and actions

6 Contents

Reading

Learning vocabulary

Writing

Getting ready for the exam

Building grammar knowledge

Listening

Developing exam strategies

Speaking

Understanding how the exam works

The AQA GCSE French exam is divided into four main subject areas, called **Contexts**. This book is divided up in the same way, with colour-coding to help you know where you are. Each Context is divided into two **Topics**, making a total of eight Topics to study during the course.

| Lifestyle | Leisure | Home and environment | Work and education |

The exam is divided up according to the four **Language Skills**: Listening, Speaking, Reading and Writing. Each one of these has its own separate exam, either in the form of an end-of-course paper or as a Controlled Assessment.

Writing (30%) (Controlled Assessment)

Listening (20%) (Exam)

Speaking (30%) (Controlled Assessment)

Reading (20%) (Exam)

AQA GCSE French

📖 Reading

The Student Book contains plenty of French reading material on the kind of subjects that come up in the GCSE exam. A headphones icon means the texts are also recorded so that you can compare the spoken and written word. The activities that follow the reading passages are similar to the types of questions you'll encounter in the exam.

🎧 Listening

Some activities only have a headphones icon. This means they're for developing listening skills and you won't see the words written down. The recordings are available from the Kerboodle book – just click on the icon next to the activity. A few of these recordings also exist as video, to help to bring the French language alive.

🗨 Speaking

Your ability to speak in French accounts for 30% of your final mark. In every Topic there are activities that are designed to build up the skills you need for your Speaking Controlled Assessment while using the language you have just learnt.

✏ Writing

Many students think that Writing is the hardest part of the exam, but it doesn't have to be if you are properly prepared. Each Topic contains carefully structured tasks that will help you to develop the skills you need to maximise your grade.

V Learning vocabulary

You can't get away from the fact that vocabulary has to be learnt in order to do well in the exam, so we are giving you help with this in various different ways.

- Vocabulary lists – For each section where new language is introduced there is a list of up to 20 useful words that come up in the tasks. There are also recordings to help you learn to pronounce each word correctly. Why not start by learning these?
- Vocabulary tasks – Every Foundation spread starts with a vocabulary activity. You might work

on these together as a class, or you can use them for practice and revision at home.

- Context lists – AQA have made lists of words that come up in their exams, one for each of the four subject areas or Contexts. We have put these lists in Kerboodle and added English translations.
- Interactive activities – If you learn well by getting instant feedback, why not try out the vocabulary builder in Kerboodle?

G Building grammar knowledge

Understanding grammar is the key to building your own phrases. AQA GCSE French helps you to consolidate your grammar knowledge in a logical way.

- Grammar boxes outline the grammar points you need to know for the exam.
- Activities next to the boxes provide instant practice, before you have had time to forget what you have just read.
- Interactive grammar activities in Kerboodle give you more practice.
- There is a Grammar section with verb tables at the back of the Student Book, to refer to whenever you need to.

> **Using *avoir mal à***
>
> To say something hurts, use the correct part of *avoir* followed by *au, à la, à l'* or *aux* and the name of the part of the body:
>
> *J'ai mal au pied.* – My foot hurts.
>
> *Grammaire* page

Language structure boxes

These tables provide the scaffolding you need to construct different sentences for Speaking and Writing. On Kerboodle you will find editable versions matched to most of the Student Book Topics, allowing you to get creative by adding your own ideas and vocabulary items.

Je mange	souvent / rarement /
Je fais	quelquefois / régulièrement
Je me couche Je me lève	assez / très
Pour me relaxer, je	lis / fais du sport / regarde la télé.

 **Lien**

Accessing Higher Student Book pages

Where you see this link icon in your book, this means you can access Higher reading and writing practice and cover some new grammar points directly from your Foundation Kerboodle Book.

Developing exam strategies

Getting a good grade at GCSE French is not just about how much you know; it is also about how you apply this knowledge in the exam. Throughout the book you will find strategy boxes that are linked to exam-type activities. Read them carefully and use the suggestions to help you improve your grade.

> **Use pictures to help you focus**
>
> The pictures in questions 1 and 2 tell you whereabouts in the advert to focus. The fact that for both questions there is a (3) means that each time there is only one item that is not mentioned. Make sure you write down three letters each time.
>
> *Stratégie 1a*

Getting ready for the exam

At the end of each Context, you will find an Exam Practice section. There are four of these in the book. They give you:

- further practice in the sort of Reading and Listening questions you will meet in the exam
- recaps on Reading and Listening strategies, plus a few new ones
- some sample tasks for Speaking and Writing Controlled Assessments, with example answers
- exam technique advice to explain everything you need to know about AQA Controlled Assessments
- some Grade boosters to tell you what you need to do to push up your grade.

> **Grade booster**
>
> To reach grade C, you need to ...
>
> - Write longer sentences using appropriate linking words fairly accurately, e.g. for bullet point 1: *Je m'entends bien avec ... parce que ... et ... Par contre, je n'aime pas ... car ... et quelquefois ...*

 **kerboodle**

Kerboodle offers an innovative, blended range of products to help engage teachers and students alike. It can be purchased as a whole learning solution or in parts, depending on the needs of each school, college, department and learner.

Kerboodle for AQA GCSE French includes differentiated resources focused on developing key grammar, vocab, listening, reading and writing skills. These engaging and varied resources include videos of native speakers, self-marking tests, listening activities with downloadable transcripts, interactive vocabulary builders, practice questions with study tips and comprehensive teacher support.

Our AQA GCSE French Kerboodle resources are accompanied by online interactive versions of the Student Books. All your Kerboodle resources are embedded to open directly from the book page.

Where appropriate there are links to support Groundwork and Higher activities.

Find out more at www.kerboodle.com

Log into Kerboodle at live.kerboodle.com

Numbers 1–20, ages, days of the week and seasons

1 📖 🎧 **G** Match the phrases with the correct photos.

1 J'ai trois ans.   3 Il a un an.
2 J'ai vingt ans.   4 Il a quinze ans.

1	un	11	onze
2	deux	12	douze
3	trois	13	treize
4	quatre	14	quatorze
5	cinq	15	quinze
6	six	16	seize
7	sept	17	dix-sept
8	huit	18	dix-huit
9	neuf	19	dix-neuf
10	dix	20	vingt

Saying your age

Remember you need to use *avoir* when saying how old you are.

Tu as quel âge? How old are you?
J'ai quinze ans. I am fifteen.
Elle a seize ans. She is sixteen.
Il a dix-huit ans. He is eighteen.

Grammaire page 187

2 💬 Work with a partner. Take turns to read out the phone numbers on the screen. Note that in French, phone numbers are said in pairs of digits, as they are shown: if the figure 27 is part of a phone number, you would say *vingt-sept*, not *deux, sept*.

3a ✏️ Solve the anagrams to find the correct days of the week.

1 dinlu   3 diuje
2 madichen   4 drinvede

4-19-07-15-11
2-03-18-12-20
8-16-13-05-09
5-01-14-06-17
7-19-15-02-08
9-05-17-20-12

3b ✏️ The letter 'e' has been deleted throughout the word snake. Divide it into the four seasons, as shown in the *Vocabulaire,* and add the missing letters, with accents if required.

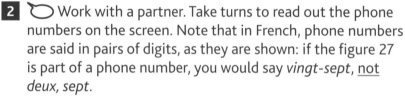

lundi	Monday	*vendredi*	Friday	*au printemps*	in spring
mardi	Tuesday	*samedi*	Saturday	*en été*	in summer
mercredi	Wednesday	*dimanche*	Sunday	*en automne*	in autumn
jeudi	Thursday			*en hiver*	in winter

Months, birthdays and time

1

Marion:	Mon anniversaire, c'est au mois de décembre.
Pierre:	Le vingt-cinq décembre?
Marion:	Non, le quinze décembre. Et toi?
Pierre:	Moi, c'est le dix janvier.

2

Charles:	Mon anniversaire, c'est le quatorze avril. Et toi?
Chloé:	Euh … Moi, c'est le premier octobre.
Charles:	Le premier octobre? C'est aujourd'hui! Bon anniversaire!

janvier	January
février	February
mars	March
avril	April
mai	May
juin	June
juillet	July
août	August
septembre	September
octobre	October
novembre	November
décembre	December
Bon anniversaire!	Happy birthday!

1a 📖 🎧 **G** Look at the two conversations above and write the four dates digitally, for example 25/12, in the order they occur.

1b 📖 🎧 💬 Read the conversations in pairs. Then have a similar conversation about your own birthdays.

2 📖 🎧 Match each sentence with the corresponding clock.

1 Il est cinq heures.
2 Il est midi moins cinq.
3 Il est huit heures vingt.
4 Il est une heure et demie.
5 Il est trois heures et quart.
6 Il est onze heures moins le quart.

A B C D E F

> **Dates in French** *Grammaire* page 192
>
> To say dates in French, use:
> *le* + number + month.
> *le six janvier*
> (literally) the six January
> The only exception is for the first day of each month:
> *le premier avril*
> (literally) the first April

3a 📖 🎧 **G** Reorganise the sentences below into chronological order, and write the times digitally (1–6).

et quart	quarter past	*midi*	midday
et demi(e)	half past	*minuit*	midnight
heures	o'clock, hours	*moins le quart*	quarter to

Exemple: 6 07h15

1 Le soir, nous mangeons vers dix-neuf heures quarante-cinq.
2 Les cours finissent généralement à dix-sept heures.
3 Je prends mon petit déjeuner à sept heures vingt.
4 En général à vingt-deux heures trente, je dors.
5 J'arrive au collège à huit heures trente.
6 Je me lève à sept heures quinze.

3b ✏️ Adapt the sentences in activity 3a to describe your own typical school day. Write them in the correct order.

> **Time** *Grammaire* page 192
>
> ■ To ask the time, you can say:
> *Quelle heure est-il?* (formal)
> *Il est quelle heure?*
> *Quelle heure il est?*
> ■ A typical reply is:
> *Il est midi / deux heures et demie.*
> ■ To say when something happens / is happening, use *à* to introduce the time:
> *Je me lève à sept heures.*

Classroom equipment and colours

description	prix	coloris
Stylo GEL	2,50 € (les 2)	*bleu, rouge, vert, violet, noir*
crayon à papier	2 € (les 6)	*noir*
gomme	0,45 €	*rose, orange, jaune*
calculatrice SOLAIRE	15 €	*gris, noir*
règle plastique souple	1,20 €	*rouge, jaune*
cahier papier recyclé	3 €	*blanc*

SPÉCIAL RENTRÉE

blanc(he)	white
bleu(e)	blue
un cahier	notebook
un crayon	pencil
une calculatrice	calculator
un dictionnaire	dictionary
une gomme	eraser
gris(e)	grey
jaune	yellow
un livre	book
noir(e)	black
une règle	ruler
rose	pink
rouge	red
un stylo	pen
une trousse	pencil case
vert(e)	green
violet(te)	purple

1a 📖 🎧 Can these items be bought from the catalogue above?

1

2  **3**  **4** **5**  **6**

1b 💬 Work with a partner. Partner A chooses from the items above and describes what she / he is looking for. Partner B guesses the correct number. Then swap parts.

Exemple: **A** Je voudrais un crayon jaune et un stylo gris.
B C'est le numéro 3.

2a 🖊 **G** Copy the text and fill in each of the gaps with *un*, *une* or *des*. Make the adjectives agree when necessary.

Je voudrais _____ calculatrice gris_____, _____ cahier et _____ dictionnaire. Je vais aussi commander _____ stylos (_____ stylo bleu_____ et _____ stylo rouge_____), _____ trousse jaune_____, _____ règle vert_____, _____ crayons et _____ gommes.

2b 🖊 Adapt the text above to say what <u>you</u> would like to order.

Saying 'an' or 'some' — **Grammaire** page 174

- How to say 'a(n)'/'some':

  un stylo   a pen
  une gomme   an eraser
  des crayons   (some) pencils

Although you can leave out 'some' in English, you have to include *des* in French.

- When using adjectives, make them agree with the nouns when necessary.

  un stylo vert   a green pen
  une gomme verte   a green eraser

Numbers and dates

1a 📖 🎧 **G** Replace the following digits with words from the vocabulary list. Translate the sentences into English.

> Mon père a 53 ans.
> J'ai économisé 99 euros …
> Ma grand-mère a 84 ans!
> Il y a 27 élèves dans ma classe.
> Mon nouveau jean a coûté 68 euros.
> Mon frère a regardé 75 matchs de foot.

1b 💬 Work with a partner. Partner A reads one of the numbers from the posts above. Partner B reads the corresponding sentence. Then swap parts.

Exemple: **A** Vingt-sept.
　　　　　B Il y a 27 élèves dans ma classe.

2 📖 🎧 Read the text in the bubble, then complete the quantities required for each ingredient – using digits.

> Pour ce gâteau, il faut cinq cents grammes de pommes, deux cent cinquante grammes de farine, cent vingt-cinq grammes de beurre et cent grammes de sucre.

3a ✏️ Rewrite the following years using digits.

1 deux mille quatorze
2 mille neuf cent soixante-huit
3 mille neuf cent quarante-cinq
4 mille sept cent quatre-vingt-neuf
5 mille neuf cent quatre-vingt-seize

3b 💬 Work out how to say the year you were born in French.

> Je suis né en _____ .

> Je suis née en _____ .

Grammaire *page 192*

Numbers

70 is literally 60, 10 (*soixante-dix*)

71 is literally 60 and 11 (*soixante et onze*)

72 is literally 60, 12 (*soixante-douze*)

And so on.

80 is literally 4 20s (*quatre-vingts*)

81 is literally 4, 20, 1 (*quatre-vingt-un*)

And so on.

Use *mille* (the word for 1000) when saying years in French.

1995: *mille neuf cent quatre-vingt-quinze*

2013: *deux mille treize*

27	vingt-sept
30	trente
40	quarante
50	cinquante
53	cinquante-trois
60	soixante
68	soixante-huit
70	soixante-dix
71	soixante et onze
75	soixante-quinze
80	quatre-vingts
81	quatre-vingt-un
84	quatre-vingt-quatre
90	quatre-vingt-dix
91	quatre-vingt-onze
99	quatre-vingt-dix-neuf
100	cent
999	neuf cent quatre-vingt-dix-neuf
1000	mille
2000	deux mille

1.1 G On mange et on boit

Objectifs

Describing food and drink that you like

Contents and quantities

Listening for detail

A

un rôti de bœuf

4 côtelettes d'agneau

un poulet

2 morceaux de saumon

2 biftecks

B

3 poires

un demi-kilo de carottes

250g de haricots verts

un kilo de pommes de terre

un chou-fleur

C

un litre de lait

250g de beurre

un pot de crème

un morceau de fromage

200g de jambon

D

un paquet de café

un paquet de riz

une brique de jus d'orange

un litre d'eau minérale

une bouteille de vin

1a 📖 🎧 Look at the four shopping lists. Answer in English.

1   Which item in list **A** would you not buy at the butcher's?

2   How many items in list **B** would you buy from the fruit stall?

3   How many items in list **C** would you buy from the cold meat section of the supermarket?

4   Which item in list **D** might form part of a main course?

1b 📖 🎧 Which three items in the English list below do <u>not</u> appear in the French shopping lists?

salmon	eggs
butter	milk
rice	chicken
bread	cauliflower
ham	pasta

Contents and quantities *Grammaire*

Words expressing contents and quantities are followed by *de* (*d'* before a vowel), even when the word that follows is plural: *un litre d'eau (a litre of water), une boîte de tomates (a tin of tomatoes), une tranche de saucisson (a slice of salami), beaucoup de fruits (a lot of fruit).*

Also learn about using *au, à la, à l', aux* for foods and flavours.

See page 26 ➡

2 **G** Match the phrases to the pictures. Then copy the sentences and fill in each gap with the correct word.

1   _____ de légumes

2   un _____ de biscuits

3   un _____ de gâteau

4   une _____ de jus d'orange

5   _____ de fromage

6   une _____ de pizza

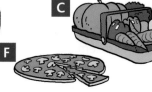

bouteille	beaucoup	tranche	morceau
	100 grammes	paquet	

3a 🎧 Listen to Section A. Five people are talking about what they usually have for lunch. Choose the correct picture for each person.

1 Marc   2 Sophie   3 Joël   4 Viviane   5 Ahmed

3b 🎧 Listen to Section B. The same people are talking about what they have for breakfast. Match the beginnings and endings of the sentences.

1 Marc has bread and jam and	a	tea.
2 Sophie has cereal and a glass of	b	milk.
3 Joël has cereal and	c	coffee.
4 Viviane has a cup of	d	orange juice.
5 Ahmed has bread, cheese and a glass of	e	hot chocolate.

4 🗨 Work with a partner. Prepare answers to the following questions, then take turns to ask and answer. Use the language structure box to help you. (You will find more food vocabulary on page 28.)

1 Qu'est-ce que tu prends au petit déjeuner?
2 Qu'est-ce que tu aimes manger à midi?
3 Qu'est-ce que tu bois à midi?
4 Est-ce que tu aimes les desserts?

Je prends	du pain (grillé) avec de la confiture / des céréales / un fruit.
Je mange	
Je bois	du café / une tasse de thé / un jus d'orange / un verre de lait.
J'aime	les pâtes / les pizzas.
Je n'aime pas	les sandwichs au fromage / au jambon.
Je préfère	le Coca / le jus de fruits / le chocolat chaud.
J'adore	la glace au chocolat / à la vanille.
	les tartes aux pommes / aux fraises.

> **Listening for detail**
>
> It is tempting to guess answers in this type of activity, but be careful. While some may seem obvious, there is often more than one possible answer, so you must listen carefully. Do not be put off if the speakers use a few words that you do not recognise. Focus on listening for the details that you need. This advice is even more important when you are listening for details in a much longer passage.

Stratégie 3a–3b

Qu'est-ce que tu prends au petit déjeuner?

Je prends des céréales et je bois une tasse de thé. Et toi?

1.1 F   Des régimes différents

Je ne suis pas végétarienne car je mange du poulet, mais je n'aime pas d'autres viandes. Je préfère le poisson. Mon père, Bernard, ne mange pas de desserts sucrés parce qu'il est diabétique, mais ma mère, Adrienne, adore les gâteaux et le chocolat. Elle essaie d'y résister. Elle ne veut pas être grosse, mais c'est difficile.

Mon frère, Christophe, travaille tard le soir, et achète souvent du fast food pour son dîner, mais il sait que c'est mauvais pour la santé. Ma sœur, Amélie, aime faire la cuisine et elle adore les fruits.

Quelquefois, le dimanche, nous mangeons ensemble, et Amélie prépare un poulet rôti et une salade de fruits. C'est bien car toute la famille peut en manger et c'est un repas sain.

1a 📖🎧 Read Caroline's blog about her and her family's eating habits. Match the names to the pictures.

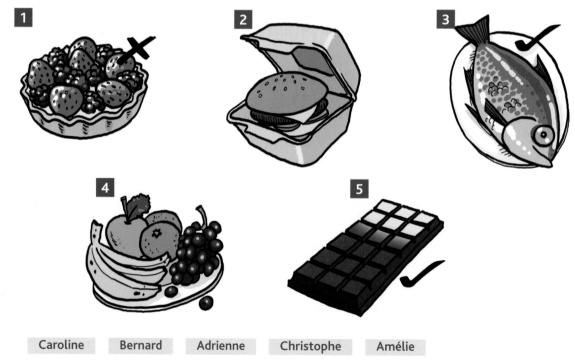

Caroline   Bernard   Adrienne   Christophe   Amélie

1b 📖 🎧 Read Caroline's blog again. Who …

1 does not eat red meat?
2 cooks chicken for the family?
3 can eat cakes but tries not to?
4 eats late in the evening?
5 has a diet affected by a medical condition?

2 **G** Choose the correct form of the verb to complete these sentences.

1 Elle **bois / boit / boire** souvent du jus d'orange.
2 Vous **aime / aimes / aimez** le fast food?
3 Tous les soirs, ils **mange / manges / mangent** de la viande.
4 J'**adore / adores / adorer** les fruits.
5 Ils **boire / boit / boivent** trop de vin.
6 Nous **déteste / détestons / détestez** les légumes.
7 Je **prend / prends / prenez** du café au petit déjeuner.

Grammaire

Present tense of -er verbs, boire and prendre

Most French verbs are -er verbs and follow the same pattern as aimer.

aimer = to like

singular	plural
j'aime	nous aimons
tu aimes	vous aimez
il / elle / on aime	ils / elles aiment

Boire (to drink) and prendre (to take) are irregular verbs and do not follow this pattern. Look them up in the verb tables on pages 193–197 and make a table similar to the one above for each of them.

Also revise how to say 'some' in French.
See page 27 ➡

3a 🎧 Listen to Section A. Match the countries to the topics mentioned.

1	Canada	a	a diet lacking variety
2	Niger	b	a spicy stew
3	Ivory Coast	c	obesity
4	Morocco	d	malnutrition

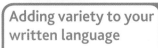

3b 🎧 Listen to Section B. Lucie is talking about her eating habits in Guadeloupe. Which three sentences are true?

1 Traditional cooking in Guadeloupe is generally healthy.
2 Her father is a fisherman.
3 She says that she has coffee for breakfast.
4 She has a banana every day for lunch.
5 They usually eat rice with their evening meal.
6 She often chooses a healthy dessert.

4 ✏️ Write a short paragraph about your eating habits and those of three other people you know. Give reasons.

J'	aime	les fruits		c'est bon pour la santé.
Je	n'aime pas	les légumes		c'est mauvais pour la santé.
Mon père	adore	la viande	car	c'est un plat sain.
Ma mère	déteste	le chocolat	parce que	c'est délicieux.
Mon frère	préfère	les frites		je suis / il est / elle est végétarien(ne).
Ma sœur		les pizzas		ça a un goût horrible.
Mon ami(e)		les boissons sucrées		

Stratégie 4

Adding variety to your written language

Try to vary your language so as to not overuse certain words. As well as the words in the table, you can include language that is used in the other activities on these pages: *je prends, je bois, il achète, en général, souvent*, or words from the vocabulary on page 28.

 **Lien**

1.1 Higher is available in the Higher book.

1.2 G Les parties du corps

Normalement je commence avec le corps, la tête et les cheveux. Puis je dessine les jambes, les pieds, et après ça, les bras et les mains. Ensuite, c'est les oreilles, les yeux et le nez et enfin, je dessine la bouche.

'Portrait du père de l'artiste' par Paul Cézanne

'Self Portrait' par Picasso

1a 📖 🎧 Read the description of the order in which the artist paints a portrait. Complete the sentences in English.

1 The artist starts with the body, the head and the _____.
2 Next he adds the _____ and the _____ before drawing the arms and hands.
3 He draws the eyes after he has added the _____ and before the _____.
4 Finally he draws the _____.

1b 📖 🎧 Which portrait above is being described in each sentence?

1 On voit les jambes.
2 On ne voit pas les mains.
3 Il porte un bonnet sur la tête.
4 Il tient un journal dans les mains.
5 On voit seulement l'oreille droite.
6 On voit le nez, mais pas les pieds.

2 **G** Here are six more words for parts of the body. Copy them and fill in each gap with the correct French word for 'the'. Check in a dictionary if you're not sure.

1 _____ dos
2 _____ genou
3 _____ gorge
4 _____ œil
5 _____ dents
6 _____ ventre

Checking the gender of nouns

Some of the words here are used in the plural form, but when you use them in the singular you will need to know if they are masculine or feminine. Check in a dictionary if you're not sure.

e.g. **doigt** *n.m.* finger
     poitrine *n.f.* chest

Then use your knowledge of the rules to decide whether to use *le*, *la* or *l'*.

Some bigger dictionaries give more information about the words.

See page 171 ➡

Stratégie 1b

How to say 'the'

masculine: *le nez*

feminine: *la tête*

before a vowel: *l'oreille*

plural: *les mains*

Also learn about different uses of *le, la, l', les*.   See page 26 ➡

Grammaire page 174

3a 🎧 Listen to Section A, a description of another painting that shows four people and two animals. Which four sentences are true?

1 There is a woman with dark hair.
2 She is touching the dog's ear.
3 The girl is holding the man's hand.
4 She doesn't like dogs.
5 The cat is mostly white.
6 It is sitting on the boy's knees.
7 The boy is stroking the cat's head.

3b 🎧 Listen to Section B. Choose the picture (A–E) that shows who is speaking each time (1–5). To help you, listen for the parts of the body they mention.

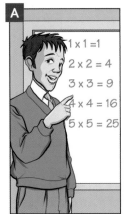
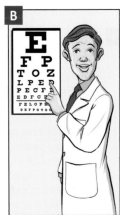

4 ✏️ Write labels for the numbered parts of the girl's body. Then write sentences about four other parts that you <u>can't</u> see, using the words on this page.

Exemple: *On ne voit pas <u>les yeux</u>.*

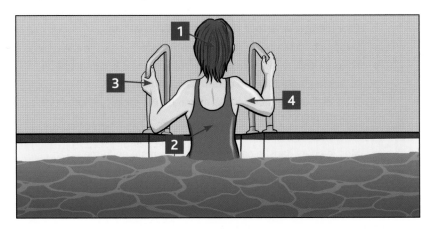

1.2 F   Le bien-être

Objectifs

Describing a healthy lifestyle

Present tense of *faire* and *dormir*

Using negatives

1 **V** Sort the words and phrases below into the four groups shown in the grid.

se coucher	se relaxer	l'activité physique	un régime équilibré

courir sur place   dormir   boire de l'eau régulièrement   le gymnase   le sommeil

faire la grasse matinée   les jeux vidéo   éviter les sucreries   lire un magazine

une alimentation saine   écouter de la musique   la natation

Avez-vous la forme?

A

B

C

1

Deux semaines au Centre Blairot pour 20 euros. Offre spéciale d'introduction.

Deux visites par semaine à notre gymnase, c'est exactement ce qu'il vous faut pour vous aider à garder la forme. Ici, pendant une visite d'une heure, vous pouvez faire du cyclisme, comme sur la photo, et aussi courir sur place.

2

3 paquets de sachets "Relax" pour le prix de 2 paquets. Offre spéciale jusqu'à vendredi.

Vous ne dormez pas très bien? Vous avez peut-être une vie stressante? Chaque nuit, avant de vous coucher, il faut boire une tasse de notre infusion. Pour garder la forme, nous recommandons huit heures de sommeil par nuit. Notre boisson va vous aider à dormir, et à vous réveiller le matin plein d'énergie.

3

L'auteur va signer cette nouvelle bible anti-stress. Venez dans notre magasin entre 10 et 11 heures samedi!

Voilà sept idées pour éliminer le stress:

- Pour me relaxer, je joue de la guitare ou de la flûte.
- De temps en temps, je lis un bon livre.
- Le week-end, je fais souvent des promenades à la campagne.
- Je fais la grasse matinée de temps en temps.
- Tous les jours, je me lève à la même heure, parce que la routine est importante pour moi.
- Je mange équilibré et j'évite les matières grasses et les sucreries.
- Moi, je cours dans le parc, comme ça je reste en forme.

Achetez le livre *Mille idées pour éliminer le stress* et trouvez des possibilités qui vont transformer votre vie et vous aider à vous relaxer.

2a 📖 🎧 Read the adverts 1–3 and match them to the photos A–C.

2b 📖 🎧 In which adverts are the following mentioned?

a une boisson chaude

b se lever tard

c faire du vélo

d manger sain

e deux heures d'exercice par semaine

f une solution quand on est stressé.

Stratégie 2b

Using the vocabulary lists

Refer to the vocabulary (pages 28–29) to help with new words.

The lists of words on those pages are the ones that are likely to be in the reading and listening exams, so you need to learn them!

You might like to download the audio file to help you with the pronunciation. Try covering the English words and testing yourself, or asking a friend to test you.

---

3 **G** Work with a partner. Choose *faire* or *dormir* to fill each gap, then decide what the verb ending should be. Write down the missing word.

1 Il est sportif. Il _____ du sport tous les jours.

2 Je me couche à dix heures et je _____ huit heures.

3 De temps en temps, elles vont au centre commercial où elles _____ du shopping.

4 Vous êtes fatigué! Est-ce que vous _____ bien?

5 Ma sœur et moi, nous _____ dans la même chambre.

6 Tu _____ ton lit le matin?

Grammaire *page 195*

Present tense of *faire* and *dormir*

Faire is an irregular verb.

***faire* = to make or do**

singular	plural
je fais	nous faisons
tu fais	vous faites
il / elle / on fait	ils / elles font

Dormir is also irregular. Find it in the verb tables on page 195 and draw a table like the one above to help you learn it.

Also learn about adverbs of frequency.

See page 27 ➡

4a 🎧 Listen to Section A of Docteur Bernard's advice. Copy the sentences and fill in each gap with the correct word.

1 C'est une bonne idée de faire du sport _____.

2 Si vous n'aimez pas le sport, vous pouvez faire des _____.

3 Le sport vous aide à éviter les _____ cardiaques.

4 Pour combattre le stress, il est important de bien _____.

5 Il ne faut pas se _____ trop tard.

promenades

coucher

maladies

régulièrement

dormir

copains

4b 🎧 Listen to Section B. Which items in the list does the doctor mention as potentially positive (**P**) or negative (**N**)? Which ones does she not mention (**?**)?

1 blogs   3 salt   5 alcohol   7 playing sport

2 conversation 4 fruit   6 drinking water

---

5 💬 How healthy is your lifestyle? Work with a partner. Prepare answers to the following questions, then take turns to ask and answer.

■ Tu fais souvent de l'exercice?

■ Qu'est-ce que tu fais pour te relaxer?

■ Est-ce que tu dors bien?

■ À ton avis, es-tu en bonne forme?

Tu fais souvent de l'exercice?

Oui, je fais de la natation. Et toi?

Stratégie 5

Using negatives

To develop your speaking, you can use negative forms. In other words, you can say what you don't eat and so on: *je ne mange pas de viande, je ne dors pas bien, je ne me couche pas de bonne heure.*

🔗 **Lien**

1.2 Higher is available in the Higher book.

1.3 G Les maladies et les solutions

Objectifs

Describing ailments and giving solutions

Using *avoir mal à*

Predicting answers when listening

1a 📖🎧 Match each complaint with the correct picture.

1 Ouille! J'ai mal aux oreilles.
2 Aïe, aïe, aïe! J'ai mal aux dents. Oh, là, là!
3 J'ai mal au ventre, j'ai mal au cœur, j'ai envie de vomir.
4 J'ai un gros rhume et j'ai mal à la gorge. Ça ne va pas très bien.
5 J'ai mal au genou et j'ai mal au bras. Je suis tombé de vélo hier!
6 J'ai mal à la tête et au dos. J'ai de la fièvre. J'ai la grippe.

1b 📖🎧 Copy the sentences and fill in each gap with the correct word.

1 Vous avez mal aux dents? Allez chez le _____ .
2 Tu es tombé de vélo? Voilà un _____ .
3 Tu as mal aux oreilles? Va chez le _____ .
4 Tu as mal à la tête? Prends de l'_____ et va au lit.
5 Vous avez un rhume et mal à la gorge? Prenez ces _____ et du sirop.
6 Vous avez mal au ventre? Prenez ces comprimés et buvez beaucoup d'_____ .

médecin

aspirine

eau

dentiste

pastilles

sparadrap

2 **G** Match the beginnings and endings of the sentences.

1 J'ai mal à   a   gorge.

2 Tu as mal au   b   rhume.

3 Il a mal aux   c   la tête.

4 Vous avez mal à la   d   bras.

5 Elle a un   e   oreille.

6 J'ai mal à l'   f   grippe.

7 Il a la   g   yeux.

3a 🎧 Listen to the five people in Section A saying what's wrong. Choose the correct advice for each of them.

a   Make sure you wear your sunglasses!

b   The toilets are over there. Hurry!

c   Oh dear. Go and wash your knee.

d   Go and buy some new shoes.

e   Don't lift that heavy package!

3b 🎧 Listen to the advice in Section B, then copy and complete the sentences about what's wrong. The sentences are in the same order as the advice.

1 J'ai mal aux _____ .

2 J'ai mal à la _____ .

3 J'ai mal à la _____ .

4 J'ai de la _____ .

5 J'ai un _____ .

4 🗨 Work with a partner. Partner A says what's wrong, using language from Activity 1a and the grammar box. Partner B gives appropriate advice, using the answers from Activity 1b. Then swap parts.

Grammaire *page 187*

Using *avoir mal à*

To say something hurts, use the correct part of *avoir* followed by *au*, *à la, à l'* or *aux* and the name of the part of the body:

*J'**ai** mal au pied.* – My foot hurts.

*Tu **as** mal à la tête?* – Do you have a headache?

*Il **a** mal à l'œil.* – He has a pain in his eye.

*Vous **avez** mal aux oreilles?* – Do you have earache?

See page 194 of the verb tables for all the forms of *avoir*.

Also learn about the imperative.

See page 26 ➡

Stratégie 3b

Predicting answers when listening

Before listening, it is a good idea to look at the activity for clues that will help you predict the possible answers: *j'ai mal aux …* tells you that you will need a plural word to complete the sentence. Think about what word that could be and then see which one best fits what you hear.

J'ai envie de vomir.

Va aux toilettes!

1.3 F On parle de l'alcool, du tabac et de la drogue

cigarettesbièrefumeurcidrealcooldroguesdurestabacnon-fumeurcannabiscompriménédroguesdoucesvin

1 Ⓥ Separate the words in the snake. Sort them into three groups: *boire*, *se droguer* or *fumer*. Add the English meanings.

Les opinions des jeunes

Georges, 17 ans

On commence avec des cigarettes et de la bière. Plus tard on essaie le whisky, la vodka et les drogues dures. L'alcool et les drogues sont dangereux parce que c'est trop facile de devenir dépendant.

Fatima, 17 ans

Je ne bois pas d'alcool parce que c'est contre ma religion. J'ai essayé les cigarettes, mais je n'ai pas aimé le goût. Ça ne me dit rien.

Pauline, 16 ans

L'alcool est une drogue mais c'est une drogue légale et il est facile d'acheter du cidre dans les supermarchés. Je bois avec mes copines pour être sociable. Il est plus facile de parler aux garçons quand on a bu, on est moins timide.

Victor, 16 ans

Je bois pour oublier mes problèmes au lycée. Je me sens très stressé en ce moment à cause des examens. Quand je bois de la bière, je me relaxe et je me sens bien. Je sais que c'est mauvais pour la santé mais je ne peux pas résister à l'alcool, surtout le samedi soir quand je suis avec mes amis.

2a 📖 🎧 Read Georges' and Fatima's opinions. Who mentions:

1. low and high strength alcohol?
2. having tried cigarettes?
3. the taste of tobacco?
4. hard drugs?
5. addiction?

2b 📖 🎧 Read Pauline's and Victor's opinions, then copy and complete these sentences in English.

1. Pauline thinks it's easy to get hold of _____.
2. She drinks with her _____.
3. After drinking, she finds that she becomes less _____.
4. Victor drinks to forget his problems at _____.
5. When he drinks he feels _____.

3 **G** 🗩 Work with a partner. Partner A reads out a sentence and Partner B gives the negative version, using the expression in brackets. Then swap roles.

1 Je fume. (**ne … jamais**)
2 Mon père boit beaucoup d'alcool. (**ne … plus**)
3 Je bois du Coca quand je suis avec mes amis. (**ne … que**)
4 J'aime le goût du vin. (**ne … pas**)
5 Le tabac aide à combattre le stress. (**ne … personne**)
6 Être en bonne santé coûte cher. (**ne … rien**)

4a 🎧 Listen to Section A. Decide if these six people drink alcohol (**A**), use drugs (**D**) or express a negative opinion (**N**).

1 ____   2 ____   3 ____   4 ____   5 ____   6 ____

4b 🎧 Listen to Coralie and Félix in Section B. Choose the correct English sentence for each speaker.

1 **Coralie**
  a I am a heavy smoker.
  b Cigarettes calm my nerves.
  c My parents don't know I smoke.

2 **Félix**
  a I still smoke from time to time.
  b I think my friends smoke to appear more grown-up.
  c I think cigarettes are very expensive.

Making verbs negative

Put *ne* (or *n'*) before the verb and a negative word after it.

Je ne fume pas. – I don't smoke.

Je ne fume plus. – I don't smoke any more.

Les fumeurs ne respectent personne. – Smokers don't respect anyone.

Je ne fume jamais. – I never smoke.

Ça ne me dit rien. – That does not interest me.

Je ne fume que cinq cigarettes par jour. – I only smoke five cigarettes a day.

Also learn about expressions with *avoir*.   *See page 27* ➡

Grammaire *page 188*

---

5 🖉 You are taking part in a survey on an online forum. Write your answers to the questions, giving reasons for your views.

◀	⌂			🔍 Buscar	

Qu'est-ce que tu en penses?

1 Est-ce que c'est un problème si on fume cinq cigarettes par jour?
2 Est-ce qu'il est facile d'arrêter de fumer?
3 Est-ce que l'alcool est mauvais pour la santé?
4 Boire une ou deux bières avec des amis, c'est sociable ou stupide?
5 Est-ce que le cannabis est dangereux?

Giving reasons for your views

Always try to justify your opinion by using a connective such as *parce que* or *car*.

If you want to qualify your view, you can say 'I know that …': *Je sais que l'alcool est dangereux.*

You could also say 'I think that … but …': *Je pense que l'alcool est dangereux, mais j'aime le goût.*

Stratégie 5

À mon avis, c'est	un problème	parce que / qu'	il est facile de devenir dépendant.
Je pense / crois que c'est	facile	car	après on risque d'essayer les drogues dures.
	difficile		on le fait pour être comme les autres / être adulte / se relaxer.
	dangereux		on peut devenir violent.
	stupide		
	sociable		toutes les drogues sont dangereuses.

 **Lien**

1.3 Higher is available in the Higher book.

G Health

1 Choose the correct form of *au, à la, à l', aux* for each food item.

1 une glace **au** / **à l'** / **à la** vanille
2 une omelette **au** / **aux** / **à la** champignons
3 une sauce **à l'** / **à la** / **au** orange
4 un gâteau **aux** / **au** / **à la** café
5 la soupe **au** / **à l'** / **aux** légumes
6 un sandwich **aux** / **à la** / **au** poulet

> ### Using *au*, *à la*, *à l'*, *aux* for foods and flavours
> You have already come across these words meaning 'to the' or 'at the', e.g. *au cinéma*. They are also used to describe the ingredients or flavour of foods. Use the right one: *au* (masculine), *à la* (feminine), *à l'* (before a vowel), *aux* (plural).
>
> *une glace **au chocolat***   a chocolate ice cream
> *une tarte **aux pommes***   an apple tart
>
> *Grammaire*   page 189

2 Translate these sentences into English.

1 Elle a les yeux bleus.
2 Je déteste le poisson, mais j'adore les frites.
3 Le tabac est mauvais pour la santé.
4 Le chien a les oreilles noires.
5 L'exercice est essentiel.
6 J'aime le café mais je n'aime pas le thé.

> ### Different uses of *le, la, l', les*
> In French you often need to use *le, la, l'* or *les* when we don't say 'the' in English.
> When talking about likes or dislikes:
> *Elle n'aime pas les chiens.*   She doesn't like dogs.
> When referring to abstract things:
> *Le régime est très important.*   Diet is very important.
> When describing someone's appearance:
> *Il a les cheveux longs.*   He has long hair.
>
> *Grammaire*   page 174

3 Choose the correct form of the verb to complete each sentence.

1 Tu as la grippe? **Reste / Restez / Prends** au lit et **buvez / bois / prenez** beaucoup d'eau.
2 Vous avez un rhume? **Allez / Prenez / Prends** ce sirop et **restez / reste / buvez** à la maison.
3 Vous avez mal aux oreilles? **Allez / Mets / Mettez** un bonnet, et **allez / va / mettez** chez le médecin.
4 Tu es tombé et tu as mal au genou? **Lavez / Bois / Lave** -toi la jambe et **mettez / prenez / mets** -toi un sparadrap.

> ### The imperative
> Use the imperative to give advice.
> **Informal singular (the *tu* form):**
> *Va chez le dentiste.*
> *Prends de l'aspirine.*
> *Bois beaucoup d'eau.*
> *Mets un bonnet.*
> **Formal or plural (the *vous* form):**
> *Allez chez le médecin.*
> *Buvez du thé.*
> *Mettez vos lunettes de soleil.*
>
> *Grammaire*   page 185

4 For each of the items pictured, write a sentence starting with *Je voudrais* (I would like) followed by *du, de la, de l'* or *des* and the name of the item. Use the word snake to help you.

How to say 'some'

The French words for 'some' or 'any' are *du* (masculine), *de la* (feminine), *de l'* (before vowels) and *des* plural). Note that most food nouns ending in *e* are feminine, and that 'pasta' is always plural: *des pâtes*.

Grammaire page 174

Exemple:  *Je voudrais de la soupe.*

eaufraisesgâteaupâtespouletsaladesoupe

1  **2** **3** 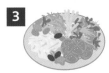 **4**  **5**  **6**

5 Put the sentences (1–6) in order, from the least to the most frequent. Copy the expression of frequency in each case.

1 Je fais de temps en temps la grasse matinée.
2 Je mange tous les jours des légumes.
3 Je mange rarement des gâteaux.
4 J'écoute toujours mes parents.
5 Je fais souvent du sport.
6 Je ne fume jamais.

Adverbs of frequency

The most common adverbs of frequency are:

de temps en temps – from time to time

ne … jamais – never

rarement – rarely

souvent – often

toujours – always

tous les jours – every day

Grammaire page 177

6 Choose the correct form of *avoir* or *être* to complete each sentence. Then translate the sentences into English.

1 Je n' **ai / est / a** pas d'alcool chez moi, car je **ai / suis / est** musulman.
2 Tu n' **as / es / et** pas d'énergie, parce que tu **ai / es / est** fatigué.
3 Elle **a / ai / est** très malade, elle **a / est / ont** le cancer du poumon.
4 Nous **avons / ont / sommes** trop de travail et nous **avons / êtes / sommes** très stressés.
5 Vous n' **avez / est / êtes** pas en bonne santé et vous **a / avez / êtes** mal au cœur.
6 Elles **avons / ont / sont** envie de prendre des drogues, mais les drogues **est / ont / sont** dangereuses.

Expressions with *avoir*

Avoir normally means 'to have': *jai beaucoup d'énergie* (I have lots of energy), but in certain expressions it can mean 'to be': *j'ai faim* (I am hungry). Learn the expressions below:

avoir … ans – to be … years old

avoir froid / chaud – to be cold / hot

avoir faim – to be hungry

avoir soif – to be thirsty

avoir raison – to be right / correct

avoir envie de – to want (to do something)

Grammaire page 187

Health

Topic 1.1 You are what you eat

1.1 G On mange et on boit ➡ *pages 14–15*

le	bœuf	beef
la	bouteille	bottle
les	céréales (f)	cereal
les	champignons (m)	mushrooms
le	chou-fleur	cauliflower
la	côtelette	cutlet
le	déjeuner	lunch
la	fraise	strawberry
les	frites (f)	chips
la	glace	ice cream
les	haricots verts (m)	green beans
le	jus	juice
le	lait	milk
les	légumes	vegetables
le	morceau	piece
le	paquet	packet
le	petit déjeuner	breakfast
la	poire	pear
la	pomme de terre	potato
le	poulet	chicken
la	soupe	soup
la	tasse	cup
la	tranche	slice
le	verre	glass

1.1 F Des régimes différents ➡ *pages 16–17*

la	boisson	drink
	bon(ne)	good
la	cuisine	cooking
	cultiver	to cultivate, to grow
	délicieux(-euse)	delicious
le	dîner	dinner
	ensemble	together
	épicé(e)	spicy
	essayer	to try

Learning new vocabulary

As you work through Topic 1, refer to these vocabulary pages to help you find out what new words mean. There is one list for each sub-topic.

To help you to learn the words, try covering the English words and testing yourself, or asking a friend to test you.

You might like to download the audio file to help you with pronunciation. Find ways of learning that work for you, such as spotting connections with English: *les frites* is like 'fries'. How many other connections can you find?

le	goût	taste
	gros(se)	fat
	malade	ill
	mauvais(e)	bad
	pauvre	poor
le	plat	dish
le	poisson	fish
	quelquefois	sometimes
le	repas	meal
le	riz	rice
	rôti(e)	roast
	sain(e)	healthy
la	santé	health
	sucré(e)	sweet
	végétarien(ne)	vegetarian
la	viande	meat

Topic 1.2 Healthy and unhealthy lifestyles

1.2 G Les parties du corps ➡ *pages 18–19*

la	bouche	mouth
le	bras	arm
	caresser	to stroke
les	cheveux (m)	hair
le	corps	body
la	dent	tooth
	dessiner	to draw
le	dos	back
le	genou	knee
la	gorge	throat
la	jambe	leg

la	main	hand
le	nez	nose
l'	œil (m) (pl. les yeux)	eye(s)
l'	oreille (f)	ear
le	pied	foot
	tenir	to hold
la	tête	head
le	ventre	stomach
	voir	to see

1.2 F Le bien-être ➡ *pages 20–21*

l'	alimentation (f)	diet
se	coucher	to go to bed
	courir	to run
	de temps en temps	from time to time
	dormir	to sleep
	équilibré(e)	balanced
	éviter	to avoid
la	grasse matinée	lie-in
au	lieu de	instead of
la	maladie	illness
	même	same
le	régime	diet
	régulièrement	regularly
le	sel	salt
le	sommeil	sleep
	souvent	often
les	sucreries (f)	sweet things
	tard	late
	tous les jours	every day

Topic 1.3 Dealing with ailments, tobacco, alcohol and drugs

1.3 G Les maladies et les solutions
➡ *pages 22–23*

l'	aspirine (f)	aspirin
	avoir envie de	to want
le	bonnet	hat
	boire	to drink
le	cœur	heart
le	comprimé	tablet

le	dentiste	dentist
la	fièvre	fever
la	grippe	flu
	laver	to wash
le	lit	bed
le	médecin	doctor
	mettre	to put
la	pastille	pastille, lozenge
	prendre	to take
	rester	to stay
le	rhume	cold
le	sirop	syrup
le	sparadrap	plaster
	vomir	to vomit

1.3 F On parle de l'alcool, du tabac et de la drogue ➡ *pages 24–25*

l'	alcool (m)	alcohol
	arrêter	to stop
la	bière	beer
	cher(-ère)	dear, expensive
le	cidre	cider
	combattre	to combat, to fight
	contre	against
	coûter	to cost
	dangereux(-euse)	dangerous
	dépendant(e)	addicted
	devenir	to become
	doux(-ce)	soft
la	drogue	drug
se	droguer	to take drugs
	dur(e)	hard
	facile	easy
	fumer	to smoke
le	(non-)fumeur	(non-)smoker
	grave	serious
	interdit(e)	forbidden
le	poumon	lung
le	problème	problem
se	sentir	to feel
le	tabac	tobacco

2.1 G — Ma famille et moi

Objectifs

Talking about yourself and your family

Saying 'my', 'your', 'his', 'her'

Asking questions

1a 📖 🎧 Read the bubbles and select the matching sticky note: A, B or C?

> Tu as quel âge?

> J'ai quinze ans.

> Tu as des frères et sœurs?

> J'ai deux frères et une sœur: Lucas a quatre ans, Léo a douze ans et Marie a dix-neuf ans.

A
14 ans – 2 sœurs (4 ans et 24 ans)

B
15 ans – 3 frères (2 ans, 14 ans et 19 ans)

C
15 ans – 2 frères (4 ans et 12 ans), 1 sœur (19 ans)

1b 📖 ✏️ Copy the sentences and fill in each gap with the right age, to match the sticky notes. Write the numbers as words.

1 J'ai _____ ans. J'ai _____ sœurs. Nadia a _____ ans et Anissa a _____ ans.

2 J'ai _____ ans. J'ai _____ frères. Mehdi a _____ ans, Karim a _____ ans et Adel a _____ ans.

3 J'ai _____ ans. J'ai _____ frères et _____ sœur: Lucas a _____ ans, Léo a _____ ans et Marie a _____ ans.

2 🄖 Copy the sentences and fill in each gap with the correct French word, as indicated in brackets.

1 J'ai des problèmes avec _____ parents. (**my**)

2 Quel âge a _____ sœur? (**your**)

3 Comment s'appelle _____ frère? (**your**)

4 Où habitent _____ grands-parents? (**her**)

5 _____ chat est noir et blanc. (**my**)

6 _____ cousine s'appelle Nathalie. (**her**)

Saying 'my', 'your', 'his', 'her' · **Grammaire**

	masculine singular	feminine singular	plural (m and f)
my	*mon*	*ma*	*mes*
your	*ton*	*ta*	*tes*
his / her	*son*	*sa*	*ses*

If the word is masculine and singular (e.g. *frère*) and you want to say 'my', the word you need is *mon* (*mon frère* = my brother).

Also revise using *avoir* (to have).

See page 42 ➡

pages 176–177

3a 🎧 Listen and match the conversations (1–3) with the pictures (A–C).

3b 🎧 Listen again and select the correct sentence (a or b) for each conversation.

1 a J'ai une sœur qui a huit ans.
  b Ma sœur s'appelle Stéphanie.
2 a J'ai deux chiens.
  b Mes chats s'appellent Minou et Mimi.
3 a Mon frère s'appelle Louis.
  b Mon frère a neuf ans.

4 🗨 Work with a partner. Prepare answers to the following questions, then take turns to ask and answer. Use the language structure box to help you.

- Tu as des frères et sœurs?
- Quel âge a ton frère / ta sœur?
- Est-ce que tu as un animal?
- Comment s'appelle-t-il / elle?
- Comment s'appellent tes parents?

J'ai un / deux frère(s).	Il / Elle s'appelle …
	Ils / Elles s'appellent …
J'ai une / deux sœur(s).	Mon frère / Ma sœur a … ans.
J'ai un chat / chien / hamster.	Il / Elle a … ans.
Mes parents s'appellent …	

Stratégie 4

Asking questions

- Use the normal word order but make sure your voice rises at the end of the question: *Tu as des frères et sœurs?*
- Swap the subject and verb over: *As-tu des frères et sœurs?*
- Use *est-ce que*: *Est-ce que tu as des frères et sœurs?*

Tu as des frères et sœurs?

J'ai un frère mais je n'ai pas de sœur. Et toi?

Objectifs
Getting on with others
Reflexive verbs (singular)
Including adjectives

2.1 F   Ma famille et mes amis

1 **V** Match the adjectives below with their translations. Decide whether each one is in its masculine form (**m**) or its feminine form (**f**). If it does not change, write (**m or f**).

casse-pieds	*gentil*	shy	kind
compréhensive	*sympa*	lazy	sad
mignonne	*timide*	annoying	older
jaloux	*aînée*	nice	numerous
triste	*paresseux*	alone, lonely	funny
seule	*drôle*	jealous	understanding
nombreux		sweet	

On s'entend bien ou mal?

Pierre

Mon meilleur ami s'appelle Paul. Je m'entends bien avec lui. Nous avons beaucoup de choses en commun et nous aimons la même musique et les mêmes films. Paul est toujours sympa et très calme.

Amélie

Ma sœur aînée m'énerve. Elle est très égoïste et paresseuse. On se dispute souvent à cause de la télé car nous n'aimons pas les mêmes émissions. Elle n'aide pas à la maison et mes parents ne la grondent pas. Ce n'est pas juste!

Julien

En ce moment, je me dispute souvent avec mes parents. Ils ne me laissent pas sortir les soirs de semaine avec mes copains car j'ai des devoirs. Ma mère est plus compréhensive mais mon père est très strict. Je préfère sortir avec mes copains plutôt que rester à la maison.

Estelle

J'aime bien un garçon de ma classe mais je suis trop timide pour lui parler. Il est gentil et très drôle mais il est toujours avec un groupe de garçons désagréables. Je pense que nous avons des choses en commun mais il est difficile de lui parler.

2a 📖 🎧 Read the four blog entries. Write the name of the correct person for each statement.

1. _____ argues with his / her parents about going out on weekday evenings.
2. _____ and her sister argue about television programmes.
3. _____ thinks a boy in her class is kind and funny.
4. _____ has a lot in common with his best friend.
5. _____'s mother is more understanding than his father.
6. _____ can't talk to a boy she likes because she is too shy.

Lien

2.1 Higher is available in the Higher book.

2b 📖🎧 Match the beginnings and endings of the sentences.

1 Pierre et son ami Paul …
2 Amélie et sa sœur …
3 Julien pense que son père …
4 Estelle pense qu'un garçon de sa classe …
5 La sœur d'Amélie est …
6 Estelle est …

a égoïste.
b s'entendent bien.
c est trop strict.
d est gentil.
e trop timide.
f se disputent souvent.

3 🄶 Work with a partner. Partner A says the sentence, filling in the missing reflexive pronoun, and Partner B translates the sentence into English. Swap over for each sentence.

1 Ma meilleure amie _____ appelle Morgane.
2 Je _____ entends bien avec mon frère.
3 On _____ dispute tout le temps.
4 Mon beau-frère _____ appelle Jean-Claude.
5 On _____ intéresse aux mêmes choses.
6 Tu ne _____ entends pas bien avec tes parents.

> **Reflexive verbs (singular)** *Grammaire* *page 183*
>
> These verbs always have **reflexive pronouns** (*me, te, se*) before them. If the verb begins with a vowel, shorten the pronoun to *m', t'* or *s'*. Here are two examples:
>
> *se disputer avec* (to argue with) and *s'entendre bien avec* (to get on well with).
>
> Use *elle* and *lui* at the end of a sentence:
>
> *je m'entends bien avec elle* – I get on well with her
>
> *tu te disputes avec lui* – you are arguing with him
>
> Also revise adjective agreement.
> *See page 43* ➡

4a 🎧📹 Listen to and / or watch the video. Choose two words or expressions to describe the members of each person's family.

1 Florence   2 Jean-Jacques   3 Abdul   4 Liliane

a lovable
b divorced
c sense of humour
d annoying
e critical
f understanding
g separated
h strict

4b 🎧📹 Listen to and / or watch the video again. Decide who is being referred to.

1 Her parents are divorced.
2 His parents are separated.
3 His parents think he is lazy.
4 Her father has remarried.
5 She can talk to her mother.
6 He doesn't see his mother any more.

5 ✏ You are working as part of the scriptwriting team for a TV soap and you are describing a new family. In a group, decide who is in the family. Then each person describes one member of the family.

- Who is in the new family?
- What are they like?
- How do they get on with each other and why?
- What do they argue about?

> **Including adjectives** *Stratégie 5*
>
> When writing French, always try to include adjectives in your work in order to make it more individual and interesting.
>
> Remember that most adjectives in French follow the noun and you need to check you have added the correct ending (Is it masculine or feminine? Is it singular or plural?):
>
> *Elle se dispute avec sa grande sœur. Il est toujours avec un groupe de garçons désagréables.*

2.2 G Ma vie de famille

1a 📖 🎧 Copy the internet chat and fill in each gap with the correct word.

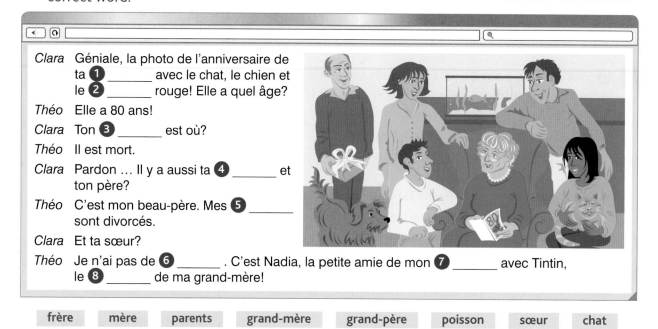

Clara Géniale, la photo de l'anniversaire de ta **1** _____ avec le chat, le chien et le **2** _____ rouge! Elle a quel âge?

Théo Elle a 80 ans!

Clara Ton **3** _____ est où?

Théo Il est mort.

Clara Pardon … Il y a aussi ta **4** _____ et ton père?

Théo C'est mon beau-père. Mes **5** _____ sont divorcés.

Clara Et ta sœur?

Théo Je n'ai pas de **6** _____ . C'est Nadia, la petite amie de mon **7** _____ avec Tintin, le **8** _____ de ma grand-mère!

| frère | mère | parents | grand-mère | grand-père | poisson | sœur | chat |

1b 📖 🎧 Match the five family members with the details given.

1	grandmother	a	divorced
2	parents	b	80
3	grandfather	c	cat
4	Tintin	d	girlfriend
5	Nadia	e	dead

2a 🎧 Listen to the four speakers' plans. Match them to the correct pictures.

2b 🎧 Listen again and complete the sentences in English.

1 I intend to …
2 I would like to have …
3 I don't intend to …
4 I would like to …

3 **G** Copy the sentences and fill in each gap with the correct word, then translate the sentences into English.

1 J'_____ l'intention de me marier.

2 Je _____ remercier mes parents…

3 J'_____ avoir beaucoup d'enfants.

4 Je ne _____ pas _____ sans voisins.

5 Elle _____ _____ un gâteau.

6 Ce couple n'_____ pas l'intention de _____!

| ai | a | divorcer | aimerais | être | manger |
| voudrais | voudrais | aimerait |

> **Grammaire** — page 187
>
> ***Je voudrais, j'aimerais** and **j'ai l'intention de** + infinitive*
>
> When *je voudrais, j'aimerais* or *j'ai l'intention de* is followed by another verb, that verb is in the infinitive.
>
> *Je voudrais acheter un chien.* – I would like to buy a dog.
>
> *J'aimerais avoir deux enfants.* – I would like to have two children.
>
> *Il a l'intention d'écrire à son père.* – He intends to write to his father.
>
> Also learn about question words. *See page 42* ➡

> **Filling gaps** — Stratégie 3
>
> To decide which word fits a gap best, look carefully at the words either side of the gap.
>
> After *j', je, tu, il*, expect to need a verb: *j'**aimerais**, je **voudrais***. Between *n'* and *pas*, you can only have a verb as in *je n'**aime** pas* or *je n'**ai** pas*. Before *l'intention*, you can only have a part of *avoir* as it is part of the expression: *j'ai l'intention de*.

4 🗨 Work with a partner. Prepare answers to the following questions, then take turns to ask and answer.

- Avec qui habites-tu?
- Est-ce que tu as un(e) petit(e) ami(e)?
- Est-ce que tu as l'intention de te marier?
- Quand voudrais-tu te marier?
- Est-ce que tu aimerais avoir des enfants?
- Tu voudrais avoir combien d'enfants?

À la maison, il y a …	mes parents / mon père / ma mère / mes sœurs.
Oui, j'ai un(e) petit(e) ami(e).	Il / Elle s'appelle …
Non, je n'ai pas de petit(e) ami(e).	
Oui, j'ai l'intention de me marier …	à l'église / en France / en Angleterre.
Non, je n'ai pas l'intention de me marier.	
Oui, j'aimerais avoir …	un enfant.
Non, je n'aimerais pas avoir d'enfants.	deux / trois enfants.

Est-ce que tu as un petit ami?

Non, je n'ai pas de petit ami.

2.2 F Est-ce que je vais me marier?

1 **V** Find the pairs. Some are opposites and some have similar meanings.

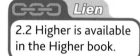
Lien

2.2 Higher is available in the Higher book.

1	un mari	a	une famille monoparentale
2	les parents	b	les enfants
3	avoir des enfants	c	un partenaire
4	une famille avec deux parents	d	divorcer
5	se marier	e	la belle-mère
6	le beau-père	f	ne pas avoir d'enfants

On parle de la vie familiale

1

Maintenant: J'apprécie la solitude. Je passe beaucoup de temps dans ma chambre devant mon ordinateur, mais je fais du baby-sitting quelquefois et ça me plaît. J'aime aussi faire des promenades toute seule. Je n'ai pas beaucoup d'amis de mon âge, mais j'aime les enfants.

2

Maintenant: Mes parents sont divorcés. J'habite avec ma mère et mes sœurs. Ma mère trouve que le mariage n'est pas nécessaire, et je suis d'accord avec elle. À mon avis, il n'est pas important de se marier pour avoir une famille. Je pense que la famille idéale, c'est une mère, un père, une fille et un garçon.

3

Maintenant: Pour moi, la religion est importante. J'ai une petite amie, et on sort ensemble depuis un an. Elle habite chez ses parents. Je ne veux pas vivre avec elle sans être marié. Je n'aime pas les enfants – ils m'énervent!

a

Le futur: Je vais trouver un partenaire très sympa et loyal, et on va vivre ensemble. On va tous les deux avoir un bon travail, donc on va avoir assez d'argent pour acheter une belle maison. Je voudrais avoir deux enfants, mais je ne vais pas rester à la maison, je vais payer quelqu'un pour les garder.

b

Le futur: Je vais me marier à l'église, peut-être dans trois ou quatre ans. Je trouve que la cérémonie du mariage est très romantique. Ça va être une journée très spéciale pour nous deux, et un bon souvenir pour toute la vie. Nous n'allons pas avoir d'enfants.

c

Le futur: Je vais acheter un appartement en ville. Je vais inviter mes amis de temps en temps, mais généralement je vais être seule. Je ne vais pas me marier, mais je vais peut-être avoir un enfant. À mon avis, une famille monoparentale n'est pas une mauvaise idée.

2a Match the different views on family life (1–3) with the plans for the future (a–c) and the correct pictures (A–C).

2b 📖 🎧 Read the views on family life and plans for the future again.
Who says the following? Write the correct combination (1–3, a–c, A–C).

1 I intend to live with my partner without getting married.
2 I want to live alone.
3 I want to get married quite young.
4 I don't want children.
5 It's not important to get married before having children.
6 I like the idea of being a single parent.

3 🄶 Transform the following sentences into the immediate future tense using *aller*.

Exemple: Il voyage en Australie. →
        Il <u>va voyager</u> en Australie.

1 Elle trouve l'amour!
2 Je me marie à l'âge de vingt-cinq ans.
3 Elle sort avec son petit ami.
4 J'ai deux enfants.
5 Tu es riche et célèbre?
6 J'adore ma femme.

> **Aller + infinitive**
> Use the verb *aller* (to go) in the present tense followed by an infinitive (e.g. *travailler*) to express future plans.
> *Je vais travailler.*   I am going to work.
> *Elle va se marier.*   She is going to get married.
> If you have forgotten the present tense of *aller*, look it up in the verb tables (page 194).
> Also revise *devoir*, *pouvoir* and *vouloir* (present tense).
> *See page 43* ➡
>
> *Grammaire page 185*

4a 🎧 Listen to the three speakers. Select the correct phrase to complete each sentence.

1 Malika's parents are going to choose …
   a her future husband.
   b her boyfriend.
   c her wedding dress.
2 Maxime would like to …
   a get married and have children.
   b get married because it's important.
   c have children without getting married.
3 Stéphanie would like …
   a to get married in church.
   b to have one child.
   c a quiet husband.
4 Stéphanie thinks that …
   a religion is not important.
   b the wedding ceremony is romantic.
   c having children is not important.

4b 🎧 Listen again. Decide who thinks the following: Malika, Maxime or Stéphanie?

1 I don't intend to get married.
2 I don't know him.
3 Religion is important.
4 I'd like to have one or two children.
5 My ideal partner is loyal.
6 I'd like to have lots of children.

5 ✏ Write a reply to this email. Give details about your life now and your plans for the future.

> Salut!
>   En ce moment, j'habite avec ma mère car mes parents sont divorcés. C'est un peu triste. Plus tard, j'aimerais avoir ma maison et habiter avec ma copine. J'ai l'intention de me marier et d'avoir trois enfants. Pour moi, le mariage, c'est important. Ma femme idéale va être généreuse et sympa.
>   Et toi? Avec qui habites-tu? Est-ce que tu voudrais te marier? Aimerais-tu avoir des enfants?

> **Adding opinions when writing**
> When writing, try to include opinions as often as you can.
> In the present tense, you can use *c'est* followed by an adjective to give a simple opinion: *c'est sympa, c'est intéressant, c'est ennuyeux.*
> In the future, you can use ça va être … (it's going to be …):
> *Ça va être super.*
>
> *Stratégie 5*

2.3 G Des problèmes sociaux

1a 📖 🎧 Read the statements and match them with the pictures.

1 Mon copain est trop gros. Il mange beaucoup de frites.
2 Un copain de mon frère n'a pas de maison. Il habite dans la rue.
3 Mon oncle ne travaille pas en ce moment. Il reste à la maison.

1b 📖 Read the statements in Activity 1a again and find the French for these words and expressions.

1 too fat
2 eats a lot
3 doesn't work
4 in the street
5 at home

2 ⓖ Copy the sentences and fill in each gap with the correct verb.

1 J'aime _____ au McDo.
2 J'_____ manger des frites et des hamburgers.
3 Je n'aime pas _____ dans la rue.
4 Je _____ rester à la maison.
5 Je préfère _____ dans un bureau.
6 J'_____ boire du Coca.
7 Je n'_____ pas aller au collège.
8 J' adore _____ des bonbons.

| dormir | travailler | déteste | aller |
| manger | adore | aime | aime |

Ⓖrammaire *page 181*

Saying you like or don't like doing something (revision)

J'aime boi**re** *du Coca.*

J'aime / J'adore mang**er** *des frites.*

Je n'aime pas dorm**ir** *dans la rue.*

Je n'aime pas all**er** *au collège.*

Je déteste rest**er** à la maison. Je préfère travaill**er**.

Also revise intensifiers (e.g. *trop de, pas assez de*).   *See page 42* ➡

3a 🎧 Listen to three people talking about social issues affecting friends or family. Identify the correct problem.

a homelessness   b obesity   c unemployment

3b 🎧 Listen again and answer the questions in English.

1 Why is his friend too fat?
2 a What does her father do at the moment?
  b How does he feel about it?
3 a Where does his cousin's friend live at the moment?
  b Why?

4 ✏ Work with a partner. You are working as part of the scriptwriting team for a TV soap based on a problem family. Describe four characters and explain their problems.

■ Who is in the family?
■ What is their problem?
■ What do they like?
■ What don't they like?
■ Give reasons.

Stratégie 4

Checking written work

Check your written work, using a dictionary and the grammar section (pages 172–192) as needed.

■ Masculine words need *le, un* or *du*. Feminine words need *la, une* or *de la* (*le* père, *la* mère).

■ With feminine or plural words, adjectives with the nouns will also have to change (*la fille est gros**se***).

■ Check also verb endings, using the verb tables (pages 193–197).

Dans la famille, il y a	une mère, deux enfants et une grand-mère, les parents, un fils et sa copine.
Le père / La mère / Le fils / La fille est	(très / assez / un peu / trop) gros(se).
Le père / Le fils / La fille / Le cousin / La cousine	ne travaille pas en ce moment.
	reste à la maison.
	n'habite pas à la maison.
	habite dans la rue.
Il / Elle aime bien / adore	rester à la maison / manger des …
Il / Elle n'aime pas / déteste	habiter dans la rue / aller au collège.
… parce que c'est	(un peu / très / assez) ennuyeux / dangereux / bon.

2.3 F On n'a pas les mêmes chances

1 **V** Match each phrase with its English translation.

1	sans domicile fixe (SDF)	a	carboard boxes
2	un logement	b	a charity
3	une organisation caritative	c	a sleeping bag
4	des cartons	d	homeless
5	un sac de couchage	e	the necessities
6	au chômage	f	a deprived area
7	les choses indispensables	g	unemployed
8	un quartier défavorisé	h	accommodation

Qu'est-ce qu'on peut faire pour aider les personnes défavorisées?

Léon habite à Paris, où il y a environ 5 000 hommes et femmes sans domicile fixe dans les rues. Il travaille pour une organisation qui s'occupe des personnes qui n'ont pas de maison. Ces personnes sont presque toujours sans travail, elles ont faim et elles n'ont pas de logement. Voici ce que dit Léon: «Mon travail, c'est d'offrir de la soupe et une tranche de pain à chaque personne malheureuse qui arrive au centre.»

Thomas travaille pour une organisation caritative. Il remplit des cartons de toutes sortes de choses pour les SDF, par exemple des sacs de couchage, du shampooing et du savon. Comme ils sont au chômage, ils n'ont pas assez d'argent pour acheter les choses indispensables de la vie. Thomas dit «Ces pauvres gens attendent avec impatience notre arrivée.»

Jules est volontaire dans un groupe sportif qui aide les jeunes des quartiers défavorisés. Il passe cinq heures par semaine à faire du sport dans les centres de loisirs d'un quartier de Paris où il y a beaucoup de familles pauvres. Grâce au sport, ces adolescents ont la chance d'avoir une vie meilleure. «La première fois, il n'y avait que cinq garçons et trois filles, mais ils ont parlé à leurs voisins et maintenant on a trente jeunes dans notre groupe. On est très populaires!» explique Jules.

2a 📖🎧 Read the article and write the name of the appropriate person for each picture (A–C).

2b 📖🎧 Which four of these sentences are true?

1 The people who come to Léon are usually unemployed.
2 Léon helps by giving the people money to buy soup and bread.
3 Thomas's charity helps by providing basic necessities for the homeless.
4 The homeless people are always happy to see the volunteers.
5 Jules earns money by working for his charity.
6 Sport gives hope to these young people.

3a **G** Copy and complete the grid for the verbs *remplir* (to fill) and *attendre* (to wait for). Follow the model in the grammar box.

remplir = to fill	*singular*	*plural*
	je _____	nous _____
	tu _____	vous remplissez
	il /elle / on remplit	ils / elles _____

attendre = _____	*singular*	*plural*
	j'_____	nous _____
	_____ attends	vous _____
	il / elle / on _____	_____ _____

Present tense of -*ir* verbs and -*re* verbs

For -*ir* verbs, take off the -*ir* and add the endings given below.

finir = to finish

singular	plural
je fin**is**	nous fin**issons**
tu fin**is**	vous fin**issez**
il / elle / on fin**it**	ils / elles fin**issent**

Find the pattern for -*re* verbs (e.g. *vendre*) in the verb tables (page 193) and make a similar table to help you learn it.

Also learn about patterns of endings for masculine and feminine nouns.   *See page 43* ➡

Grammaire   *page 182*

3b **G** Copy the sentences and fill in the gaps. First decide which verb you need from the list, then choose the correct ending.

vendre   attendre   choisir

remplir   finir

1 Je _____ des cartons de toutes sortes de choses à manger et à boire.
2 Les gens du village _____ l'arrivée du docteur de Médecins Sans Frontières.
3 Nous _____ des cartes d'anniversaire au marché pour collecter de l'argent pour une école au Congo.
4 Nathalie commence son travail avec les SDF à huit heures du soir, et elle _____ à minuit.
5 On ne _____ pas d'être sans domicile fixe: ça peut arriver parce qu'on n'a pas de travail.

🔗 **Lien**

2.3 Higher is available in the Higher book.

4a 🎧 Listen to Simon and Marie discussing various social issues. Complete the sentences by selecting a, b or c.

1 Marie thinks that the homeless people are in a difficult situation because they ...
   a have no family.   c have no help.
   b are unemployed.
2 Simon believes that the homeless must find ...
   a a job.   b a house.   c some food.
3 Marie thinks that homeless people also have ...
   a feelings.   c other problems.
   b rights.
4 Simon gives the example of ...
   a heart condition.   c disability.
   b alcoholism.

4b 🎧 Listen again and decide who said the following.

1 Charities do an excellent job.
2 Homeless people are in a difficult situation.
3 It's difficult to find a job when you are homeless.
4 Homeless people need to look for a job.
5 They have alcohol dependency issues.
6 They can suffer from a mental illness.

5 💬 Work with a partner. Discuss these statements, saying whether you agree or not.

■ Les organisations caritatives doivent aider les SDF.
■ Les SDF doivent chercher du travail.
■ Les SDF choisissent d'habiter dans la rue.
■ Il est difficile de trouver du travail quand on est SDF.

Agreeing / disagreeing in a discussion

To agree use: *c'est vrai / tu as raison / je suis d'accord / exactement / justement.*

To disagree use: *c'est faux / tu as tort / je ne suis pas du tout d'accord / certainement pas.*

Stratégie 5

Relationships and choices

1 Copy the sentences and fill in each gap with the correct form of *avoir*.

1 J'_____ quatorze ans.
2 Tu _____ des frères et sœurs?
3 J'_____ une sœur et un frère.
4 Ma sœur _____ huit ans et mon frère _____ douze ans.
5 J'_____ un chien. Il _____ trois ans.
6 Est-ce que tu _____ un animal?

Grammaire page 187

Using *avoir* (to have)

As well as using *avoir* when saying if you have brothers and sisters, remember that you also need to use it when saying how old people are.

Tu as quel âge? – How old are you?
J'ai quinze ans. – I am fifteen. (Literally, 'I have 15 years.')
J'ai un frère. – I have one brother.
Elle a une sœur. – She has one sister.

2 Match the French and the English. Then copy the sentences and fill in each gap with the correct question word: *combien, où, pourquoi, quand* or *qui*.

1 _____ de frères et sœurs as-tu?
2 _____ as-tu l'intention de te marier?
3 _____ ne voudrais-tu pas d'enfants?
4 Avec _____ voudrais-tu te marier?
5 _____ est ton père?
6 _____ habite dans ta maison?

a Why wouldn't you want any children?
b How many brothers and sisters do you have?
c Who would you like to marry?
d Where is your father?
e When do you intend to get married?
f Who lives in your house?

Grammaire pages 188–189

Question words

Make sure you know the following words and use them to introduce questions.

combien? – how much / how many?
où? – where?
pourquoi? – why?
quand? – when?
qui? – who?

3 Copy the sentences and fill in each gap with the correct intensifier: *assez, très, beaucoup, un peu* or *trop (de)*.

1 Ma sœur est trop grosse. Elle a _____ (**a lot**) de problèmes à l'école.
2 Mon copain est _____ (**quite**) gros parce qu'il mange _____ (**too many**) bonbons et de gâteaux.
3 Mon père reste à la maison en ce moment et c'est _____ (**a bit**) ennuyeux.
4 Mon frère a un copain qui n'a pas de maison; c'est _____ (**very**) dangereux d'habiter dans la rue.

Grammaire page 178

Intensifiers

Use intensifiers to make what you say or write more interesting:

assez	quite
très	very
trop	too
un peu	a bit
beaucoup (de)	a lot (of)
trop de	too much, too many

*Ma copine mange **trop de** hamburgers et de frites; elle est **trop** grosse.*
*Il habite dans la rue; c'est **très** dangereux.*
*Mon père n'a pas de travail; il est **assez** triste.*

4 Choose the correct adjectives to complete the following sentences.

1 Sa mère est **bavard / bavarde**, mais elle n'est pas **méchant / méchante**.

2 Ta grand-mère est **triste / tristes** parce qu'elle est **seul / seule**.

3 Il a des parents **riche / riches** et **célèbre / célèbres**.

4 J'ai une copine très **gentil / gentille** mais **timide / timides**.

5 Mon **grand / grands** frère est **paresseux / paresseuses**.

6 Ses **petits / petites** sœurs sont **pénible / pénibles**.

7 Mon frère **aîné / aînée** est très **égoïste / égoïstes**.

8 Elle a des grands-parents **pauvre / pauvres** mais très **gentils / gentilles**.

Grammaire · pages 174–175

Adjective agreement

Adjectives have different endings depending on whether they describe masculine, feminine, singular or plural nouns. Add *-e* if the noun is feminine, and add *-s* if it is plural. They usually go after the noun:

une fille intelligente   a clever girl

des enfants gentils   kind children

If the adjective already ends in *-e*, there is no need to add another one:

un garçon timide   a shy boy

une fille timide   a shy girl

Some adjectives, including *petit*, *grand* and *joli* usually go before the noun:

ma grande sœur   my big sister

---

5 Choose the correct form of *devoir*, *pouvoir* and *vouloir* each time. Then find the correct translation and complete it.

1 Je ne **veux / voulons** pas me marier avec lui.

2 Tu ne **dois / doit** pas être méchant avec ton copain.

3 Il ne **devez / doit** pas bavarder avec ses copains.

4 Elle ne **veut / veux** pas habiter chez sa mère.

5 Nous ne **veulent / voulons** pas divorcer.

6 Vous ne **peut / pouvez** pas vous entendre.

7 Ils ne **peuvent / pouvons** pas avoir d'enfants.

a _____ can't get on.

b _____ can't have children.

c _____ don't want a divorce.

d _____ don't want to marry him.

e _____ doesn't want to live with her mother.

f _____ mustn't be mean to your friend.

g _____ mustn't gossip with his friends.

Grammaire · page 187

Devoir, *pouvoir* and *vouloir*: present tense

devoir = to have to

singular	plural
je dois	nous devons
tu dois	vous devez
il / elle / on doit	ils / elles doivent

pouvoir = to be able to

singular	plural
je peux	nous pouvons
tu peux	vous pouvez
il / elle on peut	ils / elles peuvent

vouloir = to want (to)

singular	plural
je veux	nous voulons
tu veux	vous voulez
il / elle / on veut	ils / elles veulent

---

6 Masculine or feminine? Find the odd one out in each set.

1
| alimentation | citron |
| obésité | pomme |

2
| activité | alcoolisme |
| tabagisme | tabac |

3
| désintoxication | cancer |
| relaxation | spécialité |

Grammaire · page 173

Masculine and feminine nouns

When learning a new noun, always learn whether it is masculine or feminine. There are patterns to help you remember the correct gender.

All words ending in *-isme* are masculine: *l'alcoolisme*, *le tabagisme*.

Most fruit items ending in *-e* are feminine:

la banane, la cerise, la fraise, la poire, la pomme.

Words ending in *-tion* are usually feminine: *l'alimentation*, *la dégustation*.

Words ending in *-ité* are usually feminine: *l'obésité*, *la spécialité*.

Relationships and choices

Topic 2.1 Relationships with family and friends

2.1 G Ma famille et moi ➡ *pages 30–31*

le	chat	cat
le	chien	dog
ma	cousine (f)	my cousin
	habiter	to live
ma	sœur	my sister
mon	frère	my brother
mes	parents	my parents

2.1 F Ma famille et mes amis ➡ *pages 32–33*

	aîné(e)	older
	casse-pieds	infuriating, a pain
	célibataire	single
les	choses en commun (f)	things in common
	compréhensif(-ve)	understanding
	désagréable	unpleasant
	se disputer	to argue
	égoïste	selfish
	énerver	to annoy
	s'entendre bien / mal avec	to get on well / badly with
	gentil(le)	kind
	gronder	to reprimand
	jaloux(-ouse)	jealous
	laisser	to allow
	même	same
	mignon(ne)	cute, sweet, pretty
	nombreux(-euse)	numerous
	paresseux(-euse)	lazy
	seul(e)	alone
	sortir	to go out
	souvent	often
	sympa	nice
	timide	shy
	tranquille	quiet, calm
	triste	sad

Topic 2.2 Future plans regarding marriage / partnership

2.2 G Ma vie de famille ➡ *pages 34–35*

l'	anniversaire (m)	birthday
le	beau-père	stepfather
	divorcer	to divorce
	drôle	funny
l'	église (f)	church
l'	enfant (m/f)	child
	j'ai l'intention de	I intend to
	je voudrais	I would like
	j'aimerais	I would like
	loyal(e)	loyal, faithful
	manger	to eat
le	mari	husband
se	marier	to get married
	mort(e)	dead
le / la	partenaire	partner
le / la	petit(e) ami(e)	boyfriend / girlfriend
le	poisson rouge	goldfish
	remercier	to thank

2.2 F Est-ce que je vais me marier?
➡ *pages 36–37*

l'	amour (m)	love
la	belle-mère	stepmother
	célèbre	famous
	devenir	to become
	ensemble	together
	être d'accord avec	to agree with
la	famille monoparentale	single-parent family
	garder	to look after
	rencontrer	to meet
	sans	without
la	solitude	solitude, being on one's own
le	souvenir	memory
	vivre	to live

Topic 2.3 Social issues: family, friends and society

2.3 G Des problèmes sociaux ➡ *pages 38–39*

	aller	to go
le	*bureau*	office
	dormir	to sleep
	ennuyeux(-euse)	boring
le	*fils*	son
	rester	to stay
la	*rue*	street
	travailler	to work
	trop	too

	résoudre	to solve
le	*sac de couchage*	sleeping bag
le	*SDF (sans domicile fixe)*	homeless person
le	*trottoir*	pavement
	utîle	useful
la	*vie*	life
le	*voisin*	neighbour

2.3 F On n'a pas les mêmes chances
➡ *pages 40–41*

	alcoolisme (m)	alcoholism
l'	*argent (m)*	money
l'	*automobiliste (m)*	car driver
	avoir faim	to be hungry
	avoir raison	to be right
	avoir tort	to be wrong
le	*carton*	cardboard box
	choisir	to choose
le	*chômage*	unemployment
les	*choses indispensables*	necessities
	défavorisé(e)	deprived
	déprimé(e)	depressed
l'	*équipe (f)*	team
	être d'accord	to agree
la	*femme*	woman
l'	*homme (m)*	man
	jeune	young
le	*logement*	accommodation
la	*maladie*	illness
	malheureux(-euse)	unhappy, unfortunate
	malheureusement	unfortunately
	meilleur(e)	better
l'	*organisation caritative*	charity
	pauvre	poor
le	*quartier*	area, district
	remplir	to fill

Foundation – Exam practice

Bien se préparer aux examens

Comment ne pas paniquer?

A Prenez un bon petit déjeuner!

B Faites de l'exercice!

C Révisez!

D Mangez bien!

E Dormez bien!

F Préparez vos affaires!

G Écoutez de la musique!

H Buvez de l'eau!

---

1 Look at the speech bubbles surrounding a panicky Pauline. Sort the advice into three groups: 1 Organisation, 2 Leisure and 3 Diet.

Total = 8 marks

Tu peux être bien préparé pour les examens si ...

La veille de l'examen:

Tu ne révises pas à la dernière minute, mais ...

a Tu continues à faire des activités que tu aimes (sport, loisirs ...).

b Tu limites les visites chez les copains: le stress se communique et les copains vont parler de l'examen!

c Le soir, tu manges léger, par exemple: assiette de pâtes, poulet, yaourt, fruit.

d Tu prépares ton sac et tu penses à emporter le matériel nécessaire (stylos, calculatrice) et les documents importants.

Le jour de l'examen:

e Tu manges bien avant de quitter la maison: du pain, des biscottes ou des céréales, un fruit, du lait ou un yaourt, et une boisson (thé, café, chocolat ...).

f Tu ne quittes pas la maison au dernier moment. Comme ça, tu vas arriver calme.

g Tu manges quelque chose pendant la matinée (barre de céréales, carrés de chocolat, biscuits ...).

h Tu ne paniques pas pendant l'examen: tu vas avoir le temps de lire ta copie avant la fin de l'examen. À l'oral: parle calmement, articule bien.

---

2 📖 Read the advice for the day before and the day of an exam. Decide which piece of advice (a–h) fits with each of the categories below.

1 Preparing equipment
2 Having a good breakfast
3 Preventing friends from making you worry more
4 Allowing enough time to get to school
5 Staying calm during the exam
6 Making time for leisure
7 Eating sensibly the night before
8 Eating an energy-boosting snack during the morning

Total = 8 marks

3a 🎧 Listen to Section A, the introduction to the interview with Thomas, a young sportsman. Which five of the following sports does he mention?

| football | rugby | badminton | basketball | tennis |
| swimming | athletics | judo |

Total = 5 marks

3b 🎧 Listen to Section B. In what order does Thomas mention the things represented in the pictures?

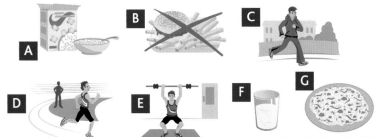

Total = 7 marks

3c 🎧 Listen again and note the time at which each of the pictured activities occurred.

Exemple: A *07h30*

Total = 7 marks

Total for Reading and Listening = 35 marks

Using what you know

At first glance, you may be put off by the length of the text and the number of unfamiliar words. However, you don't need to understand every word to be able to complete the task. For example, item g) in the advice contains a number of new words, but the words *matinée* and *manger* tell you that it deals with eating during the morning, so it fits with category 8.

Look out for cognates and near-cognates as well (words that are the same as or similar to English) as they will provide more clues to understanding.

Stratégie 2

Anticipating what is in the recording

Before listening to the recording, consider what words you are likely to hear linked to each picture. Remember, it may not be the word for the actual item shown, but something connected, e.g. for picture A he may refer to breakfast in general, rather than cereal. This technique works for other sorts of questions as well, e.g. in 3a he may talk about the activity (swimming) or the location (pool), so don't just listen for the words given, but ones that are connected.

Stratégie 3b

Foundation – Speaking

Une vie saine

You are talking to your French friend Adrien about your lifestyle.
He wants to know:

1. if you are in good health
2. if you eat healthily
3. if you exercise regularly
4. if you have a stressful lifestyle
5. if you smoke
6. if you drink alcohol.
7. !

! Remember, you will have to respond to
something that you have not yet prepared.

(i)nfo

Important information:
This sample task is for practice
purposes only and should not
be used as an actual assessment
task. Study it to find out how to
plan your Controlled Assessment
efficiently to gain maximum
marks and / or work through it
as a mock exam task before the
actual Controlled Assessment.

---

1. **If you are in good health**
   - say that you are usually in good health
   - mention the last time you weren't well
   - say what you did about it
   - say that generally you have a healthy lifestyle

Stratégie

Start your plan. Write a maximum of six words for each
of the bullet points 1–7.

Here are some suggested words for bullet point 1:
aller, grippe, médecin, pharmacie, médicaments, sain.

Remember that the maximum number of words allowed
in your plan is 40.

Although *aller* does not by itself indicate that you are in
good health, it reminds you that it is the correct verb to
use to say that you are well. Use words in your plan that
will help you to remember what to say next and will also
help you speak accurate French. See Exam technique S2.

---

2. **If you eat healthily**
   - say what you like to eat and drink
   - say what you don't eat or drink and why
   - say if you think that you have a healthy diet
   - say what you think is an ideal diet

Stratégie

Suggested words for your plan: *manger, boire, matin,
midi, soir, sainement.*

Give details about what you eat and drink for
breakfast, lunch and evening meal. Use different verbs
to avoid repetition of *manger* and *boire*: *je prends,
il y a, j'aime, je n'aime pas.*

Use different words in your plan. The repetition of
manger, for example, might confuse you on the day
you do the assessment.

---

3. **If you exercise regularly**
   - say which sports you play
   - say when, where and with whom
   - say whether you usually walk or cycle to
     various places
   - say what you intend to do to get fitter

Stratégie

Suggested words for your plan: *jouer, faire, pied, vélo,
avenir, natation.*

If you can use the word 'play' a sport in English, use
jouer au + sport: *je joue au basket.* If you can't, use
faire du / de la / de l' + sport: *je fais de l'athlétisme.*

Show initiative by developing the last point: say
precisely what you are going to do to get fitter,
explain why and say how frequently you will do
it, whether you plan to join a club, etc. See Exam
technique S10.

You can add grammatical markers to your plan, e.g.
à l'avenir. It suggests that you should talk about what
you intend to do in the future in terms of exercise.

4 If you have a stressful lifestyle
- say whether you work too hard
- say whether you sleep well
- say what stresses you out
- say what you do to avoid stress

Use fewer than six words if possible in your plan. Here, four words are probably enough to remind you of what you should be talking about. You may appreciate the luxury of more than six words when dealing with another bullet point!

Suggested words for your plan: *travailler*, *dormir*, *stresser*. Add a maximum of two words to this list.

Use *de … heures à … heures* to say that you work / sleep 'from … to …'

Start your response to the last sub-division of bullet point 4 with:

Pour ne pas être stressé, je …

5 If you smoke
- say whether you smoke
- say whether you have friends who smoke
- say why you think young people start smoking
- say why it is foolish to start smoking

Suggested words for your plan: *fumer*, *jeunes*, *commencer*. Add a maximum of three words to this list.

Use different ways of expressing your opinion: *à mon avis … / je pense que … / je trouve que …*

Use *commencer à* + infinitive to say 'start to' + verb.

Use *il est bête de …* to say 'it is foolish to…'

6 If you drink alcohol
- say whether you drink alcohol
- say what you think of the price of alcohol
- say whether you think people aged under 18 should be allowed to drink alcohol
- say what you think the problem is with young people and alcohol

Suggested words for your plan: *cher*, *interdit*, *alcool*. Add a maximum of three words to this list.

Use *il est interdit de* + verb to explain what is not allowed. Say whether you agree with the law.

Use *trop* for 'too much'.

7 ! At this point you may be asked …
- if you take drugs.
- what you have done recently to improve your fitness.
- how you intend to change your lifestyle in order to improve your health.
- about the importance of peer group pressure in trying to have a healthy lifestyle.

Choose which **two** options you think are the most likely, and for each of these, note down **three** different ideas. In your plan, write three words for each of the two most likely options.

For the third sub-division of bullet point 7 you might choose *vélo*, *fruits*, *dormir*. Learn these two options using your reminder words. See Exam technique S3.

Remember to check the total number of words you have used. It should be 40 or fewer.

 **Lien**

Higher sample assessment tasks for this Context can be found in the Higher book.

Foundation – Writing

Les rapports avec les autres

You are writing to your French friend about your relationships with family and friends and also about your choices for the future. You could include:

1. how you get on with your family
2. details of the person you get on best with
3. what you like to do with that person
4. what happened last time you went out as a family
5. details about your friends
6. where you intend to live in the future
7. what you plan to do when you leave home.

info

Important information:
This sample task is for practice purposes only and should not be used as an actual assessment task. Study it to find out how to plan your Controlled Assessment efficiently to gain maximum marks and / or work through it as a mock exam task before the actual Controlled Assessment.

---

1 How you get on with your family
- say who is in your family
- say who you get on with (or don't get on with) and why
- say who you have arguments with and why
- ask your friend how he / she gets on with his / her family

Stratégie

Start your plan. Here are some suggested words for bullet point 1: *famille – membres, s'entendre, raison, disputes, question.*
Start off with *dans ma famille, il y a …*
Use *je m'entends bien avec …, je ne m'entends pas bien avec …* to say that you get on (or not) with someone. Add *parce que* and write a reason. See Exam technique W8.
Remember that verbs can only be used in the infinitive or the past participle in your plan.

---

2 Details of the person you get on best with
- say who he / she is, his / her name and age
- say what he / she looks like
- say what his / her personality is like
- say why you get on well

Stratégie

Suggested words for your plan: *Jane, apparence physique, personnalité, raisons.*
Remember that if you describe a girl or a woman using adjectives, the adjectives have to be made feminine, e.g. *grande, belle.*
Use the correct form of *avoir* to say his / her age, mention her eye and hair colour, i.e. *il / elle a … ans / les yeux / les cheveux …* See Exam technique W10.

---

3 What you like to do with that person
- say what activities you do together
- talk about your favourite activity
- say what you like but he / she doesn't like and vice versa
- say how often you go out together

Stratégie

Suggested words for your plan: *cinéma, mon / son activité préférée, ensemble.*
You can use *on* or *nous* to mean 'we': *on va* means the same as *nous allons.*
Vary the ways in which you give your opinion: *j'aime … / ce que j'aime / ce qui me plaît / mon activité préférée, c'est …*
Use *… fois par semaine / mois* to express frequency.

4 What happened last time you went out as a family

- say when you went out and how you travelled
- say where you went
- say what you did
- say what you thought of it

Suggested words for your plan: *quand, moyen de transport, où, activités*. Add a maximum of two words to this list.

Use the perfect tense. With *être* verbs, start with *nous sommes*. With *avoir* verbs, start with *nous avons*.

Use *j'ai aimé* and *je n'ai pas aimé* to introduce what you enjoyed and didn't enjoy. Show that you know the imperfect tense by using *C'était* + adjective to say what it was like.

5 Details about your friends

- say who they are
- say what you like doing with them
- give details about your best friend
- give details of an outing with your best friend

Suggested words for your plan: *qui, activités, ensemble*. Add a maximum of three words to this list.

Use *mon meilleur ami* or *ma meilleure amie* to introduce your best friend.

You could deal with the last sub-division of bullet point 5 either by recounting an outing that has already taken place: *samedi, nous sommes allés …* or by looking forward to an outing: *samedi, nous allons aller …*

Include the words *dernière sortie* or *prochaine sortie* in your plan. See Exam technique W12.

6 Where you intend to live in the future

- say when you intend to leave home
- say where you intend to live
- say how you will keep in touch with your family
- say how often you will visit them

Suggested words for your plan: *quand, où*. Add a maximum of four words to this list.

Use *à l'âge de … ans, je …* to say at what age you intend to leave home.

Use various ways of referring to a future event: *je vais / je voudrais / j'aimerais / j'espère / j'ai l'intention de*. All are followed by a verb in the infinitive.

Use *garder le contact* (to keep in touch) and *rendre visite à* (to visit someone).

7 What you plan to do when you leave home

- say whether you would like to take a gap year
- say whether you intend to get married
- say whether you would like to have children
- conclude by saying how important family and friends are to you

Add a maximum of six words to your plan.

Use *une année sabbatique* for 'a gap year'.

Use *se marier* for 'to get married'. Take care! With reflexive verbs, if you use *je*, you also have to use *me*.

Remember to check the total number of words you have used in your plan. It must be 40 or fewer.

Lien

Higher sample assessment tasks for this Context can be found in the Higher book.

Exam technique – Speaking

S1 Responding to the bullet points

In a Speaking task, there are likely to be between three and seven bullet points on the task you are given to prepare. One of the bullet points will be the unpredictable element and will appear as an exclamation mark. The teacher will ask you questions based on these bullet points. You could break down the bullet points into sub-divisions, as in this course book, to help you find interesting details to talk about, if your teacher has not already done it for you. It is important that you respond to every question / bullet point in the exam to gain as many marks as possible.

S2 The Speaking plan

You are allowed to write a maximum of 40 words in your plan. Those words can be in French or English. Choose them carefully so that your plan works well as a reminder of what you want to say. Try to use a maximum of six words per bullet point. Remember that you are not allowed to use conjugated verbs (i.e. verbs with an ending other than the infinitive or the past participle) in your plan. Visuals, codes, letters or initialled words, e.g. *j ... s ... a ...* for *je suis allé*, are not allowed.

S3 Preparing for the **!**

The exclamation mark (often the last bullet point) is there to test you on something that you have not prepared. As you cannot predict exactly what you are going to be asked, it is often referred to as 'the unpredictable element'. However, the unpredictable is often predictable! Ask yourself: what question would logically follow the questions I have already answered? Practise guessing what the unpredictable bullet point might be about. You are likely to come up with two or three possibilities. Prepare answers to cover those possibilities. Practise your possible responses. When you are asked the question, focus on the meaning of the question itself to make sure you understand it and then give your full answer.

Grade booster

To reach grade D, you need to ...

■ Give a reasonable amount of information that is sometimes developed. When you feel that the language you are using is relatively simple, e.g. for bullet point 3 of the sample Controlled Assessment on page 48, add extra information, such as 'I walk to school every day and it takes 20 minutes. It isn't far.'

■ Use sentences that are generally simple but occasionally more complex, e.g. for bullet point 5, you may want to learn one or two complex structures that you know you can use accurately: *Les jeunes commencent à fumer parce que ... On risque de devenir accro.*

To reach grade C, you need to ...

■ Offer some evidence of an ability to sustain a conversation and occasionally show initiative, e.g. for bullet point 6, give relevant information that has not been requested, such as your own reasons for not drinking alcohol.

■ Express points of view and sometimes develop them, e.g. for bullet point 2, give your opinion using different phrases: *à mon avis / je pense que / je crois que / j'aime / je n'aime pas / je trouve que,* etc. Develop some of your answers using *car / parce que.*

Aiming for Higher? You need to ...

■ Show a range of vocabulary and an ability to use some complex sentences, e.g. for bullet point 4, learn a few phrases that will impress the examiner: *Ce qui me stresse, c'est ... Pour ne pas être stressé, je ...*

■ Answer without hesitation and extend responses beyond the minimum, e.g. for bullet point 1, say you generally have a healthy lifestyle. Explain aspects of that lifestyle that are not dealt with later on in the task, e.g. 'I go to bed early. I don't take drugs.'

Exam technique – Writing

W1 Help available

Your teacher is allowed to discuss each task with you in English, including the kind of language you may need and how to use your preparatory work. You can have access to a dictionary, your French books, Kerboodle and internet resources. This is the stage when you will prepare your plan using the Task Planning Form.

When you actually perform the task, you can have access to a dictionary. You will also have the task itself, your plan and your teacher's feedback on your plan, i.e. the Task Planning Form. You cannot use your exercise book, course book or any drafts you may have written to help you practise.

W2 The Writing plan

In your Writing plan you can write a maximum of 40 words. Visuals, conjugated verbs or codes are not allowed.

Use your plan to remind yourself of what you should be writing next. Although it is more helpful to you to write French words in your plan, you can also use English words. Try to divide the 40 words equally between the six to eight bullet points of the task. Don't go over your allowance of 40 words.

W3 AQA administration

For the writing part of your exam, you have to do two different tasks (at two different times). When your teacher has taught you the necessary language for you to complete a task, you will be given the task to prepare. You may be asked to prepare a plan using the Task Planning Form. You will get some feedback on your plan from your teacher at that point. You will then prepare your final version, under the direct supervision of your teacher.

You will have 60 minutes to complete each task. You will work in exam conditions and will not be allowed to communicate with others.

Grade booster

To reach grade D, you need to ...

- Express points of view and sometimes develop them, e.g. in your answer to bullet point 3 of the sample Controlled Assessment on page 50, name your favourite activity and develop the point by explaining how often you do it and where, when, etc.

- Show evidence of some variety of vocabulary and structures, e.g. for bullet point 7, vary your vocabulary to say what you would like to do, choosing between *j'aimerais / j'espère / j'ai l'intention de / je voudrais* + infinitive. Make sure you learn key words and phrases for the task, e.g. 'a gap year' (*une année sabbatique*), 'to get married' (*se marier*).

To reach grade C, you need to ...

- Write longer sentences using appropriate linking words fairly accurately, e.g. for bullet point 1: *Je m'entends bien avec ... parce que ... et ... Par contre, je n'aime pas ... car ... et quelquefois ...*

- Where the instruction is open-ended, e.g. for bullet point 5, communicate clearly quite a lot of relevant information. You could add how long you have known your friends for, how you became friends, how often you see one another, etc.

Aiming for Higher? You need to ...

- Show that you can use a variety of structures, including verb tenses, with reasonable accuracy, e.g. for bullet point 4, show that you can use the perfect tense. Use it with verbs that require *avoir* and also *être*. Try to include a reflexive verb too. Use a negative sentence in the perfect tense.

- Errors are likely to occur in more complex sentences. Write simple French accurately, e.g. for bullet point 2 you are asked to write simple sentences (age, eye colour, hair, personality features). Focus on accuracy.

3.1 G   Mes passe-temps et mes vêtements

Objectifs

Talking about sports, leisure activities and clothes

Using *jouer à*, *jouer de* and *faire de*

Giving longer answers to questions

1a 📖 🎧 Read about each person's activities and find the correct symbols for each one.

«Je fais de l'athlétisme et je joue au foot.»
Nadia

«Je joue du piano et de la flûte.»
Alice

«Je joue de la guitare. L'été, je fais de la voile.»
Théo

«Je ne joue pas d'un instrument de musique. Je fais du judo et du skate.»
Mehdi

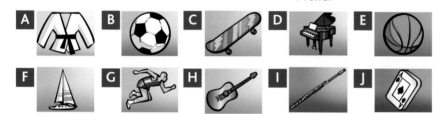

1b 🗨 **G** Work with a partner. Partner A chooses one of the symbols from Activity 1a. Partner B asks questions to find which one it is. Then swap parts.

Exemple: **A** Tu fais du judo?   **B** Non.   **A** Tu joues du piano?

2a 📖 🎧 Find the correct clothes (A–G) to match the speech bubbles (1–3).

1 Quand je joue dans mon orchestre, je porte une robe violette et des chaussures marron.

2 Quand je fais du sport, je porte un short bleu et des baskets blanches.

3 Quand je fais du skate, je porte un pantalon gris et un sweat rouge.

2b ✏ Copy the sentences and fill in the gaps according to the pictures.

1 Quand je _____ au basket, je porte un _____ vert, un sweat _____ et des _____ noires.

2 Quand je joue _____, _____ …

3 **G** Copy the sentences and fill in each gap with the correct word. Use the grammar box to help you.

1 Tu joues au foot ou _____ basket?

2 Je fais _____ karaté et je joue _____ guitare.

3 Nadia fait _____ athlétisme ou _____ skate?

4 Mehdi joue _____ flûte et _____ piano.

5 Je _____ du judo et je _____ de la batterie.

6 Tu _____ du skate et tu _____ au tennis?

4a 🎧 Listen, then complete the English statements about the speakers' leisure activities.

1 Nathalie asks Seydi about _____. He plays _____.

2 Seydi asks Nathalie about _____. She says she plays the _____.

3 Amélie prefers _____ to _____. She talks about _____.

4 Martin doesn't do _____. He plays the _____.

4b 🎧 Listen again, then choose the best phrase to sum up each speaker's attitude to what they are talking about.

1 Seydi …
   a hates it.   c loves it.
   b is passionate about it.

2 Natalie …
   a hates it.   c quite likes it.
   b is passionate about it.

3 Amélie …
   a likes it.   c hates it.
   b dislikes it.

4 Martin thinks it's …
   a okay.   c boring.
   b great.

5 💬 Work with a partner. Imagine you are celebrities. Interview each other about spare time activities and clothes.

Tu fais du sport?

Oui, je joue au foot et je fais du skate. J'adore ça!

Qu'est-ce que tu portes quand tu fais du skate?

Tu joues …?	Je joue	au basket / au foot / au golf / au hockey / au rugby.	J'adore ça!
		à la pétanque / aux cartes / aux échecs.	C'est cool / super / fantastique!
		du clavier / du piano / du violon.	C'est ma passion!
		de la batterie / de la flûte / de la guitare.	Je n'aime pas ça!
Tu fais …?	Je fais	du judo / du karaté / du skate / du sport.	Je déteste ça!
		de la musique / de la natation.	
		de l'athlétisme / de l'équitation.	
Qu'est-ce que tu portes?	(Je porte)	un chapeau / un jean / un maillot de bain / un pantalon / un short / un sweat.	
		une chemise / une robe.	
		des baskets (f) / des chaussettes (f) / des chaussures (f).	

Grammaire page 187

Using *jouer à*, *jouer de* and *faire de*

■ To talk about playing games, use ***jouer*** + *au / à la / à l' / aux*: *je joue / tu joues au tennis / à la pétanque / aux cartes*.

■ To talk about playing musical instruments, use ***jouer*** + ***du / de la / de l' / des***: *je joue du violon / de la batterie / des percussions*.

■ To talk about other sports or pastimes, use ***faire*** + ***du / de la / de l' / des***: *je fais / tu fais du karaté / de la natation / de l'équitation*.

Also revise negatives.

See page 66 ➡

Stratégie 5

Giving longer answers to questions

Rather than answering questions with just *oui* or *non*, give a fuller picture. If you answer 'yes', say how or why, including an opinion:

– *Tu joues d'un instrument musical?*

– *Oui, je joue du piano et de la guitare. J'adore ça! C'est fantastique!*

If you answer 'no', explain why. Then use *mais* (but) or *par contre* (on the other hand) to expand:

– *Tu fais du sport?*

– *Non, je n'aime pas ça, mais je fais de la musique. Je joue …*

3.1 F Qu'est-ce que tu as fait?

1 **V** Sort these activities into three groups: music, sport, or cinema.

J'ai vu un dessin animé.	J'ai chanté dans une chorale.
J'ai fait de la planche à voile.	J'ai joué du violon.
Je suis arrivé au ciné en bus.	Je suis tombé cinq fois à la patinoire.
J'ai écouté de la musique sur mon lecteur mp3.	J'ai aimé les acteurs.
J'ai acheté les billets.	Je suis rentré du concert à minuit.
J'ai fait du patinage.	Je suis allé au stade.

LES VACANCES DE FÉVRIER

Qu'est-ce que les jeunes de 16 ans ont fait pendant les vacances de février? Nous avons interviewé cinq filles et garçons, qui nous ont donné des réponses très variées.

Alexandre chante dans une chorale, et il a chanté presque tous les jours. Le soir, il est rentré chez lui et il a joué du violon.

Amina est allée quatre fois, à la piscine olympique. À chaque fois, elle a nagé pendant deux heures.

Julie est allée six fois au centre-ville, et elle a vu deux films de guerre, un film romantique et trois films policiers pendant la semaine. Et le soir, elle a regardé des films d'horreur en DVD.

Maxine a fait du cheval en Espagne avec sa sœur. Elle avait peur parce que l'année dernière elle est tombée, mais cette fois il n'y a pas eu de problèmes.

Guillaume a récemment fêté son anniversaire, et il a reçu beaucoup d'argent. Il est allé au centre commercial avec ses copains et il a acheté une nouvelle tablette tactile.

2a 📖🎧 Read the text and write the name of the person who is interested in each of these activities.

1 le cinéma
2 l'informatique
3 l'équitation
4 la musique
5 la natation

2b 📖🎧 Note whether each of these statements is true (**T**), false (**F**) or not mentioned (**?**) in the article.

1 Alexandre played the trumpet every evening.
2 Julie enjoyed the romantic film.
3 Guillaume has recently celebrated his birthday.
4 Amina spent four hours in the water.
5 Maxine went abroad.

3a **G** With a partner, copy the sentences and fill in each gap with the correct part of *avoir* or *être*.

1 Je ___ arrivé à midi.
2 Tu ___ travaillé dans le jardin?
3 Nadine ___ allée au cinéma.
4 Marc ___ fini ses devoirs.

est	a	suis	as

3b **G** Copy the sentences and fill in each gap with the correct past participle.

1 J'ai ___ aux cartes.
2 Est-ce que tu as ___ la télé?
3 Ta sœur est ___ à la patinoire?
4 Il a ___ son anniversaire.

est regardé	tombée	joué	fêté

4a 🎧 Listen to Section A. Marc is talking about last weekend and next weekend. Choose the correct sentence endings.

1 Marc went to the **shopping centre / beach / swimming pool**.
2 He was accompanied by his **parents / friends / grandparents**.
3 Before swimming they watched **football / played sports / sunbathed**.
4 Marc's favourite rugby team **is Toulouse / plays in Toulouse / drew with Toulouse**.
5 Next weekend he's going **to the beach / to see his parents / to Bordeaux**.

4b 🎧 Now listen to Sections A and B. Copy and complete the grid with the activities each speaker mentions. Give as many details as you can.

	last Saturday	last Sunday	next weekend
Marc			
Nadia			

5 ✏️ Write an account of an exciting weekend, including:
- where you went
- who went with you
- at least four activities
- your opinions on how much you enjoyed them.

Samedi dernier	je suis parti(e)	avec mon copain / ma copine / ma famille.
	je suis allé(e)	au concert / à la piscine / à la patinoire.
J'ai trouvé ça	marrant / fantastique / amusant / relaxant.	

Grammaire — *pages 183–184*

The perfect tense with *avoir* and *être* (singular)

You use the perfect tense to describe actions or events that took place in the past. To form the perfect tense, use the present tense of *avoir* and the past participle. With *-er* verbs, the past participle ends in *-é*, with *-ir* verbs it ends in *-i*.

j'ai joué	I played
tu as fini	you finished
il / elle a fait	he / she did

être verbs

The perfect tense of some verbs (especially verbs of movement) is formed with the present tense of *être* instead of *avoir*. The past participle then agrees with the subject of the sentence, e.g. *elle est arrivée* (she arrived / she has arrived).

être	past participle
je suis	*allé(e), arrivé(e), monté(e)*
tu es	*rentré(e), resté(e), tombé(e)*
il / elle est	*parti(e), sorti(e)*

Also revise negatives with the perfect tense.

See page 67 ➡

Stratégie 5

Using the present and perfect tenses together

Use more than one tense in your writing to add interest and gain credit. Contrast what you normally do (present tense) with something different you did in the past (**perfect tense**):

Normalement / D'habitude le week-end, je reste à la maison ou je vais en ville, mais samedi dernier je suis parti(e) à la plage avec mon copain.

⊂⊃ Lien

3.1 Higher is available in the Higher book.

3.2 G Mon argent et mes dépenses

Objectifs

Talking about pocket money and spending

Adjectives before nouns

Memorising numbers

1a 📖 🎧 Read the statements and match each of them with the correct items of clothing (A–H).

MES VÊTEMENTS PRÉFÉRÉS

Pour sortir avec mes copains, j'aime acheter des vêtements chics – une jolie jupe rayée et un petit sweat. **Stéphanie**

Moi, je préfère acheter un jean étroit et un petit tee-shirt pour les fêtes. **Elsa**

Avec mes cinquante euros d'argent de poche, je préfère acheter une belle paire de chaussures bleues pour ma fête d'anniversaire. **Amina**

Pour les grandes vacances, j'aime mieux acheter un petit short, un grand sweat à capuche et des baskets noires. **Jérémie**

Je n'aime pas acheter de vêtements neufs. Le week-end, je préfère porter mon vieux jean large et ma vieille chemise rouge. **Ben**

Pour les fêtes, je préfère acheter une belle robe courte. **Flora**

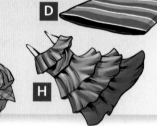

1b 📖 🎧 Read the statements again. Which three sentences below are true?

1 Stéphanie likes long skirts and green sweatshirts.
2 Elsa prefers wearing skinny jeans and a small T-shirt to parties.
3 Amina prefers to spend her money on a pair of trousers for her birthday.
4 Jérémie would rather buy sporty gear.
5 Ben's favourite weekend outfit is his old red shirt and old jeans.
6 Flora prefers a smart, long dress.

2 🇬 Copy the sentences and fill in each gap with the correct form of the adjective in brackets.

1 La _____ fille est trop mince. (**young**)
2 Il a reçu un _____ cadeau. (**small**)
3 Elles n'aiment pas les _____ magasins. (**big**)
4 C'est une assez _____ jupe. (**pretty**)
5 J'adore porter mon _____ short long. (**big**)
6 Elle a une _____ robe noire très chic. (**little**)

Adjectives before nouns

Adjectives usually come after the noun:
*Je préfère acheter un jean **étroit**.*
However, a few come before the noun:
*La **jeune** fille porte une **jolie** jupe.*
Learn the list below of adjectives that come before the noun:

beau / belle	beautiful, nice
grand / grande	big, tall
gros / grosse	big, fat
petit / petite	small, little
jeune	young
joli / jolie	pretty
vieux / vieille	old

Don't forget to add an 's' if the adjective is plural (most of the time – exceptions include e.g. *orange*, *noisette*, *marron*).

Also revise *aimer* and *détester* + infinitive.
See page 66 ➡

Grammaire (*page 175*)

3a 🎧 Listen to the four statements and match each of them with the amount of money mentioned (A–F).

Stratégie 3a

A

B

C

D

E

F

> ### Memorising numbers
>
> Students often lose marks in exams by confusing similar sounding numbers, such as:
>
> *deux / dix / douze*
> *trois / treize / trente*
> *quatre / quatorze / quarante*
> *cinq / quinze / cinquante*
> *seize / soixante*
>
> With a partner, test each other on numbers, counting how many you get right before you make a mistake.

3b 🎧 Listen again and decide whether each speaker's attitude is positive (**P**), negative (**N**) or positive and negative (**P + N**).

4a 💬 Talk about pocket money with your partner. Say:

- how much you receive
- who gives it to you
- what you think about it

> Comme argent de poche, je reçois quinze euros par semaine de mes parents (et je reçois dix euros de mes grands-parents aussi). C'est fantastique!

4b 💬 Now talk about what clothes you prefer to buy.

- Say which items of clothing you prefer to buy.
- Include adjectives of size and colour.
- Say what occasion / time they are for.

> Je préfère acheter des vêtements chics – un grand pantalon noir et un tee-shirt bleu pour ma fête d'anniversaire.

Comme argent de poche, je reçois	quinze euros par mois / quatre euros par semaine.	
Je reçois de l'argent de poche	de mes (grands-)parents / quand je fais du travail.	
C'est assez bien.		
Ça va.		
Ce n'est pas assez / suffisant.		
Pour les fêtes,	j'aime porter	un jean étroit.
Pour mon anniversaire,	je préfère mettre	un vieux jogging.
Le week-end,	j'aime acheter	un grand pantalon.
Quand je suis en vacances,		une jolie robe longue.
		une vieille chemise bleue.
		une petite jupe blanche.
		une belle paire de chaussures noires.

3.2 F Au centre commercial tout est possible!

1 **V** Sort these words into three groups: shopping centre facilities, things to buy or adjectives.

| des jouets | cinquante magasins | des vêtements | gratuit |

| des équipements de sport | un bowling | des machines à laver |

| pratique | un cinéma | nouveau | le parking | énorme |

Un nouveau centre commercial

Venez au nouveau centre commercial Clair-Soleil. Il est moderne, il est pratique, le choix est énorme et les prix sont bas!

Il y a cinq restaurants, un bowling, un cinéma et environ cinquante magasins extrêmement différents: on peut y acheter des équipements de sport, des vêtements, des frigos, des télés, des machines à laver …

Nos clients disent …

Il y a quelque chose pour toute la famille. Il y a même des jouets pour les enfants.

Carole Machin
Tout le monde parle du centre Clair-Soleil! Samedi, je vais y aller avec mon cousin. Je vais acheter un cadeau pour son anniversaire.

N'oubliez pas, pour les automobilistes, le parking est gratuit!

Thomas Deniau
Samedi dernier, je suis allé au nouveau centre commercial Clair-Soleil. C'est fantastique! J'ai pris le bus pour y aller, c'est pratique.

Nadine Lescaut
Je suis allée à Clair-Soleil samedi dernier et j'ai beaucoup aimé le choix de magasins. C'est vraiment super et donc je vais y retourner le week-end prochain.

2a 📖 🎧 Read the information on the poster. Decide whether these statements are true (**T**), false (**F**) or not mentioned in the text (**?**).

1 The prices are high.
2 There are about fifty shops.
3 The centre has a free car park.
4 Thomas went there by car.
5 Nadine liked the choice of restaurants.
6 She wants to go back to the centre.

2b 📖 🎧 Read the poster again. Copy the sentences and fill in each gap with the correct word.

offrir	recevoir
cinémas	magasins
ouvert	raisonnables
hauts	est
a	payant

1 Les prix ne sont pas _____.
2 Il y a un grand choix de _____.
3 Thomas _____ arrivé en bus.
4 Le parking n'est pas _____.
5 Carole va _____ un cadeau à son cousin.

3a 🎧 Six interviewees are talking about money and shopping. Listen to Section A and choose the correct word to complete each sentence.

1 Simon likes buying **books / DVDs / computer games**.
2 Next weekend he wants to buy presents for his **family / friends / girlfriend**.
3 David likes **big department stores / small shops / the market**.
4 He thinks the prices in small shops are **more expensive than / cheaper than / about the same as** bigger shops.
5 Nicolas likes the shopping centre because **there is plenty to do / he never tires of shopping / there are fewer people there**.

3b 🎧 Now listen to Section B and correct the mistakes in these sentences.

1 Laurie receives 20 euros a week pocket money.
2 She buys clothes, make-up and has many pairs of socks.
3 Nathan earns money by washing the windows.
4 He wants to buy himself a new bike.
5 Maude bought a new violin recently.

4 🅖 Copy the sentences and fill in each gap with the correct irregular past participle, choosing from the grammar box.

1 Il a _____ un Coca au McDo du centre commercial.
2 Tu as _____ du shopping au centre-ville?
3 J'ai _____ un bon film au cinéma.
4 J'ai _____ une publicité pour un nouveau magasin de jouets.
5 Elles ont _____ le bus pour aller au marché.
6 J'ai _____ mes nouveaux vêtements.

5 ✏ Write a paragraph for your Facebook page about your pocket money and / or earnings last week and what you spent it on.

▪ Say when you earned or received the money.
▪ Mention who gave you pocket money and how much.
▪ Give your opinion on the money you received.
▪ Say what clothes or other items you bought, where and why.

Exemple: La semaine dernière, j'ai reçu 25 euros d'argent de poche plus 15 euros de mes grands-parents – super! Alors, j'ai acheté des vêtements neufs au centre commercial: un grand sweat rouge et …

Grammaire

The perfect tense with *avoir*: **irregular verbs**

Many verbs have irregular past participles. Copy and learn the table below, making an extra column with English translations.

avoir	past participle
j'ai	eu (avoir)
tu as	lu (lire)
il a	vu (voir)
elle a	mis (mettre)
on a	bu (boire)
nous avons	pris (prendre)
vous avez	reçu (recevoir)
ils / elles ont	fait (faire)

Also learn about irregular *être* verbs in the perfect tense.
See page 67 ➡

page 183

Stratégie 5

Using emphatic language

Add weight to your opinions by using short, punchy expressions with exclamation marks to show how strongly you feel:

C'est super / fantastique / bien / moche, ça!

Je n'aime pas ça, moi!

Ça, c'est bien!

Lien

3.2 Higher is available in the Higher book.

3.3 G Vieille technologie ou nouvelle technologie?

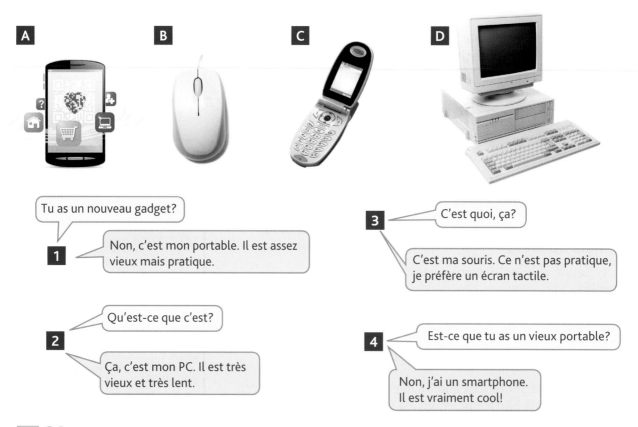

A **B** **C** **D**

Tu as un nouveau gadget?

1 Non, c'est mon portable. Il est assez vieux mais pratique.

3 C'est quoi, ça?

C'est ma souris. Ce n'est pas pratique, je préfère un écran tactile.

Qu'est-ce que c'est?

2 Ça, c'est mon PC. Il est très vieux et très lent.

4 Est-ce que tu as un vieux portable?

Non, j'ai un smartphone. Il est vraiment cool!

1a 📖🎧 Read the four conversations and match them with the illustrations.

1b 📖🎧 Now list the advantages and disadvantages of each piece of technology mentioned.

Exemple: **1** *Mobile phone: quite old, …*

2a 🎧 Listen to the four statements and match them with the devices shown.

A **B** **C** SmartTV **D**

2b 🎧 Listen again and decide whether the comments are positive (**P**), negative (**N**) or positive and negative (**P + N**).

3 Ⓖ Copy the sentences and fill in each gap with *ça*, *ce* or *c'*. Then match each sentence to the correct English translation.

1 _____ n'est pas très cher!
2 _____ n'est pas pratique!
3 _____ va?
4 _____ est trop cher.
5 Tu aimes _____?
6 _____ ne va pas!

a Are you OK?
b Do you like it?
c It's not going well!
d That's not practical!
e That's too expensive.
f It's not very expensive!

4 💬 In groups, play 'Pass the gadget!'

- Student A names a gadget.
- Student B repeats the name of the gadget and adds a detail about it.
- Student C repeats what Student B has said, adding another detail, and so on around the group.

If you get right round your group, add a second gadget and carry on!

Exemple:

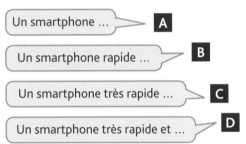

Un smartphone ... **A**

Un smartphone rapide ... **B**

Un smartphone très rapide ... **C**

Un smartphone très rapide et ... **D**

Tu as un nouveau gadget?		
Qu'est-ce que c'est / C'est quoi, ça?		
C'est	mon	smartphone / portable / ordinateur portable.
	ma	tablette / ma télé connectée.
C'est	assez pratique / très rapide / vraiment fantastique, mais ça coûte trop cher.	
Mon PC / portable / ordinateur portable	est	un peu lourd / très lent / trop vieux.

Grammaire page 180

Saying 'it' and 'that': *ce* and *ça*

Ce means 'this', 'that', 'those' or 'it', and it is usually followed by a form of *être*. It is shortened to *c'* in front of a vowel.

C'est une tablette. – It's / That's a tablet computer.

Ce sont des gadgets. – Those are gadgets.

Ça is used in various phrases:

Ça va? – Are you OK?

Ça, c'est mon smartphone. – That's my smartphone.

Tu aimes ça? – Do you like it?

Also learn about asking questions with *est-ce que* and *qu'est-ce que*.

See page 66 ➡

Stratégie 4

Adding impact to questions and statements

Remember to use intensifiers (*assez, vraiment, très, trop, un peu*) with adjectives to sharpen the focus of statements and questions: *Le gadget est assez moderne ou très vieux?*

3.3 F On peut communiquer plus facilement

1 Sort these words into three groups: *cinéma*, *TV* or *Internet / en ligne*. Then give your opinion using *j'adore les …* (love), *je déteste les …* (hate), or *les …, ça m'est égal* (indifference).

un feuilleton   un forum   un film policier   un podcast

un tweet   un film de science-fiction   un documentaire   un jeu télévisé

une page Web   une émission sportive   un film d'horreur   un film de guerre

Technomec
Je garde le contact avec mes copains et ma famille au portable et sur Internet. C'est plus rapide au portable d'envoyer des textos en train, en bus, en ville, partout. Franchement, je trouve Facebook plus intéressant pour communiquer – on peut publier des photos, des clips et des documents sans problème. Je sais qu'il y a certains dangers, mais je fais bien attention: je ne révèle pas trop de données personnelles sur mon profil Facebook.

Logicielle
Je suis d'accord avec toi, Technomec. Les textos par portable sont plus rapides (et moins chers qu'un appel!), mais j'ai horreur des réseaux sociaux comme Facebook. Franchement, je trouve que tout le monde révèle des données personnelles trop facilement. C'est dangereux pour les victimes éventuelles, par exemple les jeunes filles innocentes. Il faut faire attention quand on utilise la technologie!

Supertweeter
Je te comprends, Logicielle. Un de mes copains a dit une bêtise sur son compte Twitter – il a exprimé ses opinions politiques un peu extrêmes. On l'a accusé d'inciter au terrorisme et au racisme. Quel idiot! Mais, comme toi, Technomec, même si la confidentialité est menacée, je trouve que Facebook est plus pratique pour contacter et informer ses copains et ses parents.

2 📖 🎧 Read the three forum texts. Which four sentences below are true?

1 Technomec thinks texting is more interesting than communicating on Facebook.

2 He limits the personal information he discloses on Facebook.

3 Logicielle agrees totally with Technomec.

4 She worries about internet stalkers preying on young people.

5 She doesn't mind giving her personal details on Facebook.

6 Supertweeter finds Logicielle's views a bit on the extreme side.

7 He is not very sympathetic towards his friend, who was accused of inciting racism.

8 He still prefers to use social networks, despite the dangers.

3a 🎧 Listen to the four statements and match them with the illustrations.

A

B

C ✗

✓

D

3b 🎧 Listen again and decide whether the statements are positive (**P**), negative (**N**) or positive and negative (**P + N**).

4 **G** With a partner, make these sentences comparative by completing them with a word that matches your opinion: *plus*, *moins* or *aussi*. Say if you agree or disagree with your partner's opinion (*c'est vrai / je ne suis pas d'accord*).

Exemple: La radio est <u>plus</u> amusante que le cinéma.

1   Les télés connectées sont ____ pratiques que les ordinateurs.
2   La lecture est ____ amusante que la musique.
3   Les textos sont ____ faciles que les e-mails.
4   Les tablettes sont ____ utiles que les portables.
5   Les films romantiques sont ____ intéressants que les films d'horreur.
6   La musique est ____ relaxante que le sport.

5 🖉 With a partner, prepare statements for an online debate about the advantages and disadvantages of communication technology. One of you loves new technology, the other dislikes it.

- Pourquoi tu utilises un portable / Internet / les réseaux sociaux comme Facebook?
- Quels sont les avantages?
- Quels sont les inconvénients?

On peut	garder le contact avec les copains / la famille. envoyer des textos. publier des photos / clips / vidéos / documents.
C'est plus intéressant pour communiquer / informer.	
On révèle des données personnelles trop facilement.	
C'est l'ennemi de la vie privée / des victimes potentielles.	
On peut dire des bêtises.	
Il faut faire attention à la technologie.	

Comparative adjectives

Grammaire page 176

Use the words *plus*, *moins* or *aussi* (as), followed by an adjective, then *que* and the thing you are comparing.

La télé est moins utile qu'Internet. – TV is less useful than the internet.

C'est plus pratique. – It's more practical.

Two exceptions are: *meilleur* (better) and *pire* (worse).

Les films téléchargés sont meilleurs que les DVD. – Downloaded films are better than DVDs.

Les émissions de télé sont pires que la publicité. – TV programmes are worse than the adverts.

Also learn about using *on* to say 'we' or 'people'.   *See page 67* ➡

Justifying opinions

Stratégie 5

When you have given your opinion, it is a good idea to give a reason why you hold that view. Useful phrases for adding a reason are *parce que / car / pour cette raison / à cause de cela.* So if you say something like *les réseaux sociaux sont dangereux*, you could add *parce que la confidentialité est menacée.*

 **Lien**

3.3 Higher is available in the Higher book.

G   Free time and the media

1 Copy the sentences and fill in each gap with the correct word to make the sentence negative.

1 Tu _____ joues pas samedi?
2 Tu _____ aimes _____ la natation?
3 Nadia ne fait _____ d'équitation.
4 Amélie _____ joue pas _____ instrument musical.
5 Théo _____ adore _____ le sport.
6 Je _____ fais _____ _____ musique.

| ne | n' | pas | de | d' |

Using negatives (revision)

Remember, negative expressions such as *ne … pas, ne … plus, ne … rien, ne … que, ne … ni … ni* and *ne … jamais* fit around the verb:

Je n'aime pas ça!   I don't like that!

Tu ne joues plus? Aren't you playing any more?

After these negatives, you need to use *de* before the noun, instead of *du, de la, de l'* or *des*:

Tu fais du sport?   Do you do sport?

Non, je ne fais pas de sport? No, I don't do sport.

Grammaire *page 188*

---

2 Copy the sentences and fill in each gap with the correct word from the list (a–h).

1 Je n'aime pas _____ une robe le soir.
2 Tu _____ acheter un sweat ou un tee-shirt?
3 J'_____ mieux porter mes vieilles baskets.
4 Je _____ le look sportif: short, sweat et baskets.
5 Nathalie aime _____ porter un jean étroit.

a	aime	b	déteste	c	préfères
d	mieux	e	acheter	f	préfère
g	porter	h	n'aimes pas

Aimer and *détester* + infinitive

When *j'aime, je déteste, je préfère* or *j'aime mieux* is followed by a verb, the second verb is in the infinitive.

J'aime porter des robes. – I like wearing dresses.

Je déteste faire les magasins. – I hate shopping.

Je préfère aller à la patinoire. – I prefer going ice skating.

J'aime mieux acheter des baskets. – I'd rather buy trainers.

Grammaire *page 181*

3a Work with a partner to turn statements 1–3 into questions, first using intonation, then using *Est-ce que* or *Est-ce qu'*.

1 Tu as un smartphone.
2 Il est très rapide.
3 La télé connectée coûte trop cher.

3b Now copy questions 4–6 and fill in each gap with *Est-ce que, Est-ce qu', Qu'est-ce que* or *Qu'est-ce qu'*.

4 _____ tu achètes au centre commercial?
5 _____ la tablette est plus grande que le smartphone?
6 _____ elle est vraiment rapide?

Asking questions with *est-ce que* and *qu'est-ce que*

In French, you can make a statement into a question through intonation (using your voice). You can also change statements into questions by adding *est-ce que* (or *qu'* before a vowel) at the beginning of the sentence and a question mark at the end.

Statements:

C'est ton portable.   That's your mobile.

Il est pratique.   It's practical.

Questions:

C'est ton portable?   Is that your mobile?

Est-ce qu'il est pratique? Is it practical?

The French equivalent of 'What …' is usually *Qu'est-ce que …?*

Qu'est-ce que c'est?   What is it?

Qu'est-ce que tu veux?   What do you want?

Grammaire *page 188*

4 Rewrite these jumbled sentences with the words in the correct order.

1 Je / sortie /ne / pas / suis / hier soir
2 n' / pas / a / fait / Elle / les courses
3 n' / pas / Il / a / trouvé / ça amusant
4 n' / Tu / es / pas / tombé / sur la glace
5 à la maison / es / Tu / n' / resté / pas
6 n' / au tennis / joué / pas / ai / Je

Negatives with the perfect tense

To make a negative statement in the perfect tense, *ne / n'* comes before the form of *avoir / être* and *pas* comes straight after.

Il a regardé la télé. — He watched TV.
Il n'a pas regardé la télé. — He didn't watch TV.
Je suis sorti. — I went out.
Je ne suis pas sorti. — I didn't go out.

Grammaire · page 188

5a Copy sentences 1–4 and fill in each gap with the correct part of *être*.

1 Je _____ revenu au centre commercial à pied.
2 Il _____ mort à l'âge de quatre-vingt-cinq ans.
3 Ils _____ nés samedi dernier.
4 Tu _____ venue toute seule, Alice?

5b Now copy sentences 5–8 and fill in each gap with the correct past participle from the grammar box.

5 Elle est _____ en avril. Son anniversaire est le vingt-cinq, je crois. (**naître**)
6 Il est _____ célèbre grâce à la mode. (**devenir**)
7 Elles sont _____ au centre en bus. (**venir**)
8 Vous êtes _____ à quelle heure, Marc et Ben? (**revenir**)

The perfect tense with *être*: irregular verbs

Some of the *être* verbs have irregular past participles:

English	infinitive	past participle
to come	*venir*	*venu*
to become	*devenir*	*devenu*
to come back	*revenir*	*revenu*
to be born	*naître*	*né*
to die	*mourir*	*mort*

Remember, with all *être* verbs the past participle ending agrees with the subject (*je, tu*, etc.) in gender (masculine or feminine) and number (singular or plural):

– *Tu es née où, Amina?*

– *Je suis née à Paris, mais mes parents sont nés au Maroc.*

Grammaire · page 183

6 Replace each infinitive with the correct form of the verb. In each case, note whether *on* means 'we' or the impersonal 'you' / 'people'.

1 Qu'est-ce qu'on faire ce soir?
2 On regarder un film ensemble, si tu veux.
3 Est-ce qu'on pouvoir se faire des amis sur Internet?
4 On dire que les téléphones portables sont dangereux, mais on ne savoir pas vraiment.
5 Si on rester trop longtemps devant son ordinateur, on avoir mal aux yeux.
6 On sortir ? On aller où?

Using *on* to say 'we' or 'people'

Most French people use *on* to mean 'we' in casual speech:

On sort ce soir. – We are going out tonight.

On can also be the equivalent of 'people' or 'they' or the impersonal 'you':

On dit que c'est bien. – People say it is good.

Comment dit-on 'computer' en français? – How do you say 'computer' in French?

On peut communiquer plus facilement. – You can communicate more easily.

On is followed by the same verb ending as *il / elle*. Check the verb tables on pages 193–197 if you are unsure of the endings.

Grammaire · page 178

Free time and the media

Topic 3.1 Free time activities (at home and away)

3.1 G Mes passe-temps et mes vêtements
➡ *pages 54–55*

l'	*athlétisme (m)*	athletics
les	*baskets (f)*	trainers
	blanc(he)	white
	bleu(e)	blue
les	*chaussettes (f)*	socks
les	*chaussures (f)*	shoes
la	*chemise*	shirt
	détester	to hate
l'	*équitation (f)*	horse riding
	faire de la natation	to go swimming
	faire du sport	to do sport
	jouer à la pétanque	to play (French) bowls
	jouer au basket	to play basketball
	jouer aux échecs	to play chess
	jouer de la batterie	to play the drums
le	*maillot de bain*	swimsuit
	marron	brown
l'	*orchestre (m)*	band, orchestra
le	*pantalon*	trousers
	par contre	on the other hand
	porter	to wear
la	*robe*	dress
le	*short*	shorts
le	*sweat(shirt)*	sweatshirt
la	*voile*	sailing

3.1 F Qu'est-ce que tu as fait? ➡ *pages 56–57*

	à chaque fois	each time
	apprécier	to appreciate
	avoir peur	to be afraid
	barbant(e)	tedious, boring
la	*chorale*	choir
le	*dessin animé*	cartoon
l'	*écran (m)*	screen, monitor
	ennuyeux(-euse)	boring

	faire du cheval	to go horseriding
	fatigant(e)	tiring
	fêter	to celebrate
les	*films de guerre (m)*	war films
les	*films policiers (m)*	thrillers
les	*films romantiques (m)*	romantic films
l'	*informatique (f)*	ICT, computer studies
	intitulé(e)	entitled
	marrant(e)	funny
le	*patinage*	ice skating
la	*patinoire*	ice skating rink
	pendant deux heures	for two hours
la	*piscine*	swimming pool
la	*planche à voile*	windsurfing
	recevoir	to receive, to get
	rester	to stay
le	*violon*	violin

Topic 3.2 Shopping, money, fashion, trends

3.2 G Mon argent et mes dépenses
➡ *pages 58–59*

l'	*argent de poche (m)*	pocket money
	assez	enough
	ça va	it's okay / alright
	chic	smart
	cinquante	fifty
	la fête	celebration, festival
les	*grandes vacances (f)*	summer holidays
	j'aime mieux	I prefer
le	*jean étroit*	skinny jeans
la	*jupe rayée*	striped skirt
	mince	thin, slim
la	*paire*	pair
le	*pantalon large*	baggy trousers
	quarante	forty
	soixante	sixty
	suffisant(e)	enough, sufficient
le	*sweat à capuche*	hoodie

| les | vêtements neufs (m) | new clothes |
| | vieux / vieille | old |

3.2 F Au centre commercial tout est possible!
➡ *pages 60–61*

l'	automobiliste (m)	motorist
	c'est payant	you have to pay
le	choix	choice
le	client	customer
	devenir	to become
	donc	so, therefore
	énorme	huge, enormous
l'	équipement de sport (m)	sports equipment
	extrêmement	extremely
	gratuit(e)	free
le	jouet	toy
la	machine à laver	washing machine
le	magasin	shop
	moche	rubbish! / no good!
	mourir	to die
	naître	to be born
	nouveau / nouvelle	new
	offrir un cadeau	to give a present / gift
le	parking	car park
	pratique	practical, convenient
les	prix bas (m)	low prices
	prochain(e)	next
	tout le monde	everybody
	y	there

Topic 3.3 Advantages and disadvantages of new technology

3.3 G Vieille technologie ou nouvelle technologie? ➡ *pages 62–63*

	assez	quite, fairly
	c'est quoi, ça?	what is that?
	ça coûte	that costs
	cher(ère)	dear, expensive
l'	écran tactile (m)	touch screen
le	gadget	gadget
	lent(e)	slow
	lourd(e)	heavy

	moderne	modern, up-to-date
l'	ordinateur (m)	computer
l'	ordinateur portable (m)	laptop
	rapide	fast, speedy
la	souris	mouse
la	tablette	tablet computer
la	télé connectée	smart TV
le	(téléphone) portable	mobile (phone)
	très	very
	trop	too (much)
	un peu	a bit
	vraiment	really

3.3 F On peut communiquer plus facilement
➡ *pages 64–65*

la	bêtise	something stupid
	communiquer	to communicate
la	confidentialité menacée	confidentiality threatened
le	documentaire	(TV) documentary
les	données personnelles (f)	personal details
l'	émission sportive (f)	(TV) sports programme
l'	ennemi (m)	enemy
	exprimer	to express
le	feuilleton	TV soap (opera)
les	films d'horreur (m)	horror films
les	films de science-fiction (m)	science-fiction films
	franchement	frankly
	garder le contact	to keep in touch
	il faut faire attention	you need to be careful
	inciter	to stir up, incite
le	podcast	podcast
le	jeu télévisé	TV game
	naïf(-ve)	naive, unsuspecting
	partout	everywhere
le	réseau social	social network
	révéler	to reveal, disclose
	sinon	if not, otherwise
les	textos (m)	text messages
la	victime éventuelle	potential victim

4.1 G Deux villes à visiter

Objectifs

Places in town

How to say 'to the ...' or 'at the ...'

Improving your writing

1 **V** Find the odd one out in each list.

A
- une boulangerie
- une pâtisserie
- une librairie
- une boucherie

B
- un stade
- un musée
- une piscine
- une patinoire

C
- un restaurant
- un hôtel de ville
- une poste
- un office de tourisme

Sophie

J'habite une petite ville près de Bordeaux qui est célèbre pour le vin. Les touristes viennent ici pour visiter les caves à vin. Il y a aussi quelques petits magasins dans le centre, par exemple, une boucherie, une boulangerie et une poste, mais le supermarché est à dix kilomètres de la ville. Le soir, pour les visiteurs, il y a deux restaurants, mais pour voir un film au cinéma, il faut aller à Bordeaux. Pour les sportifs, il n'y a pas de piscine dans la ville. Il y a un stade de foot, mais c'est tout.

Éric

Moi, j'habite à Rouen. C'est une grande ville touristique et il y a un office de tourisme près de l'hôtel de ville. Les touristes descendent des cars sur le parking pour visiter la cathédrale, le musée et les restaurants. Si on aime la musique, il y a souvent des concerts au théâtre. Il y a aussi un bon centre commercial, et on peut acheter des souvenirs et des livres dans les boutiques et les petites librairies.

2a 📖 🎧 Read the texts. Which four of these places are there in Sophie's town?

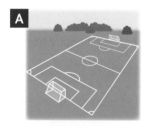

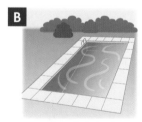

2b 📖 🗨 Work with a partner. Partner A asks whether Rouen has each of these places. Partner B gives the answer according to the places Éric mentions / doesn't mention in his text. Then swap parts.

> Est-ce qu'il y a un hôtel?

> Non, il n' y a pas d'hôtel.

a hotel	a town hall	a cathedral
a bookshop	a library	a tourist office
a theatre	a sports centre

3a 🎧 Listen to Section A. Which five places do the speakers say they do <u>not</u> have in their town or village? Note them down in English.

3b 🎧 Listen to Section B. Choose the correct place from the list for each speaker's activity.

| le théâtre | la patinoire | la station-service |
| la confiserie | le cinéma | la gare | la pâtisserie |

4 Ⓖ Copy the sentences and fill in each gap with *au*, *à la*, *à l'* or *aux*.

1 Il va loger _____ hôtel au centre-ville.
2 Est-ce que tu vas _____ magasins samedi?
3 Je fais mes achats _____ hypermarché.
4 J'achète mes légumes _____ marché.
5 Achète-moi des timbres _____ poste, s'il te plaît.
6 Nous allons acheter du saucisson _____ charcuterie.
7 Sylvie travaille _____ hospital.
8 Il y a un match de rugby _____ stade.

5 ✏ Write a short description of a town or village (real or imaginary) that is visited by tourists. Describe the facilities, and say what there is and isn't in the town.

À Édimbourg / Stratford / Springfield, il y a ...	un	marché / cinéma / restaurant / café / bar / hôtel / office de tourisme ...
Il y a aussi ...	une	piscine / église / station-service ...
	des	magasins ...
Il n'y a pas de ...		
Beaucoup de touristes aiment aller au / à la / à l' / aux ...		

> **Grammaire** *page 189*
>
> **How to say 'to the ...' or 'at the ...'**
>
> Use *au / à la / à l' / aux* to introduce the name of the place you are going to or the place where you are:
>
> *Je vais au cinéma.*
>
> *Tu vas à la patinoire.*
>
> *Elle travaille à l'hôtel de ville.*
>
> *Nous allons aux magasins.*
>
> Also learn how to say 'from the ...'
> *See page 82* ➡

> **Stratégie 5**
>
> **Improving your writing**
>
> Improve your writing grade by using negatives, e.g. *Il n'y a pas de piscine. Il n'y a pas d'hôtels. Je ne vais pas au stade.*
>
> For help with the rules on the use of negatives, see Topic 1.3 G on page 24.

4.1 F Vive les vacances!

Objectifs
Holiday choices
How to say 'to' or 'in' a country
Using language that you know

1 **V** Choose the odd one out in each set.

1 le ski nautique   la voile   la natation   la promenade en bateau   le cyclisme

2 la Chine   la France   le Portugal   la Russie   la Belgique

3 la montagne   la plage   le ski   les sports d'hiver   la neige

4 le pique-nique   le camping   l'hôtel   le logement   la villa

5 la cuisine   les glaces   le pique-nique   le restaurant   le bord de la mer

Sondage: les vacances que je préfère …

77% des Français aiment passer leurs vacances au bord de la mer, comme Valérie …

«Je pars en vacances avec ma famille. Tous les ans, on va au bord de la mer, pas loin de Bordeaux. J'adore bronzer sur la plage et nager dans la mer. L'année dernière, il faisait trop chaud.»

35% aiment passer des vacances à la campagne, comme Églantine …

«Moi, j'aime les vacances à la campagne parce que j'adore le calme et l'air est pur. Ma famille a passé des vacances en France. Mon père veut aller au Portugal mais il fait trop chaud, je crois. J'aime faire des promenades en forêt avec mes parents; j'aime aussi faire des pique-niques dans la nature. Je n'aime pas aller au bord de la mer en été car je trouve qu'il y a trop de monde sur les plages et on dit que bronzer est mauvais pour la santé.»

23% aiment partir à l'étranger, comme Guillaume …

«J'aime partir à l'étranger parce que je veux connaître des cultures différentes. La plage, ça va, mais j'aime surtout rester dans une grande ville parce que j'adore visiter les musées et les monuments historiques. L'année dernière, je suis allé en Angleterre et j'ai visité Londres. Il y avait beaucoup de choses à faire et c'était vraiment intéressant mais malheureusement il a fait mauvais presque tous les jours.»

57% aiment les sports d'hiver, comme Safina …

«Je n'aime pas partir au mois d'août, pendant les grandes vacances, parce qu'il fait souvent trop chaud. Je préfère partir à la montagne pour faire du ski. Quand je suis en vacances, j'aime me relaxer. J'aime partir avec mes amies parce que j'ai plus de liberté. Je ne m'entends pas bien avec mes parents. L'année prochaine, je voudrais aller aux États-Unis, à New York.»

2a 📖 🎧 Read the report and choose the photo that best fits each speaker's preferred holiday.

2b 📖 🎧 Read the report again. Who says the following?

1 I love peace and quiet.

2 I like sunbathing.

3 I'm interested in foreign culture.

4 Sunbathing is bad for you.

5 I think it is important to relax on holiday.

Coping with longer reading passages

Don't be put off if there are a number of words that you don't know in longer texts. Read the questions first so you can scan for the words you need. Then you can focus on these in order to complete the activity.

Stratégie 2b

3a 🎧 Listen to five people describing the holidays they like and their last holiday. Choose the correct accommodation (a–f) for each speaker (1–5). There is an extra option that you will not need.

a   a hotel by the sea.
b   a cottage in the country
c   a cottage by a lake

d   a chalet in the mountains
e   a youth hostel in city
f   camping in the mountains

3b 🎧 Listen again. Which three sentences are true?

1   Chloë went water skiing in Portugal.
2   Martin went sailing on a lake in the mountains.
3   Thérèse hired a boat in the Loire Valley.

4   Thierry went skiing with his brother.
5   Fabienne went to Brussels with her sister.
6   She likes to go sightseeing and shopping.

4 🇬 Copy the sentences and fill in each gap with *en*, *au*, *aux* or *à*.

1   Je veux aller _____ États-Unis.
2   Mes grands-parents habitent _____ Canada.
3   Je vais faire du shopping _____ New York.
4   Cette année, je vais _____ Rome _____ Italie.
5   En juillet, je suis allé _____ pays de Galles.
6   Je voudrais aller _____ Caraïbes.

How to say 'to' or 'in' a country

If you want to say 'to' or 'in' a country in French, you need to know the gender of the country. Feminine countries (*la France, l'Angleterre, l'Espagne*) take *en*.

Masculine countries (*le Portugal, le Canada*) take *au*. If the country is plural (*les États-Unis*) use *aux*. Cities take *à*.

Je vais à Londres.   I am going to London.

Also learn how to recognise some useful verbs in the imperfect tense.

See page 83 ➡

Grammaire *page 190*

---

5 🗨 Work with a partner. Prepare answers to the following questions, then take turns to ask and answer. Give reasons for your answers.

◼ Où est-ce que tu aimes partir en vacances? Pourquoi?
◼ Quelle sorte de logement préfères-tu?
◼ Qu'est-ce que tu aimes faire en vacances?
◼ Tu aimes mieux partir en vacances en famille ou avec des amis? Pourquoi?
◼ Où es-tu parti(e) l'année dernière?
◼ Comment sont tes vacances idéales? Pourquoi?

J'aime partir en Espagne	parce qu'il y fait chaud.
J'aime aller en vacances avec ma famille	parce que je m'entends bien avec mes frères.
Je préfère loger dans un hôtel.	
En vacances, j'aime aller à la plage pour bronzer et nager.	
Pour mes vacances idéales, je voudrais partir en Chine.	
L'année dernière, je suis allé(e) dans le nord de l'Espagne.	C'était vraiment intéressant.

Using language that you know

When speaking French in the exam, avoid guessing at words you do not know. Use what you are sure is correct. If you are talking about holidays, for example, and you stayed in a campsite but you forget the French for 'campsite', it is better to say *j'ai logé dans un hôtel* (I stayed in a hotel) rather than making up a word that may be incorrect.

Stratégie 5

Où est-ce que tu aimes partir en vacances? Pourquoi?

J'aime partir en Espagne parce qu'il fait chaud. Et toi?

 Lien

4.1 Higher is available in the Higher book.

4.2 G   C'est où?

Objectifs

Points of the compass and directions

Asking the way

Speaking politely

1a 📖 🎧 Look at the map and decide which three statements are true. Correct the false statements.

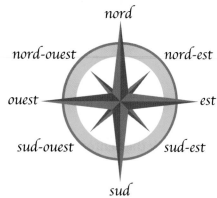

1   Calais est dans le sud de la France.
2   Bruxelles est dans le centre de la Belgique.
3   Marseille est dans le sud de la France.

4   Genève est dans l'est de la Suisse.
5   Bordeaux est dans le sud-est de la France.
6   Rennes est dans le nord-ouest de la France.

1b 📖 🎧 Find the correct sketch map for each dialogue.

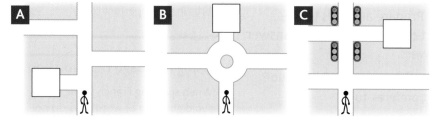

1
– Pour aller à l'hôtel de ville, s'il vous plaît?
– Allez jusqu'au rond-point, puis continuez tout droit.

2
– Où est le stade, s'il vous plaît?
– Tournez à droite aux feux.

3
– Où est le marché, s'il vous plaît?
– Prenez la première rue à gauche.

2 **G** Copy the sentences and fill in each gap with *le, la, les, au, à la* or *à l'*.

1   Excusez-moi, monsieur, où est _____ boulangerie?
2   Excusez-moi, madame, pour aller _____ église, s'il vous plaît?
3   Pardon, monsieur, pour aller _____ stade, s'il vous plaît?
4   Pardon, mademoiselle, où sont _____ toilettes?
5   Excusez-moi, madame, pour aller _____ poste?
6   Pardon, monsieur, où est _____ terrain de camping?

Asking the way

There are two ways of asking for directions in French:

1 Use *Où est …* (Where is) or *Où sont …* (Where are)

Où est la banque? – Where is the bank?

Où sont les courts de tennis? – Where are the tennis courts?

2 *Pour aller à …*

Pour aller à la gare? – Where is the station?

Remember to use the correct form of *au, à la, à l'* or *aux* with this form of question.

Also learn 'first', 'second', 'third', etc.   *See page 82* ➡

Grammaire

3a 🎧 Listen to Section A. Complete the English sentences with the correct point of the compass.

1 Marcel is going to a holiday village in the _____ of Belgium.
2 Angélique goes to stay with her grandparents in the _____ of France.
3 Ibrahim is going to a resort on the _____ coast of Morocco.
4 Julie is going to a village in the _____ of France.

3b 🎧 Listen to Section B. Match the places with the correct directions in English.

1 Post office
2 Cathedral
3 Railway station
4 Supermarket

a Left at the lights, and it is on the right.
b First left, and it is on the right near the lights.
c Right at the roundabout, then straight on.
d Right at the lights, then second left.

4 🗨 Work with a partner. Partner A asks the way to one of the places on the plan below and Partner B gives directions. Then swap parts.

> **Speaking politely**
>
> If you need to ask a stranger for help or for directions, remember to always use *vous*, and to start and end the conversation politely.
>
> Start your question with *Excusez-moi / Pardon, monsieur / madame / mademoiselle* and end it with *s'il vous plaît*. Don't forget to say *merci* at the end.
>
> *Stratégie 4*

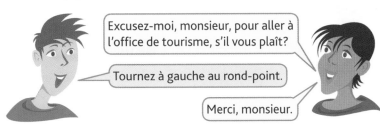

Excusez-moi, monsieur, pour aller à l'office de tourisme, s'il vous plaît?

Tournez à gauche au rond-point.

Merci, monsieur.

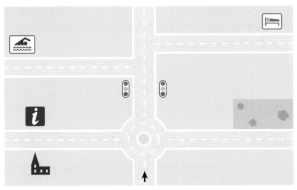

Pardon, Excusez moi,	monsieur / madame / mademoiselle,	pour aller	à l'	hôtel / office de tourisme / église,	s'il vous plaît?
		où est	au	parc,	
			à la	piscine,	
			l'hôtel / l'office de tourisme / l'église / la piscine / le parc,		
Tournez	à gauche / à droite		aux feux.		
			au rond-point.		
Allez	jusqu'aux feux		puis	tournez à gauche / à droite.	
	jusqu'au rond-point			continuez tout droit.	

4.2 F Que faire en vacances?

1 **V** Sort these words into three groups: seaside activities, places to stay or sporting facilities.

se baigner   un centre d'escalade   une colonie de vacances   des pistes cyclables

une patinoire   un dortoir   un gîte   faire de la voile   bronzer

A
L'été dernier, j'ai passé une semaine avec mes amis dans une auberge de jeunesse, près des gorges du Verdon dans le sud de la France. Nous avons fait de l'escalade et du canoë-kayak, et le vendredi nous avons fait une randonnée de 20 kilomètres! Le soir, on a mangé dans le village ou à l'auberge. Nous avons partagé un dortoir avec des garçons d'Allemagne et de Belgique. C'était super mais fatigant!

B
L'année prochaine, je pars en vacances en octobre. Je vais aller dans les montagnes du Maroc où il fait beau en automne, mais très chaud en été. Je vais faire une longue randonnée guidée avec mes amis. Des poneys vont porter nos bagages et nous allons faire du camping dans de petits villages. Nous devons acheter des provisions en route et préparer les repas. Je n'aime pas faire la cuisine!

Marcel, 17 ans

C
L'année dernière, je suis allée à Biarritz avec ma famille. Nous avons logé dans un petit hôtel près de la plage. J'ai fait du surf avec mon frère, et nous avons joué au volley-ball sur la plage. Ma mère aime se baigner et mon père fait de la voile. Des vacances idéales pour toute la famille!

Patricia, 14 ans

D
L'été prochain, je vais en colonie de vacances avec mes amis. La colonie est située à la campagne, près d'une rivière. Nous allons faire des promenades à vélo dans la forêt où il y a beaucoup de pistes cyclables. Le jeudi, nous allons visiter un parc d'attractions dans la région. Nous allons loger dans de petits chalets pour quatre personnes. Les repas sont servis dans un restaurant près des chalets. J'espère qu'il va faire beau!

2a 📖 🎧 Choose a suitable heading for paragraphs A, B, C and D from the list (1–6).

1 Hiking in North Africa
2 A holiday camp in the countryside
3 A holiday at home
4 Adventure activities in the south of France
5 Sightseeing in the city
6 A family holiday by the sea

2b 📖 🎧 Complete these sentences in English.

1 Marcel went _____ and canoeing in the *gorges du Verdon*.
2 He shared a dormitory with people from _____ and Belgium.
3 He will go to Morocco in the month of _____ .
4 Patricia's father likes _____ .
5 Next summer she will go _____ in the forest.
6 She will also visit a _____ .

Past and future time expressions

Spot the difference … When reading or listening about the things that happened at different times, be careful not to get confused between *dernier* (last), followed by past tense verbs, and *prochain* (next) followed by verbs in the future tense.

Stratégie 2a–2b

3 🅖 Copy the sentences and fill in each gap with the correct form of the verb in brackets. Look carefully at the clues at the beginning, which will help you to decide.

1   Tous les ans, je _____ en vacances en Normandie. (**aller**)
2   Il y a deux ans, nous _____ la Bretagne. (**visiter**)
3   L'année prochaine, je _____ une chambre familiale avec demi-pension. (**réserver**)
4   Hier, les enfants _____ une promenade à vélo. (**faire**)
5   La semaine dernière, nous _____ dans une grande villa. (**loger**)
6   Dans deux ans, je _____ aux États-Unis. (**voyager**)

4a 🎧 Listen to Section A. Lucas is describing his plans for a visit to Bordeaux. In what order does he mention the activities shown?

4b 🎧 Listen to Isabelle in Section B. Which three sentences are true?

1   Isabelle went away in the summer.
2   She loves winter sports.
3   Her parents went with her to stay with her uncle.
4   Her uncle lives in a small village in the mountains.
5   He owns a chalet.
6   She went skiing with her cousin.
7   One day she went ice skating.

5 ✏ Write an account of last year's holiday and your plans for this year (real or imaginary). Include information about the destination, accommodation and activities. Give your opinion.

PAST		FUTURE	
L'année dernière,	je suis allé(e) … avec …	Cette année,	je vais aller / loger …
L'été dernier,	j'ai logé dans …	L'été prochain,	
D'abord, / Puis, / Le lendemain,	j'ai fait / joué / visité / mangé …	Au début, / Ensuite, / Après ça,	je voudrais faire / jouer / visiter …
C'étaient les vacances les plus amusantes / relaxantes / ennuyeuses de ma vie.		J'espère passer des vacances sportives / intéressantes / relaxantes.	

Grammaire pages 182–185

Perfect, present and immediate future tenses

Learn how to use verbs in the perfect, present and future tenses.

J'ai visité l'Italie. – I visited Italy.

Je visite l'Italie. – I am visiting / I visit Italy.

Je vais visiter l'Italie. – I am going to visit Italy.

Faire* and *aller

j'ai fait > je fais > je vais faire

je suis allé > je vais > je vais aller

Also learn about using *faire* and *jouer* for past and future activities.   *See page 83* ➡

Stratégie 5

Expressions of sequence

When you are writing in the past or future tenses, use adverbs to structure what you want to say.

D'abord and *au début* both mean 'first' or 'at the beginning'. *Ensuite* and *après* mean 'next' or 'afterwards'.

You can also use times of day (*le matin, l'après-midi, le soir*), days of the week or *le lendemain*, 'the next day'. Don't forget *hier* and *demain*: 'yesterday' and 'tomorrow'.

 *Lien*

4.2 Higher is available in the Higher book.

4.3 G Les moyens de transport

1 ⓥ Unjumble these French words for means of transport.

1 olév
2 uotvier
3 edpi
4 noiva
5 autbae
6 nitar

2a 📖🎧 Read the speech bubbles to find out how each of ten students travels to school, then find the pie chart that shows the results for the group.

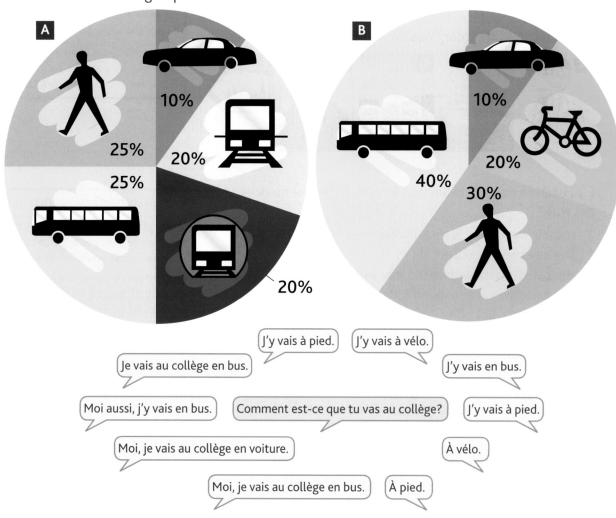

A

10%
25%
20%
25%
20%

B

10%
20%
40%
30%

J'y vais à pied.

J'y vais à vélo.

Je vais au collège en bus.

J'y vais en bus.

Moi aussi, j'y vais en bus.

Comment est-ce que tu vas au collège?

J'y vais à pied.

Moi, je vais au collège en voiture.

À vélo.

Moi, je vais au collège en bus.

À pied.

2b 📖🎧 Which three of the following means of transport, that you might use during a holiday, are **not** featured in either pie chart?

en métro   en avion   en voiture
en bateau   en train   à moto

3 **Ⓖ** Copy the sentences and fill in each gap with *en* or *à*.

1 Je vais voyager _____ train et _____ vélo.

2 Je préfère voyager _____ TGV, mais je voyage souvent _____ car.

3 Mon père va au travail _____ métro et _____ pied.

4 Les touristes vont en Corse _____ bateau ou _____ avion.

5 Voyager _____ moto est plus dangereux que les voyages _____ voiture.

How to say 'by' a means of transport

To describe how you travel, you usually use *en*, e.g. *en voiture* (by car).

Exceptions: *à pied* (on foot), *à vélo* (by bike), *à moto* (by motorbike) and *à cheval* (on horseback).

Memory tip: if you can get inside the means of transport, use *en*. If not, use *à*.

Also learn about *y* meaning 'there'. *See page 82* ➡

Grammaire

4a 🎧 Listen to Section A. Match the means of transport (A–E) with each speaker (1–5).

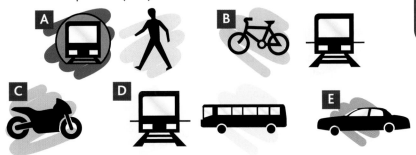

4b 🎧 Listen to Section B. Match the destinations mentioned (1–5) with the means of transport used (a–e).

1 Canada   a boat

2 Morocco   b plane and car

3 Switzerland   c bike

4 Spain   d train and bus

5 Brittany   e car

5 🗨 In groups of four, draw lots to see who will ask each of the questions below. Ask ten people the question you have been allocated, then draw up a pie chart to show the results.

Comment est-ce que tu voyages au collège?

J'y voyage …

Comment préfères-tu voyager de ta ville à Londres?

Je préfère y voyager …

Comment est-ce que tu vas au centre-ville?

J'y vais …

Comment préfères-tu voyager pendant tes vacances?

Pendant mes vacances, je préfère voyager …

Using intonation when asking questions

When questions start with a question word, French people tend to let their voice fall, but then rise at the end. Listen to the questions at the start of listening activities, as examples, and try to do the same when you ask a question.

Stratégie 5

4.3 F Les excursions

1 **V** Sort these words into four groups: air travel, road travel, train travel or travel by sea. (Some words fit in more than one category.)

| le vol | la salle d'attente | les feux rouges | un horaire |

| un sens interdit | l'autoroute | stationner | le quai |

| composter | le bateau | le port | la gare routière |

| la gare SNCF | l'aéroport | l'hôtesse de l'air | le trottoir |

Une visite à Québec

L'été dernier, nous avons passé des vacances chez ma tante au Canada. Un jour, nous sommes allés à la ville de Québec en train. Nous sommes partis de la maison à neuf heures et le voyage a duré environ quarante minutes. C'est une des villes les plus historiques du Canada, et il y a beaucoup de choses à faire.

Le matin, nous avons visité le Vieux-Québec. Mes parents aiment l'histoire et les arts, et ils sont allés au musée des Beaux-Arts, mais mon frère et moi, nous avons fait du shopping dans les petits magasins. C'était la fête musicale d'été et il y avait beaucoup de musiciens dans les rues. C'était très pittoresque. Après une pause-café, nous avons visité la cathédrale de Notre-Dame et la Citadelle de Québec avec nos parents. C'est le monument le plus célèbre de la ville et il y a de belles vues du sommet.

L'après-midi, nous avons fait une promenade en bateau sur la rivière. C'était très intéressant. Puis mon père et mon frère sont allés en métro au stade municipal pour regarder un match de base-ball. Ma mère et moi, on a décidé d'aller au parc aquarium de Québec. Nous y sommes allées en bus. Il y avait beaucoup de poissons et d'animaux des océans. Pour moi, c'était la meilleure visite du jour. Enfin, nous avons pris un taxi pour la gare. Mon père et mon frère sont arrivés du stade en taxi aussi, cinq minutes avant le départ du train, pour rentrer chez ma tante.

Lola, 14 ans

2a 📖 🎧 Read the text and match the pictures to the family members.

1 Lola and her brother
2 Lola and her mum
3 her brother and her dad
4 the whole family

2b 📖 🎧 Which three sentences are true?

1 They arrived in Quebec at 9.00 in the morning.
2 The musicians were taking part in the spring music festival.
3 There are good views from the Citadelle.
4 The boat trip in the morning was interesting.
5 Lola thought the visit to the aquarium was the best part of the day.
6 They all went to the railway station by taxi.

3 **G** Copy the sentences and fill in each gap with the correct French phrase, as indicated in brackets

1 Les TGV sont les trains _____. (**fastest**)
2 La plage de La Baule est _____ d'Europe. (**longest**)
3 Le Concorde était l'avion _____ du monde. (**fastest**)
4 Nous avons mangé dans _____ restaurant de la ville. (**best**)
5 Je passé mes vacances dans _____ maison de la région. (**prettiest**)
6 Est-ce que la tour Eiffel est le monument _____ de Paris? (**most visited**)

| la plus longue | le plus rapide | le meilleur |
| les plus rapides | le plus visité | la plus jolie |

> ### Superlative adjectives
>
> **Grammaire** page 176
>
> To say 'the most', use *le / la / les plus* + adjective:
>
> *C'est la plus belle chambre.* – It is the most beautiful room.
>
> To say 'the best', use *meilleur / meilleure / meilleurs / meilleures*:
>
> *C'est le meilleur camping.* – It is the best campsite.
>
> Also learn about the *tu* form of the imperative.
> *See page 83* ➡

4a 🎧 Listen to the advice given in Section A and complete these sentences in English.

1 You can get a taxi from the _____ to go to the _____.
2 Bus number _____ will take you to the _____.
3 You can visit the main sights on _____ with a guide from the _____.
4 A journey of _____ minutes by _____ will take you to the beach.
5 The metro station to go to the _____ is 100 metres from the _____.

4b 🎧 Listen to Section B and match the English answers (a–e) with the French questions that you hear (1–5).

a The nearest underground station is opposite the post office.
b Ten euros for adults and six euros for children.
c You can get a bus from outside the hotel.
d To book tickets for the helicopter trip.
e About two hours.

> ### Using intensifiers
>
> **Stratégie 5**
>
> Use intensifiers to add variety to your written language, e.g. *très* (very), *trop* (too), *assez* (quite), *vraiment* (really).
>
> *Le voyage était assez confortable, mais trop long.* – The journey was quite comfortable but too long.

5 ✏ Describe a day out while on holiday (real or imaginary). Write about how you travelled, what the journey was like, the activities you did and things you saw. Give reasons and opinions.

Un jour, je suis allé(e)	à un parc d'attractions / à une forêt /… au centre-ville / au bord de la mer / …		
J'ai voyagé	en voiture / en bus / en train / …	parce que	c'est pratique / rapide / pas trop cher.
Le voyage a duré On est partis à / on est arrivés à	(environ) … heures.		
On a	fait une excursion en car. fait une promenade en bateau. fait du cheval. loué des vélos.	C'était (vraiment) amusant / fatigant / casse-pieds.	
On a visité un château / des monuments / une ferme / le théâtre / …		Je l'ai trouvé intéressant / ennuyeux / agréable.	

Lien
4.3 Higher is available in the Higher book.

Holidays

1 Choose the correct form to complete each sentence: *du, de la, de l'* or *des*.

1 Il va partir **du / de la / de l'** musée à cinq heures.
2 Allô! J'appelle **de la / du / des** gare.
3 Le bus va arriver **de la / de l' / du** centre commercial.
4 Les touristes partent en car **du / de l' / de la** hôtel.
5 Nous sommes en route **du / de la / des** magasins au restaurant.
6 Les enfants sont rentrés **de l' / de la / du** école.

> ### How to say 'from the ...'
> The French for 'from' is *de*. Also remember that:
> - *de + le* changes to *du*
> - *de + la* remains *de la*
> - *de + l'* remains *de l'*
> - *de + les* changes to *des*
>
> *J'appelle du bureau.* – I am calling from the office.
>
> *J'arrive de l'aéroport.* – I am coming from the airport.
>
> **Grammaire** page 174

2 Copy the sentences and fill in each gap with the correct French word, according to the instructions in brackets.

1 L'appartement est au _____ étage. (**5th**)
2 Prenez la _____ rue à gauche. (**1st**)
3 C'est la _____ maison à droite. (**3rd**)
4 Il habite au _____ étage de l'immeuble. (**6th**)
5 Aujourd'hui, c'est le _____ jour de mes vacances. (**4th**)
6 C'est la _____ rue à gauche. (**2nd**)

> ### 'First', 'second', 'third', etc.
> The word for first is *premier(-ière)*. To change other numbers from 'two' to 'second', from 'three' to 'third', etc., add *-ième*: *deuxième, troisième*.
>
> For numbers ending in e, the e is removed before adding the ending, e.g. *quatre → quatrième*.
>
> **Grammaire** page 192

3 Match the questions with the answers, then translate the answers into English.

1 Comment est-ce que tu vas au collège?
2 Comment préfères-tu voyager de ta ville à Londres?
3 Comment voyage-t-elle en Espagne?
4 Comment préfère-t-il aller à Paris?

a Il préfère y aller en voiture.
b Elle y voyage en avion.
c Je préfère y aller en train.
d J'y vais en bus.

> ### Y meaning 'there'
> You will often come across the pronoun *y*, which means 'there'.
>
> *J'y vais en bus.* – I go there by bus.
>
> *J'y ai voyagé en avion.* – I travelled there by plane.
>
> *Je préfère y aller en train.* – I prefer to go there by train.
>
> **Grammaire** page 179

4 Copy the sentences and fill in each gap with the correct verb in the imperfect.

1 Il y _____ du soleil à Marseille.
2 J'ai dormi sous la tente. C'_____ amusant!
3 Hier, il _____, alors je suis allée au musée d'art moderne.
4 Je ne suis pas sortie parce qu'il _____ trop froid.
5 Je ne suis pas allé à la plage, car il _____ mauvais temps.
6 Il _____ quand je suis arrivée dans les Alpes. C'_____ beau!

> avait   était   était   faisait
> neigeait   pleuvait   faisait

> ### The imperfect tense
> Use the imperfect tense to describe what something was like in the past.
>
> *C'était super!* It was great!
> *Il faisait froid.* It was cold.
> *Il y avait du soleil.* It was sunny.
> *Il pleuvait.* It was raining.
> *Il neigeait.* It was snowing.
>
> **Grammaire** page 184

5 Copy the sentences and fill in each gap with the correct form of *jouer* or *faire*.

1 Demain, je _____ du vélo, mais samedi prochain je _____ au tennis.
2 Samedi dernier, j'_____ au basket et j'_____ de la natation.
3 Pendant les vacances, l'été dernier, mes parents _____ de la voile, et mon frère et moi, nous _____ au volley-ball.
4 En colonie de vacances, l'année prochaine, nous _____ de l'escalade, et les petits enfants _____ au foot.

> vont jouer   ai fait   avons joué   vais faire
> ai joué   vais jouer   allons faire   ont fait

> ### *Faire* and *jouer* for past and future activities
> When describing activities that you have done or plan to do, don't forget to use *jouer* with games that you play, and *faire* with other sports and activities. Remember that *faire* is an irregular verb. Check it in the verb tables on page 195.
>
> Use the perfect tense to talk about past activities:
> *Hier, **il a joué** au rugby.*
>
> Use the immediate future (present tense of *aller* + *jouer* / *faire*) to talk about future activities:
> *Demain, **il va faire** du cheval.*
>
> **Grammaire** page 187

6 Underline the imperative (command) in the following sentences, then translate each one into English.

Exemple: <u>Achète</u> les billets! *Buy the tickets!*
1 Visite le port!
2 Loue un vélo!
3 Va au guichet!
4 Prends un bus!
5 Mange le fromage de la ferme!
6 N'oublie pas le pourboire pour le guide!

> ### The imperative (*tu* form)
> Use an imperative (command) when giving orders or instructions.
>
> Use the *tu* form when speaking to someone your own age or someone you know very well. This is usually the *tu* form of the present tense. However, with -*er* verbs, remove the *s* at the end.
> *Tu vas à la piscine.* You go to the swimming pool.
> → *Va à la piscine!* Go to the swimming pool!
>
> **Grammaire** page 185

Holidays

Topic 4.1 Holiday possibilities and preferences

4.1 G Deux villes à visiter ➡ pages 70–71

la	bibliothèque	library
la	boucherie	butcher's
la	boulangerie	baker's
la	cathédrale	cathedral
la	cave	cellar
le	centre commercial	shopping centre
la	confiserie	sweet shop
l'	église	church
la	gare	railway station
l'	hôtel de ville (m)	town hall
la	librairie	bookshop
le	marché	market
le	musée	museum
l'	office de tourisme (m)	tourist office
la	patinoire	ice rink
la	pâtisserie	cake shop
la	piscine	swimming pool
le	stade	stadium
la	station-service	filling station
le	théâtre	theatre

4.1 F Vive les vacances! ➡ pages 72–73

	à l'étranger	abroad
l'	alpinisme (m)	mountaineering
l'	auberge de jeunesse (f)	youth hostel
le	bord de la mer	seaside
	bronzer	to sunbathe
la	campagne	countryside
le	Canada	Canada
les	Caraïbes	Caribbean
la	Chine	China
l'	Espagne (f)	Spain
les	États-Unis	United States

la	forêt	forest
le	gîte	holiday cottage
le	logement	housing, accommodation
	louer	to hire
la	montagne	mountain
les	monuments historiques (m)	historic monuments / sights
le	pays de Galles	Wales
la	plage	beach
la	voile	sailing

Topic 4.2 Where you've been and where you're going

4.2 G C'est où? ➡ pages 74–75

	à droite	to the right
	à gauche	to the left
la	Belgique	Belgium
la	Bretagne	Brittany
la	côte	coast
l'	est (m)	east
l'	étage (m)	floor, storey
les	feux (m)	traffic lights
	jusqu'à	as far as
le	Maroc	Morocco
le	nord	north
l'	ouest (m)	west
	premier(-ière)	first
le	rond-point	roundabout
la	rue	street
	situé(e)	situated
le	sud	south
la	Suisse	Switzerland
	tourner	to turn
	tout droit	straight on

4.2 F Que faire en vacances? ➡ *pages 76–77*

	à l'heure	on time
d'	abord	first of all
les	bagages	luggage
se	baigner	to bathe
le	client	customer
le	canoë-kayak	canoeing
la	colonie de vacances	holiday camp
	au début	at the beginning
la	demi-pension	half board
le	dortoir	dormitory
	ensuite	next
l'	escalade (f)	rock-climbing
le	lendemain	the next day
	loger	to live, to stay
l'	oncle (m)	uncle
le	parc d'attractions	theme park
	partager	to share
la	piste cyclable	cycle track
le	propriétaire	owner
la	randonnée	walk/hike

Topic 4.3 What to see on holiday and getting around

4.3 G Les moyens de transport ➡ *pages 78–79*

en	avion	by plane
en	bateau	by boat
le	bureau	office
en	bus	by bus
en	car	by coach
la	Corse	Corsica
	dangereux(-euse)	dangerous
en	métro	by underground
à	moto	by motorbike
à	pied	on foot
	souvent	often
en	TGV	by high speed train
en	train	by train

le	travail	work
à	vélo	by bicycle
en	voiture	by car
le	voyage	journey
	voyager	to travel

4.3 F Les excursions ➡ *pages 80–81*

l'	autoroute (f)	motorway
	avant	before
	célèbre	famous
	composter	to punch (a ticket)
	coûter	to cost
le	départ	departure
	devant	in front of
	durer	to last (a period of time)
	enfin	finally
	environ	about
la	fête	festival
le	guichet	ticket office
	pittoresque	picturesque
le	pourboire	tip
	pratique	practical
le	quai	platform
la	salle d'attente	waiting room
le	sens interdit	no entry
la	station de métro	underground station
	stationner	to park
le	syndicat d'initiative	tourist information office
le	trottoir	pavement
le	vol	flight
la	vue	view

Foundation – Exam practice

info

These pages give you the chance to try GCSE-style practice exam questions at grades D–C, based on the AQA Context of Leisure.

Lien

Higher practice exam questions (grades B–A*) are available at the end of this Context in the Higher book.

Femme | Bébé | Enfant | **Jeune 10–18** | Homme | Chaussures | Sport | Accessoires

Offres de la semaine!

De nouveaux prix pour une semaine seulement! Désirez-vous profiter de ces offres? Vous avez 7 jours!

Cliquez sur la description pour voir la photo.

1 Veste grise en laine garçons
16,44€

6 Gilet long filles, en laine, ceinture, sans manches
10,46€

2 T-shirt, coton, manches longues garçons
15,90€

7 Chemise blanche en polyester garçons, manches longues
6,96€

3 Chaussures noires en cuir filles
10,00€

8 Jean noir en coton garçons, slim
13,69€

4 Jean bleu filles, standard
15,00€

9 Parka filles, capuche
16,47€

5 T-shirt coton filles, manches longues
7,14€

10 Sweat à capuche garçons
7,96€

Christophe – un client satisfait

Je déteste aller dans les magasins! J'ai donc comparé vos prix à ceux des grands magasins en ville, et quand j'ai vu les résultats, j'ai choisi ces vêtements par Internet. Pour moi, il est important de trouver des articles de bonne qualité, mais qui ne sont pas trop chers. Et, en plus, j'ai fait des économies, car je n'ai pas payé le bus pour aller faire mon shopping. J'ai fait mes achats en ligne mardi après-midi. Mon frère aussi a acheté des vêtements. Il a choisi un jean et un pull. Jeudi matin, ils sont tous arrivés à la maison. Quel service de qualité! Je vais revenir sur ce site web, avant de partir en vacances en juillet.

Merci!
Christophe (étudiant, Bordeaux)

1a 📖 Look at the clothes shopping website and answer these questions in English.

1 For how long are these offers available?
2 What happens if you click on the description of an item?
3 How much would you pay for the item with a belt?
4 What sort of material is the grey jacket made of?
5 What colour is the shirt?
6 How much are the shoes?
7 Whose jeans are the most expensive?
8 How much is the hoodie?

Total = 8 marks

1b 📖 Read the message sent in by Christophe. Complete the sentences in English.

1 Before deciding to buy from the website, Christophe ___.
2 His two main considerations when buying clothes are ___.
3 He also saved money because ___.
4 The order included clothes for ___.
5 The clothes arrived ___ after ordering.
6 He expects to use the website again before ___.
7 He probably does not have much money because ___.

Total = 8 marks

Use your knowledge of English

Many of the words in Christophe's message are cognates or near-cognates (words that are the same as or similar to English). This should help you work out the meaning of what he has written.

Stratégie 1b

2a 🎧 Listen to the whole conversation, and put Solange's weekend activities (A–E) in the order that she mentions them.

A B C D E

Total = 5 marks

2b 🎧 Now listen again in detail. Which three sentences are true?

1 Delphine travelled home by coach.
2 She was met by her father.
3 Solange's mother thinks her shoes are too dangerous.
4 On Saturday evening they went to a party.
5 Solange didn't do her homework because she was ill.
6 Delphine has to revise for a test in geography.

Total = 3 marks

Think ahead before listening

Look at the sentences in advance and work out which part, if any, is likely to be wrong, e.g. in sentence 1 it is likely to be the means of transport.

Stratégie 2b

Total for Reading and Listening = 24 marks

Foundation – Speaking

En vacances

You are on holiday in France. You have agreed to take part in a survey about holidays.

Your teacher will play the part of the person carrying out the survey and will ask you the following:

1 personal details

2 details about your accommodation

3 why you chose the area

4 what you did yesterday

5 what you have planned for today

6 where you intend to spend your next holiday

7 !

! Remember, you will have to respond to something that you have not yet prepared.

> **ⓘnfo**
>
> **Important information:**
> This sample task is for practice purposes only and should not be used as an actual assessment task. Study it to find out how to plan your Controlled Assessment efficiently to gain maximum marks and / or work through it as a mock exam task before the actual Controlled Assessment.

---

1 Personal details
- say your name, age and nationality
- say how you travelled and when you arrived
- say how long you are staying for
- give details about your family

Stratégie
> Start your plan. Write a maximum of six words. Here are some suggested words for bullet point 1 of the sample task: *nom, âge, nationalité, voyager, rester, famille*. Remember that the maximum number of words allowed in your plan is 40.
> Remember that *j'ai* = 'I have' and *je suis* = 'I am'. However, you should use *j'ai* when saying your age. For saying how you travelled and how you arrived, use the perfect tense, e.g. *j'ai voyagé, je suis arrivé(e)*.

---

2 Details about your accommodation
- say where your hotel is situated
- describe the hotel facilities
- describe your room
- say what you think of the standard of the accommodation

Stratégie
> Suggested words for your plan: *se trouver, près, piscine, chambre, lit*.
> Show initiative when you describe the hotel facilities, e.g. mention a swimming pool, say that you like swimming, say that you go swimming at home every week, say you are generally quite sporty, that you also like playing tennis, etc. See Exam technique S10.

---

3 Why you chose the area
- say why you chose the area
- say what you enjoyed visiting last time you came
- compare it to your own area at home
- say which area you prefer

Stratégie
> Suggested words for your plan: *choisir, temps, aimer, plage, préférer, raison*.
> Show that you can use the perfect tense, e.g. *j'ai choisi …* as well as the present tense, e.g. *parce que d'habitude, il fait beau*
> Keep the comparison simple, e.g. *dans ma ville, il n'y a pas de …*

4 What you did yesterday
- say where you went yesterday morning
- say what you thought of it
- say what you did for the rest of the day
- say what others in your family did

> Suggested words for your plan: *hier, aller, après-midi, soir*. Add a maximum of two more words to this list.
> When giving your opinion, use *j'ai aimé …* and *je n'ai pas aimé …*
> Vary your vocabulary. Use different verbs for different people, e.g. *aller, rester, visiter, faire* in the perfect tense.
>
> **Stratégie**

5 What you have planned for today
- say what your own plans for today are
- say why you chose those activities
- say what you will do if it rains
- say what others in your family want to do today

> Suggested words for your plan: *sortir, copains, courses*. Add a maximum of three words to this list.
> Use *je voudrais / j'aimerais* + verb in the infinitive to explain your own plans.
> Use *s'il pleut* to introduce what you will do if it rains.
> Use *mon frère / ma sœur / mes parents instead of je* to introduce what others would like to do.
>
> **Stratégie**

6 Where you intend to spend your next holiday
- say where you intend to spend your next holiday
- say why you have chosen that particular destination
- say how long you would like to go for
- say what you would like to do / visit there

> Suggested words for your plan: *Espagne, soleil*. Add a maximum of four words to this list.
> Use a variety of ways to introduce a future event, e.g. *j'ai l'intention de / j'espère / je voudrais / je vais / j'aimerais*.
> All of these phrases are followed by a verb in the infinitive, e.g. *j'ai l'intention d'aller …*
> Develop your answer by mentioning the weather, the seaside, the activities, etc. See Exam technique S9.
>
> **Stratégie**

7 ! A conclusion to the survey might be …
- what you think of the facilities on offer.
- how the resort could be made more appealing to various groups of people: adults, teenagers, families with young children, etc.
- whether what is on offer is good value for money.
- what your ideal holiday would be like.

> Choose which **two** options you think are the most likely, and for each of these, note down **three** different ideas.
> In your plan, write three words that illustrate each of the two most likely options, e.g. for the second suggestion here (how the resort could be made more appealing to various groups), you might choose *adultes, jeunes, familles*.
> Prepare for the two options you have chosen using your reminder words. See Exam technique S3.
> Remember to check the total number of words you have used. It should be 40 or fewer.
>
> **Stratégie**

 **Lien**
> Higher sample assessment tasks for this Context can be found in the Higher book.

Foundation – Writing

Mes loisirs

You are writing an email to your French friend Sabine, who has asked you:

1. what you do with your free time when you stay in
2. what you do when you go out
3. how much money you receive and from whom
4. how you like spending your money
5. if you have a mobile phone
6. if you are interested in fashion
7. if you are sporty.

> **ⓘnfo**
>
> **Important information:**
> This sample task is for practice purposes only and should not be used as an actual assessment task. Study it to find out how to plan your Controlled Assessment efficiently to gain maximum marks and / or work through it as a mock exam task before the actual Controlled Assessment.

---

1. **What you do with your free time when you stay in**
   - talk about music you listen to and / or play
   - mention TV and what you watched last night
   - say what you like doing on the computer
   - mention the last time you had a friend to visit

> **Stratégie**
>
> Start your plan. Suggested words for your plan: *musique, télé (hier), ordinateur (activités), inviter*.
> Use the present tense for the very first sentence: *j'écoute / j'aime* écouter …
> Use the perfect tense for the second sub-division suggested here: *j'ai regardé* …
> Use *j'ai invité … chez moi* to say you had a friend to visit.

---

2. **What you do when you go out**
   - say where you go and when
   - say who you go with
   - say what you did the last time you went out
   - say what time you had to be back in and what you thought of that

> **Stratégie**
>
> Suggested words for your plan: *Cirencester, week-end, copains, dernier, retour, opinion*.
> Use *j'ai dû rentrer à* … to say when you had to be back. Use *c'était* … to say what you thought of having to be back in at that time.
> Sometimes proper nouns (e.g. Cirencester, Sabine, Odeon) are the best way of summarising what you want to say. Don't be afraid of using them in your plan. See also Exam technique W2.

---

3. **How much money you receive and from whom**
   - say how much money you receive each week
   - say whether it is pocket money or whether you earn it
   - say whether you think it is enough
   - compare how much pocket money you get with what your brothers / sisters / friends get

> **Stratégie**
>
> Suggested words for your plan: *recevoir, argent, gagner, assez, comparaison, frère*.
> Use *me donne* to say 'gives me' and *gagne* for 'earn'. Use *reçoit / reçoivent* when writing about what others get (but *je reçois*).

4 How you like spending your money
- say how much you regularly save and what for
- say what you usually buy with your money
- say how you spent your money last month
- say what you would do if you won the lottery

Stratégie

Suggested words for your plan: *économiser, raison, acheter, loterie*. Add a maximum of two words to this list.
Use *économiser* for 'save'.
Start the last sub-division for bullet point 4 with *Si je gagnais à la loterie, je voudrais …* You can also use *j'aimerais*.
Use a dictionary to help with vocabulary you want to use that you don't know. See Exam technique W1.

5 If you have a mobile phone
- say whether you have a mobile phone and when you got it
- say what you do with it
- say how much you spend monthly on using your mobile
- say what you think of your mobile

Stratégie

Suggested words for your plan: *portable, Internet, dépenser*. Add a maximum of three words to this list.
Use *je paie / ça coûte / je dépense* to say how much you spend. The word for 'pounds' is *livres*.
Give your opinion and explain it, using longer sentences that include link words. See Exam technique W9.

6 If you are interested in fashion
- say what clothes you like wearing
- say whether fashion is important to you
- mention a fashionable item you bought recently
- say why it is difficult to keep up with fashion

Stratégie

Suggested words for your plan: *vêtements, mode*. Add a maximum of four words to this list.
Use *à la mode* for 'in fashion'.
Remember that fashion can be about things other than clothes, e.g. jewellery, bags, etc.

7 If you are sporty
- say which sports you like and dislike
- say whether you walk and / or cycle in order to keep fit
- say whether your diet helps your fitness
- say whether it is important to play sport and be fit

Stratégie

Add a maximum of six words to your plan.
Use *jouer au* + sports to say which sports you play.
If you want to say 'it is important to play + sport' use *il est important de jouer* + sport. Note that the second verb is in the infinitive, e.g. *jouer, faire*.
Remember to check the total number of words you have used in your plan. It must be 40 or fewer.

 *Lien*

Higher sample assessment tasks for this Context can be found in the Higher book.

Exam technique – Speaking

S4 Help available

Your teacher is allowed to discuss each task with you in English, including the kind of language you may need and how to use your preparatory work. You can have access to a dictionary, your French books, Kerboodle and internet resources. This is the stage when you will prepare your plan using the Task Planning Form.

You will then give this to your teacher, who will give you feedback on how you have met the requirements of the task.

When you actually perform the task, you will only have access to your plan and your teacher's comments (i.e. the Task Planning Form).

S5 AQA adminstration

For the Speaking part of your exam, you have to do two different tasks (at two different times). One of the tasks will be recorded and sent to a moderator. Each task will last between four and six minutes.

When your teacher thinks that you have been taught the language you need and feels that you are ready, you will be given the task to prepare. It could be a task designed by the AQA Examination Board or a task designed by French teachers in your school.

S6 Marking of the tasks

Your teacher will mark your work. A moderator (i.e. an examiner) will sample the work of your school and check that it has been marked correctly. A senior examiner will check the work of the moderator. This complicated but secure system ensures that candidates are given the correct mark.

The Speaking part of your exam counts for 30% of the French GCSE. Each task is marked out of 30 marks. As there are two Speaking tasks, the total number of marks available for Speaking is 60.

For each task, the marks are divided in the following way, with the maximum number of marks available shown in each case: 10 marks for Communication, 10 marks for Range of language and Accuracy, 5 marks for Pronunciation and Intonation, 5 marks for Interaction and Fluency.

Grade booster

To reach grade D, you need to …

■ Express opinions when the occasion arises, e.g. bullet points 3, 4 and 6 of the sample Controlled Assessment on page 88. Find different ways of giving your opinion, e.g. *je préfère / j'ai aimé / je pense que c'est…*

■ Sometimes develop your answers, e.g. for bullet point 4, mention several activities. Add extra information such as where, when, and what it was like.

To reach grade C, you need to …

■ Show a reasonable range of vocabulary and avoid repeating the same words. Here are some over-used verb phrases: *il y a / c'est / je voudrais / je suis allé*. If you have used them already, try to think of alternatives.

■ Include the three time frames, e.g. present tense for bullet points 1 and 2, past tense for bullet points 3 and 4. Use the immediate future for bullet point 6: *L'année prochaine, je vais aller aux États-Unis*. Use *j'aimerais / j'ai l'intention de* + infinitive for bullet points 5 and 6.

Aiming for Higher? You need to …

■ Develop about half of your answers. Make a point of explaining what you are saying, e.g. for bullet point 4, say what you did and why you chose to do that.

■ Show some initiative. Aim to do so several times, e.g. for bullet point 5, say what you are going to do and why, what you don't want to do and why.

Exam technique – Writing

W4 Responding to the bullet points

In a Writing task, there are typically between six and eight bullet points. All bullet points are written in English. Although you have to write a response to the title of the task, it is recommended that you deal with every bullet point that is given below it so that you don't miss out any important information.

W5 Using different tenses

In order to obtain grade C, you need to demonstrate that you can use more than one tense. You might refer to the present and the past, or you might refer to the present and the immediate future, e.g. *je vais* + infinitive. As you don't know exactly which combination will be best for the task that you will be given, it is a good idea to make sure that you know how to write about present, past and future events.

W6 How much to write

For grades G–D, you should produce 200–350 words across the two tasks (i.e. 100–175 words per task). Although there is flexibility, aim to write approximately 20 words per bullet point.

For grades C–A*, you should produce 400–600 words across the two tasks (i.e. 200–300 words per task). Although there is flexibility, aim to write approximately 40 words per bullet point.

You may produce a draft, but this is for your use only. Your teacher cannot comment on it and you cannot have access to any draft when you write the final version.

Grade booster

To reach grade D, you need to …

- Use longer sentences linked by *et / mais / car / parce que*, e.g. for bullet point 4 of the sample Controlled Assessment on page 91. 'I save … because …', and for bullet point 6, 'I like wearing … but …'

- Try to give a fair amount of information. Give yourself a target number of words for each bullet point, e.g. 25 to 30 words.

To reach grade C, you need to …

- Work out where you are going to use tenses other than the present, e.g. past for bullet point 1 (what I did last night).

- Try to vary your vocabulary. For bullet point 5, avoid repeating *mon portable*. Use *mon téléphone* or pronouns, e.g. *je l'utilise, il me coûte*, as alternatives.

Aiming for Higher? You need to …

- Give your point of view and explain it, e.g. for bullet point 3, say that you don't receive enough pocket money and say why you feel that way.

- Write a response to the title of the task that gives relevant and detailed information. Stick to your plan.

5.1 G — Chez moi

De:	Rose
À:	Théo
Sujet:	Ma nouvelle maison

Au rez-de-chaussée, il y a l'entrée, un petit salon et une super grande cuisine! Il y a aussi des toilettes et puis l'escalier pour monter au premier étage où il y a un grand salon et la chambre de mes parents. Au deuxième étage, il y a ma chambre, la chambre d'Émilie et puis la salle de bains.

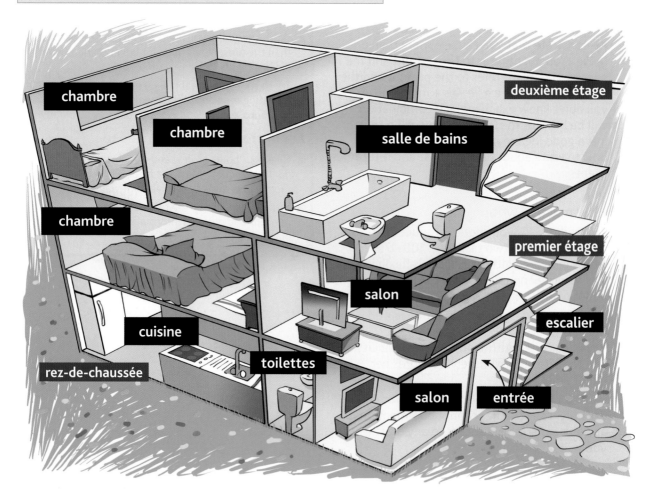

chambre · chambre · salle de bains · deuxième étage · chambre · premier étage · salon · escalier · cuisine · toilettes · rez-de-chaussée · salon · entrée

1a 📖🎧 Read Rose's email about her new house, then decide which three statements are true.

1 There is a small lounge on the first floor.
2 Rose's bedroom is on the second floor.
3 Émilie's bedroom is on the first floor.
4 The bathroom is on the second floor.
5 Rose's parents' bedroom is on the second floor.
6 The toilet and the kitchen are on the ground floor.

1b 📖 🎧 Read Rose's email again, then match each question (1–5) with the correct answer (a–e).

1 Où est la chambre des parents?
2 Il y a combien de chambres?
3 Il y a combien de salons?
4 Où est la salle de bains?
5 Où sont les toilettes?

a Il y en a trois.
b Il y en a deux.
c Au rez-de-chaussée.
d Elle est au premier étage.
e Elle est au deuxième étage.

2a 🎧 A French visitor will be staying at Jane's house for the next few days. Listen to her showing her guest Marie round the house (Sections A and B). Copy the grid and list in English all the rooms on each floor in Jane's house.

ground floor	
first floor	

2b 🎧 Listen to Section C and note from the list which items are in Marie's bedroom.

a bed	bookshelves	a wardrobe	a TV
a computer	a chest of drawers	a mirror
a desk	posters	a guitar

3 🄶 Copy the sentences and fill in each gap with *il* or *elle*.

1 Le salon? _____ est au rez-de-chaussée.
2 La chambre de Marie? _____ est au premier étage.
3 L'ordinateur? _____ est sur le bureau.
4 La commode? _____ est derrière la porte.
5 Le bureau? _____ est devant la fenêtre.

4 🖊 Your parents are welcoming a young French visitor to your home next week. Help them prepare what they are going to say when they show the guest round the house. Write a description of your own house.

Au rez-de-chaussée,	il y a …	
Au premier étage,		
La salle de bains	est	à côté de …
Ta chambre		en face de …
Elle est assez		grand(e) / petit(e).
Dans ta chambre, il y a …		

Using *il* or *elle* for 'it'

Il and *elle* can mean 'it' as well as 'he' and 'she'. Use *il* for a masculine word (*le / un / mon / ton / son*) and *elle* for a feminine word (*la / une / ma / ta / sa*):
Comment est ta maison?
Elle *est grande.*

Also practise how to use prepositions correctly.
See page 106 ➡

Grammaire page 178

Making the task manageable

Divide the activity into manageable chunks, e.g. when describing your house, you could write one sentence about each floor, each room, the garden, etc. Write sentences using familiar vocabulary, and keep them quite simple so you know that the language you are using is correct.

Stratégie 4

5.1 F Ma maison

Objectifs

Different types of homes

Using *depuis*

Qualifiers and intensifiers

1 **V** Choose the correct word to match each definition (1–7).

1 On y dort.

2 On y prépare le repas.

3 On y va pour faire du ski.

4 On le prend pour monter au sixième étage par exemple.

5 On s'y lave.

6 C'est une machine qui fait la vaisselle.

7 La salle à manger, la chambre et la cuisine en sont.

la salle de bains	des pièces	la cuisine
la chambre	l'ascenseur
un lave-vaisselle	à la montagne

LOCATIONS VACANCES

A **Le Barroux:** Maison récente avec vue sur la campagne – pour six personnes – chambres (il y en a trois) – piscine privée – à huit cents mètres du village. Grand jardin, cuisine, séjour, salle de bains, WC. Confort, machine à laver, lave-vaisselle, four à micro-ondes, frigo, congélateur, télévision, lecteur DVD. 750 euros par semaine.

B **Nice:** Appartement au rez-de-chaussée – trois pièces pour quatre personnes. Deux chambres, une salle de bains, WC, salon, cuisine. Les habitants actuels y habitent depuis six ans. Commerces 4 km. Plage 500 m. 600 euros par semaine.

C **Chamonix:** Chalet de montagne. Vue extraordinaire du Mont Blanc. Cinq pièces pour six personnes. Trois étages, quatre chambres, deux salles de bains. Très récent. Assez grande terrasse, balcon, sous-sol.

Équipement: frigo, four, cuisinière, lave-vaisselle, micro-ondes, aspirateur, télévision. 800 euros la semaine.

D **Immeuble de luxe:** Interphone, ascenseur. Cinquième étage. Tout confort. Petite cuisine, séjour, chambre. En plein centre, à cinq minutes de l'Arc de Triomphe et à dix minutes de la Tour Eiffel. 1100 euros par semaine.

2a 📖 🎧 Read the adverts and decide which would be most suitable for each of these situations.

1 Your father would like a sea view.

2 Your brother would like a swimming pool.

3 Your mother wants to be in the countryside.

4 Your sister wants to see Paris.

5 You would prefer a holiday in the mountains.

2b 📖 🎧 Read the adverts again and note which places satisfy these situations. In some cases there are two possibilities, so write them both down.

1 There are five people in your family.
2 You want a garden.
3 There has to be a lift.
4 You want to be on the ground floor.
5 You want a dishwasher and a microwave oven.

🔗 **Lien**
5.1 Higher is available in the Higher book.

3a 🎧 Listen to the recording of a French TV programme similar to 'Location, location, location' (Sections A–D). Copy and complete the grid with one advantage and one disadvantage of each property shown to Nicolas and Marine.

	advantages	disadvantages
A		
B		
C		
D		

3b 🎧 Listen again and decide which of the four properties is Nicolas' favourite and why, and which is Marine's favourite and why.

4 🅖 Copy the sentences and fill in each gap as indicated in brackets. Then translate the sentences into English.

1 J'habite ici _____ . (**for three years**)
2 Greg habite cette maison _____ . (**for six months**)
3 J'habite mon appartement _____ . (**for a year**)
4 Nous sommes dans la salle à manger _____ . (**for an hour**)
5 Elle regarde la télé dans la salle de séjour _____ . (**for two hours**)
6 J'habite en France _____ . (**since I was born**)

5 🗨 Work with a partner. Prepare answers to the following questions, then take turns to ask and answer.

- Où habites-tu?
- Tu y habites depuis quand?
- Il y a combien de chambres?
- Quelles autres pièces y a-t-il dans la maison?
- Qu'est-ce qu'il y a dans ta chambre?
- Tu habitais où avant?
- Tu aimes ta maison?

Grammaire *page 190*

Using *depuis*

Sometimes *depuis* is translated by 'for' and sometimes by 'since'. In English we use the past tense before both these words, but in French you use the present tense before *depuis*:

J'habite ici depuis ma naissance. – I have been living here since I was born.

J'habite ici depuis six ans. – I have been living here for six years.

Also learn about *en* meaning 'of it', 'of them'.
See page 107 ➡

Stratégie 5

Qualifiers and intensifiers

When using adjectives in your conversation, remember to add qualifiers and intensifiers such as *très* (very), *un peu* (a bit), *assez* (quite), *trop* (too) and *vraiment* (really). Example: *J'habite dans une assez grande maison*.

J'habite (dans) Nous habitons dans	une (assez) grande maison (au centre-ville). un (très) petit appartement (dans un village).	
J'y habite	depuis (trois) ans / depuis ma naissance.	
Avant, j'habitais	dans le centre-ville / dans un appartement.	
Au rez-de-chaussée, Dans la salle de séjour,	nous avons / il y a	une cuisine / une salle de bains. une table / des chaises.
La maison / l'appartement	se trouve / est situé(e)	près de … / dans le centre de …
J'aime bien / Je n'aime pas	ma maison	parce qu'elle est …

Où habites-tu?

J'habite une assez grande maison au centre-ville, avec ma famille.

5.2 G Là où j'habite

1 📖🎧 Match each person with the correct pictures (two people need two pictures each, and two people need one picture each).

> J'habite un vieil appartement en centre-ville. C'est nul! Je rêve d'un chalet à la montagne …

Nadia

> J'habite à la campagne. On a une vieille maison dans un village sympa.

Mehdi

> Quand je suis chez mon père, j'habite un appartement moderne en centre-ville. Chez ma mère, c'est une petite maison individuelle dans la banlieue de Nantes.

Théo

> J'habite une grande maison au bord de la mer. C'est dans une petite ville touristique.

Rose

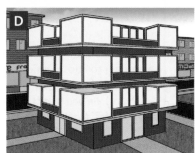

2 💬 Work with a partner. Partner A chooses to be one of the four people above. Partner B asks yes / no questions to guess who it is. Then swap parts.

Exemple:

> Tu habites un appartement? Non.
>
> Tu habites à la campagne? Oui.
>
> Tu es Mehdi?

3a 🎧 Listen to five students saying what facilities there are in their towns. Match the students' names (1–5) with the activities you can do where they live (a–e).

1 Nadia
2 Guillaume
3 Julie
4 Florent
5 Marion

a sunbathing
b playing football
c going to the market
d going to the cinema
e going ice skating

Stratégie 3a–3b

Words that introduce a contrast

Look out for key words that introduce a contrast, e.g. *mais* (but), *pourtant* / *cependant* (however), *par contre* (on the other hand).

On a une patinoire mais on n'a pas de piscine. – We have an ice rink but we don't have a swimming pool.

3b 🎧 Listen again and choose from the list what each student regrets not having in their town.

no shopping centre   no nightclubs   no sports centres
no swimming pools   nothing to do in the evenings

4 🅖 Rewrite these sentences using *on*.

1 Nous avons une patinoire.
2 Nous n'avons pas de piscine.
3 Nous allons faire les courses.
4 Nous habitons une vieille maison.
5 Nous jouons au foot.

Grammaire page 178

Using *on* to say 'we'

On is often used in French to say 'we'. The slightly more formal word for 'we' is *nous*.

On va au cinéma tous les samedis. – We go to the cinema every Saturday.

On a une piscine. – We've got a swimming pool.

On n'a pas de boîtes de nuit. – We don't have / haven't got any nightclubs.

Note that the verb that follows *on* is given the same ending as *il* or *elle*.

Also revise adjectives that are placed before nouns. *See page 106* ➡

5 🗨 Work with a partner. Ask and give details to one another about:

- where you live
- what you like about where you live
- what there is to do
- places of interest
- what is not there that you would like to see.

J'habite une ville / un village situé …

Ma maison / mon appartement est …

J'aime bien … parce que …

À …, il y a …

Cependant, il n'y a pas de …

Je trouve ça dommage parce que …

Qu'est-ce qu'il y a d'intéressant à faire là où tu habites?

Il y a un cinéma et une piscine. Cependant, il n'y a pas de patinoire.

Stratégie 5

Using the language structure boxes

Make sure you use the information given to you in the language structure box. Don't copy everything in it. Change the information given and expand on your answers by giving your opinion and reasons.

5.2 F Ma région

1 ⓥ Match the activities (1–8) with where they usually take place (a–h).

1 On peut voir un film.
2 On peut faire de la gymnastique.
3 On peut faire de la voile.
4 On peut prendre un café.
5 On peut faire les courses.
6 On peut danser.
7 On peut jouer au foot.
8 On peut faire du ski.

a au stade
b au café
c à la plage
d au centre de sports
e au cinéma
f au centre commercial
g en boîte de nuit
h à la montagne

A Clément habite une maison à la campagne près d'Orange qui est une petite ville touristique dans le sud-est. Il y habite depuis sa naissance. Il aime bien là où il est parce que c'est tranquille. Cependant, le jeudi, la ville est assez animée parce que c'est jour de marché. En été, il y a les Chorégies qui sont des spectacles de danse, de théâtre et de musique. Il y a alors de l'animation en ville parce que beaucoup de gens viennent voir ces spectacles.

B Émilie est étudiante à Montpellier qui est une grande ville universitaire située dans le sud. Elle a un petit studio à Palavas, un joli petit village au bord de la mer. Ce qui lui plaît à Palavas, c'est la plage, bien sûr. Quand elle a du temps libre, elle fait de la voile. Quelquefois, elle passe la nuit chez ses copines qui partagent un appartement au centre de Montpellier. Elle aime sortir avec elles au cinéma ou en boîte de nuit.

C Benjamin a dix-huit ans. Il travaille dans une usine dans la banlieue de Calais qui est un port dans le nord. Il habite chez ses parents dans une maison individuelle près du centre. Qu'est-ce qu'il y a à faire à Calais? Comme c'est au bord de la mer, on peut faire tous les sports nautiques, bien sûr, mais ce n'est pas une région chaude et la plage est souvent déserte. En ville, on peut faire du shopping et pour les jeunes, il y a des cafés, des centres de sports et le cinéma.

D Élodie habite à Jausiers qui est un petit village de montagne dans les Alpes. Pour ceux qui aiment le ski, c'est parfait. En hiver, il y a toujours beaucoup de neige et il fait froid. Élodie est monitrice de ski l'hiver et l'été, elle fait faire des randonnées aux touristes. Elle aime beaucoup sa vie à la montagne car elle est très sportive. Elle adore faire du VTT et de l'alpinisme.

2a 📖 🎧 Read the four paragraphs and name the town or village where these activities are possible.

1 going to a concert
2 mountain biking
3 sailing
4 going to a nightclub
5 indoor sports
6 hiking

Stratégie 3a–3b

2b 📖 🎧 Read the text again and decide whether these statements are true (**T**), false (**F**) or not mentioned in the text (**?**).

1   Clément has always lived in Orange.
2   Orange is a quiet town, particularly on Thursdays.
3   Émilie lives in Montpellier and goes to the Palavas university.
4   She has friends she goes out with in Palavas.
5   Benjamin lives with his parents in the suburbs of Calais.
6   He often goes swimming in the sea.
7   Élodie lives in a small mountain village in the Alps.
8   In the summer, she takes tourists hiking.

> ### Listening to a recording twice
>
> Before listening to a recording for the first time, read the questions you have to answer about it. Then listen and answer as many questions as you can.
>
> Before listening for the second time, focus on the questions you have not yet answered and anticipate where on the recording those answers should be. Make sure you know what type of answer is required, e.g. a number, a time, a place, a reason.

3a 🎧 🎥 Arnaud has just moved from Avignon to Vitrolles. Cécile and Julien are his new school friends. Watch the video and / or listen to the audio track. Which towns do these adjectives refer to: Avignon (**A**) or Vitrolles (**V**)?

polluée	sale	animée	touristique
	industrielle	grande	

3b 🎧 🎥 Watch or listen again. According to the conversation, which four statements refer to Avignon (**A**) and which refer to Vitrolles (**V**)?

1   It is quite a big town.
2   There are a lot of shops there.
3   There is a lot for tourists to see.
4   There is too much traffic in town.
5   There is a lot of pollution.
6   You can watch a film there.
7   There are a lot of cafés there.
8   You can go ice skating there.

4 Ⓖ 🗣 Work with a partner. Partner A asks if you can go to one of the places shown and Partner B answers. Then swap parts.

Exemple: **A**   Est-ce qu'on peut aller au cinéma?
            B   Non, on ne peut pas aller au cinéma.

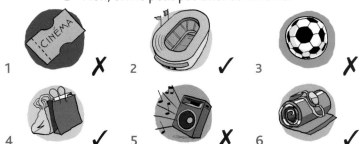

1 ✗   2 ✓   3 ✗
4 ✓   5 ✗   6 ✓

> ### Saying what you can and can't do
>
> In English, we use 'you can' or 'you can't' to mean 'people can / can't'. In the same way, the French use *on peut* and *on ne peut pas* followed by the infinitive.
>
> *On peut aller au cinéma.* – You can go to the cinema.
>
> *On ne peut pas manger ici.* – You can't eat here.
>
> Also learn more about the adjectives *vieux, nouveau, beau.* See page 107 ➡
>
> **G**rammaire *page 187*

5 ✏ Write the text for a French website, giving information about your home town or village (real or imaginary).

Exemple: *Southampton est une grande ville au bord de la mer. Elle se trouve dans le sud de l'Angleterre.*

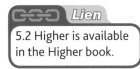

Lien
5.2 Higher is available in the Higher book.

5.3 G La routine à la maison

Je partage ma chambre avec Manon, ma sœur jumelle, et c'est l'horreur! Manon se lève à six heures et demie. Moi, je me lève à sept heures et quart.

Manon prend une douche, puis elle s'habille très lentement. Moi, je me lave, puis je m'habille et hop, je pars au collège.

Le soir, je fais mes devoirs avant le dîner. Manon fait ses devoirs après le dîner, puis elle se couche à dix heures. Moi, je regarde la télé et puis je lis ou j'écoute de la musique dans ma chambre. Mais Manon n'est pas contente: elle veut dormir. Ça m'énerve!

1a 📖 🎧 Read what Alice says about her twin sister, then decide whether each picture (A–F) shows Alice or Manon.

1b 💬 Work with a partner. Compare your daily routines.

Je me lève à sept heures et quart. Et toi?

Moi, je me lève à …

Spotting time references

Where there are time references, you usually need to understand them in order to answer a question. They might be actual times, e.g. *six heures et demie*, or words that indicate a time, such as *le soir, après, puis, ensuite*.

Stratégie 1a–1b

2 **G** Who in your family does the household chores? Write your answers in complete French sentences.

Grammaire *page 187*

Faire + household chores

To say that you do (or don't do) certain household chores, use the verb *faire*, e.g. *la vaisselle* (the washing up), *la cuisine* (the cooking), *les courses* (the shopping), *le ménage* (the housework).

je fais (I do), *tu fais* (you do), *il fait* (he does), *elle fait* (she does)

To say that you don't do …, add *ne … pas* around the part of *faire*: *Je ne fais pas la vaisselle.* – I don't do the washing up.

Also revise how to use reflexive verbs. See page 106 ➡

3a 🎧 Listen to Julien talking about household chores. Find the correct picture for each sentence you hear (1–6).

3b 🎧 Listen again and identify the family member who does each chore.

4 🗩 Work with a partner. Exchange information about:

1 your daily routine (what time you get up, have breakfast, etc.)
2 what you (and others in your family) do to help at home.

Qu'est-ce que tu fais pour aider à la maison?

Je fais la vaisselle. Et toi?

À quelle heure est-ce que tu	te lèves?
	prends le petit déjeuner?
Qu'est-ce que tu fais / ton frère / ta sœur fait pour aider à la maison?	
Je me lève à … Je vais au collège à …	
Je fais	la vaisselle / la cuisine / le ménage / les courses.
Je mets la table. Je range ma chambre.	
Mon frère / ma sœur	fait la vaisselle / met la table / range sa chambre.

5.3 F Les jours de fête à la maison

Objectifs

Celebrations

Common imperfect expressions

Including negatives

1 ⓥ Match the special occasions (1–7) with their definitions (a–g).

1	Le réveillon	a	C'est une fête musulmane, à la fin du Ramadan.
2	Le jour de Noël	b	C'est le jour où on se dit: «Bonne année».
3	Un anniversaire	c	C'est une fête qu'on fait le trente et un décembre.
4	Le jour de l'An	d	On fait la fête pour célébrer le jour où on est né.
5	La fête des Mères	e	C'est une fête chrétienne, au printemps.
6	Le jour de Pâques	f	C'est le vingt-cinq décembre.
7	La fête de l'Aïd	g	C'est le jour où on dit: «Bonne fête, maman».

La tradition de l'Aïd el-Fitre

Le mois de Ramadan est fini. C'est enfin la fête de l'Aïd el-Fitre. Pendant le Ramadan, on n'a pas le droit de manger pendant la journée, seulement le soir et tôt le matin.

Pour la fête de l'Aïd el-Fitre, traditionnellement, les hommes portent leurs plus beaux vêtements et les femmes préparent des plats cuisinés pour l'occasion.

Hommes et femmes rendent visite à leurs amis et à leur famille. Certaines familles préfèrent sortir ou se promener plutôt que de rendre visite aux oncles et aux cousins.

Les enfants savent bien que c'est aussi leur fête et reçoivent des cadeaux de toutes sortes.

C'est un jour où on va à la mosquée parce que c'est une fête religieuse.

La plus grande partie de la journée, cependant, se passe en famille autour de la table. On mange, on boit (mais on ne boit pas d'alcool) et on s'amuse. C'est une occasion joyeuse que tout le monde apprécie.

2a 📖🎧 Read the text and decide whether these statements are true (**T**), false (**F**) or not mentioned in the text (**?**).

1 Eid is celebrated just before the period of Ramadan.
2 During Ramadan, eating is not allowed during the daytime.
3 For Eid, people visit their friends and their relatives.
4 Some families prefer staying at home, however.
5 Children give presents to their parents.
6 As Eid is a religious day, people go to the mosque.
7 Little time is spent around the table.

2b 📖🎧 Read the text again and answer these questions in English.

1 What do men traditionally wear for Eid?
2 How do women contribute to the day?
3 Why do children in particular like Eid?
4 What do the family actually do for most of the day?

3a 🎧 Listen to Antoine and Thomas exchanging information about their birthdays and identify the person who …

1 could not be there for Thomas's birthday.
2 paid for Thomas to have download vouchers.
3 was ill on his birthday.
4 gave Antoine a television for his birthday.

3b 🎧 Listen again and correct the mistakes in these statements.

1 Thomas did not go to school on his birthday and his friends came to his house later to play games.
2 Thomas's friends gave him a mobile phone.
3 Antoine's birthday (15th January) was a cold day with some snow.
4 Antoine spent his birthday watching television.

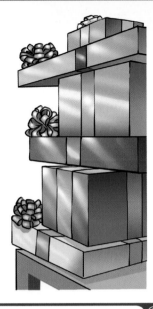

4 Ⓖ Transform these sentences so they state what things were like last year. Use the imperfect tense.

Exemple: Il fait beau pour mon anniversaire. →
    L'année dernière, il faisait beau pour mon anniversaire.

1 J'ai quatorze ans.
2 La cuisine de ma tante, c'est délicieux!
3 Je suis à la maison à Noël.
4 Il y a du monde au réveillon.
5 C'est dommage. Il est malade le jour de son anniversaire.

5 ✏️ Write a social networking site message to your friends, telling them about your birthday. Mention:

■ when your birthday is and how old you are
■ how you normally spend your birthday (where, what you do)
■ what you did for your last birthday (using the perfect tense)
■ what you thought of it (using *faire, avoir* and *être* in the imperfect tense)
■ what your favourite festival is (and why)
■ what you do / did for that festival.

Mon anniversaire, c'est le …	
Normalement, pour mon anniversaire, je …	
À mon dernier anniversaire,	j'ai reçu … / j'ai mangé … / je suis allé(e) …
C'était	génial / barbant.
Il faisait	froid / beau.
Ma fête préférée, c'est	Noël / Pâques / l'Aïd / la Saint-Valentin.
Je préfère … parce que	je reçois … / on mange … / on va …

Grammaire · page 184

Common imperfect expressions

You sometimes need to use the imperfect tense to describe what something was like, how someone was feeling or where something / somebody was. You need to learn these five by heart: *j'avais* (I had), *j'étais* (I was), *il y avait* (there was / there were), *c'était* (it was) and *il faisait chaud / froid* (it was hot / cold).

Find out more about the imperfect tense. *See page 107* ➡

Stratégie 5

Including negatives

When writing, include what you don't do as well as what you do. As well as *ne … pas*, include expressions such as *ne … jamais* (never) and *ne … plus* (no more, no longer). Include three things you don't do, never do or no longer do on your birthday.

 *Lien*

5.3 Higher is available in the Higher book.

Home and local area

1 Complete these sentences using prepositions, to say where things are in the room. (Check page 108 to find the French for 'bed', 'window', 'desk', 'wardrobe'.)

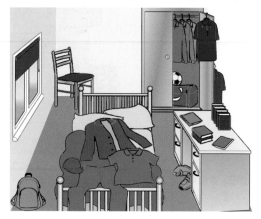

1 Les baskets sont _____ . (*in relation to the desk*)
2 Le sac de sport est _____ . (*in relation to the wardrobe*)
3 Les livres sont _____ . (*in relation to the desk*)
4 Le pantalon est _____ . (*in relation to the bed*)
5 La chaise est _____ . (*in relation to the bed*)
6 The desk is _____ . (*in relation to the window*)

Grammaire page 190

Prepositions

Devant (in front of), *derrière* (behind), *sur* (on), *sous* (under) and *dans* (in) are examples of prepositions that are easy to use.

However, when using a preposition that is followed by '*de*', e.g. *à côté de* (next to), *en face de* (opposite), note that *de* can become *du* or *des*.

Use *des* when the next word is plural:

à côté des toilettes   next to the toilets

Use *du* when the next word is masculine:

en face du salon   opposite the lounge

2 Re-order the words in these sentences so that they make sense.

1 C'est touristique ville petite une.
2 On une maison jolie habite.
3 On voiture grande a une.
4 Il y a commercial un centre grand.
5 cinéma On un petit a.

Grammaire page 175

Adjectives that go before nouns

Most adjectives in French go after the noun they describe. However, some adjectives are placed before the noun, e.g. *petit* (small), *grand* (big, large), *vieux* (old), *joli* (pretty).

Note that an -*e* is added when the adjective describes a feminine word, an -*s* is added for plural and -*es* is added for feminine plural, e.g. *joli* can also be spelt *jolie*, *jolis* or *jolies*.

3 Copy the sentences and fill in each gap using the correct form of the reflexive verb in brackets.

1 Je _____ _____ à sept heures. (**se lever**)
2 Il _____ _____ dans la salle de bains. (**se laver**)
3 Elle _____ _____ dans sa chambre. (**s'habiller**)
4 Tu _____ _____ à quelle heure? (**se coucher**)
5 Moi, je _____ _____ à dix heures. (**se coucher**)

Grammaire page 183

Reflexive verbs

Se lever (to get up), *s'habiller* (to get dressed), *se laver* (to wash) and *se coucher* (to go to bed) are all reflexive verbs.

You need to add an extra word (underlined below) each time you use a reflexive verb, e.g. *je <u>me</u> lave* (I wash), *tu <u>te</u> laves* (you wash), *il <u>se</u> lave* (he washes), *elle <u>se</u> lave* (she washes).

Note that these verb endings are the normal -*er* verb endings (present tense).

4 Match the questions and the answers using the English in brackets to help you.

1 Il y a combien de pièces dans ta maison? (*There are eight of them.*)
2 Vous avez combien de chambres? (*We have three of them.*)
3 Il y a combien de salles de bains? (*There are two of them.*)
4 Comment est le garage? (*There is none.*)
5 Vous avez un jardin? (*Yes, we have one.*)
6 Vous mettez des fleurs aux fenêtres. (*Yes, we do.*)

a Oui, on en met!
b Il y en a huit.
c Il y en a deux.
d Oui, on en a un.
e Il n'y en a pas.
f On en a trois.

Grammaire page 179

> ***En* meaning 'of it', 'of them'**
>
> *En* is used to avoid repeating a noun introduced with a number or *du / de la / de l' / des*. It goes before the verb.
>
> *Vous avez deux salles de bains? Non, on **en** a trois!*
>
> Do you have two bathrooms? No, we have three (of them)!

5 Complete the captions with the correct adjective taken from the word snake.

1 un _____ jardin

2 une _____ rivière

3 une _____ église

4 un _____ château

5 un _____ hôtel

6 un _____ escalier

vieillevieuxbelnouvelbellebeau

Grammaire page 175

> **Three adjectives: *vieux*, *nouveau*, *beau***
>
> These three common adjectives come before the noun:
>
> *un **vieux** musée* – an old museum
>
> *un **nouveau** centre commercial* – a new shopping centre
>
> *un **beau** tableau* – a beautiful painting
>
> Their feminine forms are *vieille*, *nouvelle* and *belle*:
>
> *une nouvelle piscine* – a new swimming pool
>
> They have a special form used before a vowel or a silent *h*:
>
> *un vieil homme* – an old man
>
> *un nouvel aéroport* – a new airport
>
> *un bel endroit* – a beautiful place

6 Choose the correct translation for each sentence.

1 *Je dormais quand tu as appelé.*
   a I was asleep when you called.
   b I will be asleep when you call.
2 *Avant, je ne regardais jamais la télévision.*
   a I have never watched television.
   b I never used to watch television.
3 *Elle visitait le musée quand je suis arrivée.*
   a She wanted to visit the museum when I arrived.
   b She was visiting the museum when I arrived.
4 *Il lavait la voiture tous les dimanches.*
   a He used to wash the car every Sunday.
   b He washes the car every Sunday.

Grammaire page 184

> **The imperfect tense**
>
> The imperfect tense is used to describe what something was like in the past, or what someone used to do regularly in the past. In the singular, it usually ends in *-ais* or *-ait*. You don't pronounce the final *s* or *t*.
>
> | | |
> |---|---|
> | habiter | to live |
> | j'habitais | I used to live; I lived |
> | tu habitais | you used to live; you lived |
> | il / elle habitait | he / she used to live; he / she lived |

Home and local area

Topic 5.1 Home

5.1 G Chez moi ➡ *pages 94–95*

	à côté de	next to
l'	armoire (f)	wardrobe
le	bureau	desk
la	chambre	bedroom
la	commode	chest of drawers
la	cuisine	kitchen
	dans	in
	devant	in front of
	derrière	behind
	en face de	opposite
l'	escalier (m)	staircase
l'	étage (m)	floor (1st, 2nd, etc.)
la	fenêtre	window
le	lit	bed
	monter	to go up
	montrer	to show
la	porte	door
le	rez-de-chaussée	ground floor
la	salle à manger	dining room
la	salle de bains	bathroom
le	salon	lounge
	sous	under
	sur	on
les	toilettes (f)	toilets
la	valise	suitcase

5.1 F Ma maison ➡ *pages 96–97*

l'	appartement (m)	apartment, flat
l'	ascenseur (m)	lift
l'	aspirateur (m)	vacuum cleaner
le	balcon	balcony
le	chalet	chalet
la	campagne	countryside
le	congélateur	freezer
c'est	dommage	it's a pity

	dormir	to sleep
le	four à micro-ondes	microwave oven
le	frigo	fridge
l'	immeuble (m)	block of flats
	isolé(e)	isolated
le	jardin	garden
	joli(e)	pretty
le	lave-vaisselle	dishwasher
	loin	far
la	montagne	mountain
la	pièce	room
de la	place	some space
le	repas	meal
	sauf	except
le	sous-sol	the basement
la	terrasse	patio
	vieux / vieille	old
la	vue	view

Topic 5.2 My local area

5.2 G Là où j'habite ➡ *pages 98–99*

la	banlieue	the suburbs, the outskirts
	beau / belle	beautiful
la	boîte de nuit	the nightclub
au	bord de la mer	by the seaside
	bronzer	to sunbathe
à la	campagne	in the country(side)
le	centre commercial	shopping centre
	cependant	however
	habiter	to live
	mais	but
le	marché	market
à la	montagne	in the mountains
	nouveau / nouvelle	new
	par contre	on the other hand
la	patinoire	the ice rink
la	piscine	swimming pool
la	plage	beach

	pourtant	however
	rêver de	to dream of
le	stade	the stadium
le	temps libre	free time
	touristique	touristy
la	ville	the town

5.2 F Ma région ➡ *pages 100–101*

	à demain	see you tomorrow
l'	alpinisme (m)	mountaineering
l'	animation (f)	liveliness
	animé(e)	lively
	attendre	to wait for
la	circulation	traffic
	connaître	to know
	danser	to dance
	génial(e)	great
la	maison individuelle	detached house
la	monitrice	(female) instructor
la	naissance	birth
	partager	to share
	partout	everywhere
	propre	clean
la	randonnée	hike
le	spectacle	show
les	sports nautiques (m)	water sports
	tranquille	quiet
l'	usine (f)	factory
la	voile	sailing
le	VTT	mountain bike

Topic 5.3 Routine and celebrations

5.3 G La routine à la maison ➡ *pages 102–103*

d'	abord	first of all
	après	after
	avant	before
le	beau-père	stepfather
la	belle-mère	stepmother
	ça m'énerve	it gets on my nerves
se	coucher	to go to bed
	faire les courses	to do the shopping

	faire la cuisine	to do the cooking
	faire le ménage	to do the housework
	faire la vaisselle	to do the washing up
s'	habiller	to get dressed
	hier	yesterday
se	laver	to wash
	lentement	slowly
se	lever	to get up
	lire	to read
le	matin	morning
	mettre la table	to set / lay the table
	nettoyer	to clean
	prendre une douche	to have a shower
	puis	then
	ranger sa chambre	to tidy one's room

5.3 F Les jours de fête à la maison
➡ *pages 104–105*

l'	Aïd (m)	Eid
l'	anniversaire (m)	birthday
le	cadeau	present
	célébrer	to celebrate
	chrétien(ne)	Christian
	dommage	pity
	faire la fête	to have a party, a celebration
	fêter	to celebrate
la	fête des Mères	Mothers' day
le	jour de l'An	New Year's day
la	journée	day
	musulman(e)	Muslim
	Noël	Christmas
l'	occasion (f)	occasion, opportunity
	offrir	to offer
	Pâques	Easter
le	portable	mobile phone
le	printemps	spring
	recevoir	to receive
	religieux(-ieuse)	religious
	render visite à	to visit (someone)
le	réveillon	Christmas Eve / New Year's Eve party
	télécharger	to download

6.1 G L'environnement – les causes du problème

La météo

1. Il fait du soleil dans le sud-est et une température de dix-huit degrés dans l'après-midi.

2. Dans le centre, il y a encore beaucoup de nuages et ce matin, il pleut.

3. Dans le nord-est, il fait du brouillard et il ne fait pas chaud.

4. Il fait mauvais dans le sud-ouest. Il y a beaucoup de vent.

5. Dans le nord, il neige ce matin et il fait froid.

6. Dans l'ouest, il fait beau et le ciel est bleu.

7. Il gèle dans le nord-ouest. Il fait -2 degrés ce matin.

8. Dans l'est, le soleil brille mais les nuages arrivent en fin d'après-midi.

9. Dans le sud, le beau temps continue mais il y a beaucoup de pollution dans l'air.

1a 📖🎧 Read the weather forecast. Pick out the location (north, south, east, west, etc.) in each sentence. Use it to name the right town or city on the map.

Exemple: *1 = Nice*

1b 📖🎧 Read the weather forecast again and give two details in English about the forecast for each town.

2 💬 Work with a partner. You are a weather forecaster on French TV. Take turns to say what the weather is like in each town. Use the map and some of the phrases in the forecast above to help you.

À Nice, il fait mauvais et il fait du brouillard.

À Clermont-Ferrand, il fait du brouillard et il gèle.

3 📖 Match each phrase (1–6) with the correct definition (a–f).

1	la circulation	a	les parcs et les jardins publics
2	les changements climatiques	b	quand il pleut trop, on risque d'en avoir
3	les inondations	c	on en donne au supermarché
4	un centre de recyclage	d	le temps a beaucoup changé en comparaison avec le passé
5	les espaces verts	e	les voitures et les camions, par exemple
6	les sacs en plastique	f	un endroit public pour recycler le papier, le verre, etc.

4a 🎧 Listen to these people talking about climate change and the causes of pollution. Write down the missing words for each of the following sentences.

1 The temperature is _____ .
2 There is too much traffic, especially _____ and _____ .
3 There is not enough _____ .
4 _____ are a big problem.
5 There aren't enough _____ .
6 We don't _____ enough. There aren't enough _____ .
7 There is too much _____ .
8 We travel too much by _____ and the _____ are too close to cities.
9 We use too many _____ .

4b 🎧 Listen again. Copy and complete the grid with the number of each statement (1–9) in the correct column.

about the climate	about pollution

5a 🅖 Copy the sentences and fill in each gap with *trop (de / d')* or *pas assez (de / d')*.

1 Il y a _____ voitures sur les routes.
2 Il n'y a _____ centres de recyclage.
3 On ne recycle _____ .
4 Les aéroports sont _____ près des villes.
5 Il n'y a _____ neige pour faire du ski.

5b 🅖 Translate these sentences into French using trop (*de / d'*) or *pas assez* (*de / d'*) in each sentence.

1 There is too much traffic.
2 There are not enough recycling centres.
3 We travel too much by car.
4 There are not enough parks.
5 We use too many plastic bags.

> ## Grammaire — page 178
>
> ### *Trop de* and *pas assez de*
>
> *Trop* means 'too much' or 'too many'. When it is followed by a noun, add *de* or *d'*, e.g. *trop de pluie*.
>
> *Pas assez* means 'not enough'. When it is followed by a noun, *de* or *d'* also need to be added, e.g. *pas assez de centres de recyclage*.
>
> Also learn about *moi*, *toi*, *lui*, *elle*.   *See page 118* ➡

6 🖎 Design a poster in support of an environmental organisation which highlights some of the environmental problems in our cities. Write short sentences to match the points that your illustrations are making.

Il y a trop de	circulation / …
On utilise trop	l'avion /…
On utilise trop de	sacs en plastique / …
On voyage trop	en avion / …
Il n'y a pas assez de	parcs / …

> ## Stratégie 6
>
> ### Using phrases you know
>
> Try to use French words and phrases that you have already studied and therefore know to be correct, e.g. *Il y a trop de voitures. Il n'y a pas assez de centres de recyclage.*

6.1 F Les problèmes de l'environnement

1 **V** Match the English and French phrases. Most of the French words are very similar to the English words.

1 save gas and electricity
2 floods
3 organic products
4 tornadoes and storms
5 plastic bags (or 'sacks')
6 the protection of the environment
7 recycling bottles
8 to protect the planet

a protéger la planète
b les tornades et les tempêtes
c les inondations
d la protection de l'environnement
e économiser le gaz et l'électricité
f le recyclage des bouteilles
g les sacs en plastique
h les produits bio

Notre Terre en danger

A **Tout le monde utilise trop de plastique mais il est très difficile à recycler.** Dans certains pays, il y a des montagnes de déchets. Avant, il y avait des sacs en plastique gratuits dans tous les supermarchés. Maintenant, personne ne les utilise. À la place, on prend des sacs en coton et on les réutilise.

B **Chaque année il y a de nouveaux records de températures.** Il y a de plus en plus de tempêtes et de tornades. Avant, il y avait une grosse tornade par an, maintenant il y en a plusieurs! Dans certains pays, il fait de plus en plus chaud. Les glaciers vont fondre, le niveau de l'eau va monter. Les villes et les villages près de la mer sont en danger.

C **Beaucoup d'espèces d'animaux sont en danger d'extinction.** Les usines où sont fabriqués tous les produits dont on a besoin sont responsables de la pollution de nos rivières. Elles y mettent tous leurs déchets. Les eaux polluées arrivent dans les mers et causent la mort de milliers de poissons. Notre industrie et notre agriculture causent la destruction de l'habitat des animaux, des oiseaux et des insectes.

2a 📖 🎧 Read the article and choose an English title for each paragraph (A–C).

1 Destruction of habitats
2 Recycling
3 Global warming

2b 📖 🎧 Below are five solutions. Decide which of the three problems outlined above (A–C) each one is aimed at resolving.

Vous pouvez sauver la planète …

1 en achetant des produits qui ne polluent pas les rivières.
2 en recyclant les déchets.
3 en voyageant en train, pas en avion.
4 en utilisant des sacs en coton.
5 en protégeant le monde animal.

3a 📖 🎧 Listen to Section A. Put these environmental issues into the order in which they are mentioned in the discussion.

climate change   river pollution
traffic fumes   pollution of the seas
destruction of the rain forest   extinction of wildlife

3b 🎧 Listen to Section B and answer the questions in English.

1 What does Sandrine think is the most serious environmental problem?
2 What is causing it, according to her?
3 Éric has a different cause to blame. Which one?
4 What problem does Adrien mention?
5 What do Sandrine and Adrien agree is the most serious problem?

4 🄖 Copy the sentences and fill in each gap with the correct present participle. Choose from the verbs below.

1 Mon père pollue en _____ une grosse voiture.
2 En _____ mes courses à pied, je ne pollue pas.
3 Je protège l'environnement en _____ des pommes françaises.
4 Je protège l'environnement en _____ les produits emballés dans du plastique.
5 Sascha protège l'environnement en _____ des sacs en coton.
6 Et moi, je protège l'environnement en _____ mes déchets.

faire   refuser   conduire   utiliser
acheter   recycler

5 🗨 Work in a small group. Discuss the various environmental problems mentioned on these two pages and agree on an order of importance. Then present the agreed order to the class: *le problème le plus grave, c'est …, puis c'est …, ensuite, c'est …*, etc. For each problem, suggest a way to improve the situation.

Le problème le plus grave, c'est	le changement climatique.
	la pollution des rivières et de la mer (des mers).
	la pollution de l'air.
	la destruction de l'habitat des animaux.
On peut protéger l'environnement en	faisant des pistes cyclables / recyclant les déchets.
	faisant des économies d'eau / de gaz / d'électricité.
	se déplaçant à vélo / à pied.
	n'utilisant pas de sacs en plastique.
On ne doit pas	polluer la mer / les rivières.

Stratégie 3b

Pronunciation of similar words

While listening, you will notice that although many French and English words are similar to look at, they are often pronounced quite differently. As you carry out the listening task, check the pronunciation of *-tion* (in *pollution, extinction, destruction, circulation*), *i* (in *plastique*), *é* (in *pollué*) and *è* (in *problème*).

Grammaire   *page 186*

Present participles

The present participle in French ends in *-ant*, and it is used if you want to say 'by doing something':

Je protège l'environnement en recyclant mes bouteilles en plastique.– I protect the environment by recycling my plastic bottles.

To form the present participle in French, take the *nous* form of the present tense, remove the *-ons*, and replace it with *-ant*.

Also learn about indefinite pronouns: *tout le monde* and *personne*.   See page 118 ➡

🔗 **Lien**

6.1 Higher is available in the Higher book.

6.2 G Ce que je fais pour l'environnement

En ville

Dans ma ville, il y a des pistes cyclables.

Ici, il y a une zone piétonne au centre.

Chez nous, il y a des centres de recyclage sur les parkings.

Dans ma ville, il n'y a pas de poubelles dans les parcs.

Ici, il y a un très bon système de transports en commun.

Dans ma ville, il n'y a pas de vélos à louer.

1a 📖 🎧 Read the speech bubbles. Which three statements are true?

1 There are recycling centres in car parks.
2 There are bikes to hire in town.
3 There aren't any cycle paths.
4 Public transport is very good.
5 There are dustbins in the parks.
6 There is a pedestrian area in the centre.

1b 📖 🎧 Find in the speech bubbles the French words that match these pictures.

1c 🎧 Read the statements. Are these people helpful or unhelpful to the environment?

1 Je vais au collège en voiture avec ma mère.
2 Chez nous, on économise le gaz.
3 Quand je vais en ville, j'y vais à pied.
4 À la maison, on recycle tout.
5 Je n'utilise pas le bus parce que c'est cher.

2a 🎧 Listen to what these people say they do to help the environment. Write down the missing words for each of the following sentences.

1 He goes to school _____ or _____ .
2 She recycles _____ and _____ .
3 He has a _____ rather than a _____ .
4 She uses _____ .
5 He saves _____ and _____ .
6 She never uses _____ from the supermarket.
7 He doesn't put his _____ in the _____ .

2b 🎧 Listen again and note down the negative verb phrases used by speakers 6 and 7.

3 Ⓖ Choose the correct verb form to complete each sentence.

1 Je **recycle / recycler / recyclent** les bouteilles.
2 J' **économises / économise / économisez** l'électricité.
3 Je **prend / prendre / prends** une douche au lieu d'un bain.
4 Je **vas / va / vais** au collège à pied.
5 J' **utilise / utilises / utiliser** les transports publics.
6 Je **met / mets / mettre** les déchets à la poubelle.

4 ✏️ Write your contribution to an internet forum on how to help the environment.

■ Make a list of what you do to help the environment. Mention at least three different things.
■ List the facilities that there are where you live to help people protect the environment. Mention at least three different facilities.

Pour protéger l'environnement,	j'utilise …
	j'économise …
	je recycle …
Dans ma ville / mon village,	il y a …
	il n'y a pas de …

Je forms of present tense verbs ⒼGrammaire · page 182

To say that you do something, in most cases, you say **je _____ e**, e.g. *je recycle, j'économise, j'utilise.*

However, some verbs are different. Learn these by heart: *je vais* (I go), *je prends* (I take), *je mets* (I put)

Also learn about unexpected prepositions. *See page 118* ➡

Using verbs that you know · Stratégie 4

In writing (and in speaking), use verbs that you know, as you don't know whether a verb is regular or irregular unless you have come across it before. You will avoid mistakes that way.

6.2 F   Une ville propre

1 🟍 Solve these anagrams. The definitions should help you.

1   **none péte in oz**   – c'est pour les gens à pied
2   **blue poles**   – c'est pour les déchets non recyclables
3   **yet roten**   – rendre propre
4   **re space vests**   – les parcs et les jardins publics
5   **rare quit**   – une partie de la ville

Troyes: ville propre

Ici à Troyes on a fait beaucoup pour l'environnement …

1   Le centre-ville est une zone piétonne où les véhicules sont interdits.
2   On a introduit un système de pistes cyclables.
3   On a installé des poubelles dans les espaces verts.
4   Il y a des centres de recyclage dans les parkings.

Pour recycler vos déchets …

Il y a des centres de recyclage pour les bouteilles, le papier et pour toutes sortes de choses recyclables. Cette initiative a eu beaucoup de succès: il y a trois ans, les habitants de Troyes recyclaient 10 pour cent de leurs déchets, aujourd'hui c'est 30 pour cent.

Pour avoir une ville propre …

On a installé des poubelles dans tous les espaces verts. Dans le quartier St-Julien, le club des jeunes a organisé l'opération «Nettoyage du jardin public». Ils l'ont vraiment transformé. Un grand merci à tous ces jeunes!

Pour pédaler sans polluer …

Une autre mesure qu'on a introduite dans la région est la construction de pistes cyclables. C'est surtout bon pour la santé des jeunes. On les encourage à prendre le vélo pour aller à l'école.

2a 📖🎧 Decide which symbol (A–D) goes with each numbered point (1–4) in the first section.

2b 📖🎧 Read the whole leaflet and decide whether the following sentences are true (**T**), false (**F**) or not mentioned (**?**).

1   They have installed recycling facilities.
2   Garden waste is collected from homes.
3   Young people are encouraged to cycle to school.
4   The city has done little to improve the environment.
5   There are initiatives for young people.
6   The park in St-Julien is dirty.

Recognising new words

You are often able to recognise new words from those you already know. For example, from the verb *recycler*, you can recognise the noun *recyclage*. Find the verb from the noun *pollution* and the noun from the verb *nettoyer* in the leaflet.

Stratégie 2a–2b

3a 🎧 Listen to the interviews. Match the people (1–3) with the right pictures (A–C).

1 Alex 2 Juliette 3 Zoé

3b 🎧 Who says what? Write Alex, Juliette or Zoé for each sentence.

1 I refuse plastic bags.
2 I'm doing something good for my health.
3 We had to clear up after the party.
4 I use public transport.
5 Mum used to take me to school.
6 You have to pay for a plastic bag.
7 We recycled everything.

4 **G** Copy the sentences and fill in each gap using the verb *faire* in the perfect tense. Then start each sentence with *d'habitude* (usually) instead of *hier* (yesterday) and do the activity again, this time using the present tense of the verb *faire*.

1 Hier, j'_____ du recyclage.
2 Hier, mon frère _____ des économies d'eau.
3 Hier, mes copains _____ du nettoyage.
4 Hier, nous _____ du vélo.
5 Hier, on _____ le trajet en utilisant les transports en commun.
6 Hier, mes parents _____ les courses avec des sacs en coton.

> **_Grammaire_** *page 195*
>
> **_Faire_: present and perfect tenses**
>
> It is important to be able to use the common verb *faire* (to do) correctly.
>
> ***Je fais*** *du nettoyage.* – I am doing some cleaning.
>
> ***J'ai fait*** *du nettoyage.* – I did some cleaning.
>
> If you can't remember how to form the present tense or the perfect tense of *faire,* look it up in the verb tables (page 195), or refer back to Topic 3 (page 61) and Topic 4 (page 77).
>
> Also learn how to use *on*.
> See page 119 ➡

5 🗨 Work with a partner. Prepare answers to the following questions, then take turns to ask and answer.

1 Quels sont les problèmes de l'environnement dans votre ville?
2 Est-ce que la ville fait assez pour la protection de l'environnement?
3 Personnellement, qu'est-ce que vous faites pour protéger l'environnement? Qu'est-ce que vous avez fait récemment?
4 Qu'est-ce que vous recyclez?
5 Économisez-vous l'eau? le gaz? l'électricité?

Il y a trop de …	
Il n'y a pas assez de …	
Dans notre ville,	il y a … on peut …
Moi,	j'utilise … j'économise … je recycle …
	j'ai nettoyé … j'ai fait …

Quels sont les problèmes de l'environnement dans votre ville?

Dans notre ville, il y a trop de circulation et il n'y a pas assez de pistes cyclables.

Lien

6.2 Higher is available in the Higher book.

(G) Environment

1 Copy the sentences and fill in each gap with the correct pronoun. Then translate the sentences into English.

1 _____, je fais mes courses avec des sacs en coton.

2 _____, tu utilises des sacs en plastique.

3 _____, il va à l'école en voiture.

4 _____, elle prend le bus.

5 _____, il jette ses déchets sur le trottoir.

6 _____, je mets mes déchets à la poubelle.

Elle	Lui	Lui	Moi	Moi	Toi

Grammaire pages 179–180

> ### *Moi, toi, lui, elle*
> In English, if you want to emphasise something you do, you just say it a bit more forcefully. French people put *moi* (me), *toi* (you), *lui* (him) or *elle* (her) at the beginning of the sentence.
> *Moi, je recycle.* – I recycle.
> *Lui, il recycle toutes ses bouteilles*. – He recycles all his bottles.
> *Elle, elle ne recycle rien.* – She doesn't recycle anything.
> The word for 'her' and 'she' is the same – *elle*!

2 What do these phrases mean in English? Check your answers, then learn the phrases by heart.

1 en ville

2 au centre-ville

3 à la poubelle

4 à pied

5 en voiture

6 un sac en plastique

Grammaire pages 189–190

> ### Unexpected prepositions
> Although prepositions like 'in' and 'on' are often translated as *dans* and *sur*, other French prepositions are sometimes used instead, e.g. *en ville* (in town).

3a How can we save the planet? Copy the sentences and fill in each gap with *personne ne / n'* or *tout le monde*, to describe an environmentally friendly world.

Exemple: Personne ne pollue les rivières.

1 _____ a un vélo.

2 _____ va au collège en voiture.

3 _____ utilise de sacs en plastique.

4 _____ prend des sacs en papier.

5 _____ recycle le papier.

6 _____ économise l'eau.

Grammaire page 180

> ### Indefinite pronouns: *tout le monde, personne*
> The French for 'everybody' is *tout le monde* and 'nobody' is *personne*.
> Both are followed by a verb in the singular. Note that in front of a verb, *personne* is followed by *ne* (or *n'* before a vowel).
> *Tout le monde économise l'énergie.* – Everyone saves energy.
> *Personne ne jette ses déchets ici.* – Nobody throws their rubbish away here.

3b Select sentences from Activity 3a as captions for these pictures.

A

B

C

4 Write these verb forms in French, using *on*.

1 we recycle
2 we pollute
3 we use
4 we travel
5 we go

Grammaire page 178

On

Remember that *on* is often used to mean 'we' instead of saying *nous*. Verbs used with *on* take the same endings as *il* or *elle*.
On voyage en avion. – We travel by plane.

5 Use the verb tables on page 193 to help you choose the correct form of the regular verbs in these sentences, then write whether they are in the present or perfect tense.

1 Il **joue / joues / jouent** au rugby.
   Exemple: joue – *present*
2 Je **se couche / me couche / te couches** à dix heures.
3 Nous **choisissent / choisissons / choisis** notre déjeuner.
4 Ils **a mangé / avons mangé / ont mangé** des pâtes.
5 Tu **avez attendu / a attendu / as attendu** à la gare.
6 Vous **a voyagé / avez voyagé / avons voyagé** en avion.
7 Je **descend / descends / descendez** l'escalier.
8 Elle **a fini / ont fini / as fini** ses devoirs.

Grammaire pages 193

Using regular verb tables

Many verbs in French follow one of three patterns of endings. You can usually tell from the infinitive which pattern they follow. The infinitive will either end in *-er*, e.g. *parler*; *-ir*, e.g. *finir*; or *-re*, e.g. *vendre*.

The first page of the verb tables gives examples of four tenses of these regular verbs, and you can use these to work out the endings for other verbs that follow the same pattern. There is also an example of a reflexive verb, to remind you of the extra pronoun needed with these verbs.

See pages 182–183 ➡

6a Use the verb tables to write the correct present and perfect tense forms of these infinitives.

Exemple: je – boire → je bois, j'ai bu
1 je – dire
2 il – écrire
3 nous – pouvoir
4 vous – prendre
5 ils – venir

6b Now find these future or imperfect forms of verbs in the verb tables. Note the tense used and the infinitive that they come from.

Exemple: j'irai – *future*, aller
1 j'aurai
2 elle était
3 tu devras
4 il faisait
5 ils voudront

Grammaire pages 194–197

Using irregular verb tables

There are a number of irregular verbs in French that you need to be able to use or recognise. The tables of irregular verbs on pages 194–197 enable you to see how they change in the present and perfect tenses. At Foundation level you should be able to use the present and perfect tenses and recognise, at least, the imperfect and future tenses. Make sure that you know how to use these tables, so that you can make your work as accurate as possible.

Environment

Topic 6.1 Current problems facing the planet

6.1 G L'environnement – les causes du problème ➡ *pages 110–111*

l'	aéroport (m)	airport
	beau / belle	nice, beautiful
le	brouillard	fog
le	camion	lorry
le	centre de recyclage	recycling centre
le	changement climatique	climate change
le	ciel	sky
la	circulation	traffic
le	climat	climate
le	degré	degree
l'	est (m)	east
	froid(e)	cold
	geler	to freeze
l'	inondation (f)	flood
	mauvais(e)	bad
la	neige	snow
le	nord	north
le	nuage	cloud
l'	ouest (m)	west
la	pluie	rain
	recycler	to recycle
le	sac en plastique	plastic bag
le	soleil	sun
le	sud	south
la	température	temperature
le	temps	weather
le	vent	wind

6.1 F Les problèmes de l'environnement ➡ *pages 112–113*

	affreux(-euse)	horrible
l'	avion (m)	plane
	conduire	to drive

les	déchets (m)	rubbish
la	destruction	destruction
	économiser	to save
l'	électricité (f)	electricity
	fondre	to melt
la	forêt	forest
le	gaz	gas
le	glacier	glacier
l'	habitat (m)	habitat
	monter	to go up
le	niveau	level
la	planète	planet
des	produits bio (m)	organic products
	protéger	to protect
	sauver	to save, to rescue
la	tempête	storm
la	tornade	tornado

Topic 6.2 Local issues and actions

6.2 G Ce que je fais pour l'environnement ➡ *pages 114–115*

le	bain	bath
la	bouteille	bottle
la	douche	shower
	économiser	to save
l'	électricité (f)	electricity
le	gaz	gas
	louer	to hire, to rent
	mettre	to put, to put on
le	papier	paper
le	parc	park
le	parking	car park
à	pied	on foot
la	piste cyclable	cycle path
la	poubelle	dustbin
	prendre	to take
les	transports en commun (m)	public transport

	utiliser	to use
le	vélo	bike
en	voiture	by car
la	zone piétonne	pedestrian area

6.2 F Une ville propre ➡ *pages 116–117*

le	carton	cardboard
le	club des jeunes	youth club
	emporter	to take (something with you)
l'	environnement (m)	environment
les	espaces verts (m)	parks, green spaces
	gratuit(e)	free (of charge)
l'	habitant (m)	inhabitant
	interdit(e)	forbidden
	introduire	to introduce
	marcher	to walk
	nettoyer	to clean
le	nettoyage	cleaning
	propre	clean
la	protection	protection
le	quartier	district
le	sac en coton	cotton bag
	sans	without
le	trajet	journey
le	trottoir	pavement

> ### Learning frequently used words
>
> The words given in the two 'frequently used words' lists are some of the most common words in the French language. They come up in every single GCSE Topic and you will find that it is a really good investment of your time to learn them all by heart.
>
> **Stratégie**

1 Frequently used words

alors	so, then
après	after
assez	quite, fairly
au revoir	goodbye
aussi	also
avant	before
avec	with
beaucoup	a lot
bien	well
bientôt	soon
bon(ne)	good
bonjour	hello
car	because
combien	how much
comme	as, like
comment	how
d'abord	first of all
dans	in
enfin	finally

2 Frequently used words

grand(e)	big
ici	here
mais	but
ou	or
où	where
par exemple	for example
parce que	because
petit(e)	small
plus	more
pour	for
pourquoi	why
puis	then
quand	when
que	that, which
qui	who
sans	without
souvent	often
sur	on
tout	all
très	very

Foundation – Exam practice

 info

These pages give you the chance to try GCSE-style practice exam questions at grades D–C, based on the AQA Context of Home and environment

 **Lien**

Higher practice exam questions (grades B–A*) are available at the end of this Context in the Higher book.

• Bastia

La Corse

Salut, tout le monde!

Un petit bonjour d'Erbalunga, près de Bastia, en Corse. Je suis bien arrivé, mais le voyage en bateau était long. Il y a beaucoup de travail à faire dans la maison, mais le plus important, c'est qu'après quelques problèmes, l'ordinateur marche bien! Demain, c'est mon premier jour au nouveau collège – au secours – et c'est aussi ma fête!! J'espère que mes parents n'ont pas oublié, et qu'ils m'ont acheté un cadeau!

Je voudrais avoir des nouvelles de mes copains de Lyon! Répondez-moi!

Guillaume

Salut Guillaume!

J'espère que ton premier jour au collège s'est bien passé. Ici rien n'a changé! Le prof de maths est toujours sévère. J'ai beaucoup de devoirs, alors je n'ai pas le temps de t'écrire un long message maintenant, mais parle-moi de ta nouvelle maison. Et ton village, il est comment?

Joël

1a Read Guillaume's first message since moving to Corsica and Joël's reply. Choose the correct word(s) to complete each sentence.

1 His new home is in **Bastia / Erbalunga / Lyon**.
2 He travelled to Corsica by **boat / plane / helicopter**.
3 It was important for him to get his **computer / music system / mobile phone** working.
4 He will start at his new school in **two weeks / next week / tomorrow**.
5 His first day at school is also important because it is his **birthday / name day / brother's birthday**.
6 He wants Joël to tell him about his **pets / friends / grandparents** in Lyon.
7 Joël complains about **a teacher / a friend / his parents**.
8 He has only written a short message because he has to **help at home / do his homework / go out**.

(**Total** = 8 marks)

Salut à tous mes amis!

Comment ça va à Lyon? Ici en Corse, après trois semaines, c'est le bazar! Mon père a commencé son nouveau travail dans un lycée de Bastia et moi, je vais au collège depuis deux semaines. Mon collège est très moderne, et les profs sont assez sympas. Je me suis déjà fait quelques amis en classe, alors ça va.

Le village où nous habitons est très petit. Ma mère l'aime bien, c'est si tranquille, mais le problème, c'est notre maison. C'est une jolie maison traditionnelle. Il y a trois chambres, et un grand jardin, mais il y a beaucoup de travail à faire dans la cuisine et la salle de bains. Depuis notre arrivée la douche ne marche pas (mais on peut prendre un bain!) et nous n'avons qu'un four à micro-ondes pour préparer les repas. Alors on mange beaucoup de salade!

Le maçon va commencer le travail lundi prochain. J'espère qu'on va finir avant l'arrivée de Joël en juillet. À bientôt,

Guillaume

1b 📖 Read Guillaume's reply. Match the beginnings and endings of the sentences.

1	Guillaume arrived in Corsica	a	works properly.
2	He started at his new school	b	very small.
3	Guillaume says the village is	c	two weeks ago.
4	His mother thinks the village is	d	in July.
5	The shower	e	peaceful.
6	The microwave	f	three weeks ago.
7	The builder will start work	g	does not work.
8	Joël will arrive	h	next Monday.

Total = 8 marks

Stratégie 1b

Paying attention to detail

When you do this sort of task, you can often see two possible endings to a sentence that are similar, e.g. endings **c** and **f** here. Check the detail of the text carefully before you make your choice. For example, think about tense, prepositions, gender and numbers, and make sure that they match.

2a 🎧 Joël will soon arrive at Guillaume's house. Guillaume's dad is checking that things are ready. Listen to Section A and match his questions (1–5) to the pictures below (A–E).

A
B

C

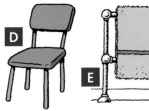
D

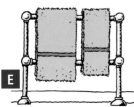
E

Total = 5 marks

2b 🎧 Joël is talking to his mother on the phone. Listen to Section B and complete the sentences in English.

1 Joël is staying by the sea and _____ the mountains.
2 He went to buy cheese at a _____ in the mountains.
3 The local beach is small and _____ .
4 There were a lot of _____ in Bastia.
5 They took bottles and _____ to be recycled.
6 The recycling centre is in the _____ part of Bastia.
7 The town centre is historic and _____ .

Total = 7 marks

Total for Reading and Listening = 28 marks

Foundation – Speaking

Chez moi

You are talking to your French friend about your house and your town. Your teacher will play the part of your friend and will ask you:

1 where you live and what your house is like
2 who lives in your house
3 what your room is like
4 about meal times
5 what you do to help round the house
6 what your nearest town is like.
7 !

! Remember, you will have to respond to something that you have not yet prepared.

> **info**
>
> **Important information:**
> This sample task is for practice purposes only and should not be used as an actual assessment task. Study it to find out how to plan your Controlled Assessment efficiently to gain maximum marks and / or work through it as a mock exam task before the actual Controlled Assessment.

---

1 Where you live and what your house is like
  - say where you live
  - say what your house is like
  - say how many rooms it has
  - talk about the garden and the garage

> **Stratégie**
>
> Start your plan. Here are some suggested words for bullet point 1: *exactement, description, pièces, jardin, garage, opinion*.
> Use *est située dans le* + county or compass direction to say where your house is located.
> Use *au rez-de-chaussée* or *en bas* for downstairs and *au premier étage* or *en haut* for upstairs.
> Use *chambres* for bedrooms and *pièces* for all other rooms.

---

2 Who lives in your house
  - say who lives in your house
  - say what they are like
  - say who you get on with (or don't get on with)
  - talk about your pets

> **Stratégie**
>
> Suggested words for your plan: *famille, personnalité, s'entendre avec, chien-détails*.
> Use *je m'entends bien avec …* to say who you get on with or *je ne m'entends pas bien avec …* to say who you don't get on with.
> If you don't have a pet, start with *je n'ai pas d'animal à la maison* and say why not.

---

3 What your room is like
  - say what your room is like
  - say whether you share your room
  - say what is in your room
  - say what you like doing in your room

> **Stratégie**
>
> Suggested words for your plan: *description-opinion, partager, mes choses, activités*.
> Show off your vocabulary. Talk about the walls, the curtains, the carpet and the furniture in your room, using adjectives to describe them.
> Use *j'ai ma propre chambre* if you don't share your room. If you have to share, use *partager* for 'to share'.
> Show initiative by saying what you do in your room when a friend visits you, e.g. play games, listen to music, etc. See Exam technique S10.

4 About meal times
- say what times meals are
- say whether you have your meals as a family
- say what your favourite meal is
- talk about the last time you went out for a meal

Stratégie

Suggested words for your plan: *quand, famille, repas préféré*. Add a maximum of two words to this list.
Use *manger en famille* to say 'to eat as a family'.
The last bullet point refers to an event in the past. See the grammar section (pages 183–184) for how to use the perfect tense, e.g. *je suis allé(e)* (I went), *j'ai mangé* (I ate).

5 What you do to help round the house
- say what you do to help round the house
- say whether you get pocket money for helping
- say what other members of the household do to help
- say how you helped last weekend

Stratégie

Suggested words for your plan: *moi, récompense, autres*. Add a maximum of three words to this list.
As the topic of helping round the house involves vocabulary hardly used in any other topic, you need to check how to say words like 'to tidy', 'dishwasher', 'washing up', etc. Take care with the pronunciation of *vaisselle*. You will gain marks for good pronunciation. See Exam technique S6.
Use *on me donne* or *je reçois …* to say what pocket money you get for helping at home.

6 What your nearest town is like
- say what the town centre is like
- say what facilities there are for young people
- say what you intend to do next time you go to town
- talk about your ideal town

Stratégie

Suggested words for your plan: *activités-jeunes*. Add a maximum of four words to this list.
Although you will inevitably use *il y a* and *c'est* in the first two sub-divisions suggested for this bullet point, try to use other verbs too, e.g. *on peut faire / voir / aller …*
Start with *le week-end prochain, j'ai l'intention de …* to say what you intend to do next time you go to town. Use other phrases that refer to future events too, e.g. *je voudrais / j'aimerais / je vais* + infinitive. See Exam technique S11.

7 ! At this point, you may be asked …
- if there are problems in your town.
- if you like living in your town.
- if you prefer living in town or in the countryside.
- if you intend to continue living in the same town or if you would like to move to another area.

Stratégie

Choose which **two** options you think are the most likely, and for each of these, note down **three** different ideas. In your plan, write three words that illustrate each of the two most likely options.
For the first suggestion you might choose: *pollution, transports, jeunes*. Learn these two options using your reminder words. See Exam technique S3.
Remember to check the total number of words you have used. It should be 40 or fewer.

 **Lien**
Higher sample assessment tasks for this Context can be found in the Higher book.

Foundation – Writing

L'environnement

Your French friend Yannick has been asked to participate in a debate on the environment at school. As he is keen to have an international perspective, he has asked you the questions below.

1 What is your local town like?

2 Are there environmental problems there?

3 What do you think the solutions to those problems are?

4 What do you do that makes environmental problems worse?

5 What are the main problems of the environment in today's world?

6 What can we as individuals do about it?

7 Should we stop going on holiday by plane?

> **(i)nfo**
>
> **Important information:**
> This sample task is for practice purposes only and should not be used as an actual assessment task. Study it to find out how to plan your Controlled Assessment efficiently to gain maximum marks and / or work through it as a mock exam task before the actual Controlled Assessment.

---

1 What is your local town like?

- say where it is situated
- describe it
- say what you think of it
- say whether you prefer to live in town or in the country

> *Stratégie*
>
> Start your plan. Here are some suggested words for bullet point 1: *où, description, opinion, préférence, ville-campagne*. Use *dans le*, e.g. *dans le Wiltshire, dans le sud-ouest*, to say where your town is situated (exception: *en Cornouailles*).
>
> To say what it is like, use adjectives such as *industrielle, historique, touristique*, etc. Use *il y a* and *il n'y a pas* to describe facilities.
>
> Develop the points you make, e.g. say what is good about your town and also what is not so good. See Exam technique W9.

---

2 Are there environmental problems there?

- say whether the town is clean or dirty
- say whether there is a lot of pollution
- say how much traffic there is in town
- say whether there is enough room for pedestrians

> *Stratégie*
>
> Suggested words for your plan: *propreté, pollution, circulation, espace piétons*.
>
> Use alternative vocabulary if you don't know a particular word, e.g. use 'not dirty' (*pas sale*).
>
> Remember you can use qualifiers such as *assez* and *très* to explain the situation more exactly.
>
> Use *piéton* for pedestrian.

---

3 What do you think the solutions to those problems are?

- say that litter should be taken home or put into bins
- say that there should be more bins and recycling centres
- say what can be done to reduce traffic in town
- say what can be done to help pedestrians

> *Stratégie*
>
> Suggested words for your plan: *poubelles, recyclage, paiement, zone piétonne*.
>
> Use *on doit* … to say what one should do and *il faut* to say what one must do.
>
> Start the third sub-division suggested here with *Pour réduire…, il faut* …

---

4 What do you do that makes environmental problems worse?
- say whether you drop litter or chewing gum
- say whether you always walk or use a bike to get to your destination.
- say whether you recycle enough
- say whether you sometimes travel by car unnecessarily

> **Stratégie**
> Suggested words for your plan: *papiers*, *transport localement*, *recyclage*.
> Add a maximum of two words to this list.
> Start the first sub-division with *Je (ne) jette (pas) …*
> To say what you recycle, use *je recycle …* and to say what you don't recycle, use *mais je ne recycle pas ..*

5 What are the main problems of the environment in today's world?
- say how the weather has changed
- mention another effect of climate change
- give some examples of some types of pollution
- talk about one of the effects of pollution

> **Stratégie**
> Suggested words for your plan: *climat*, *différentes pollutions*.
> Add a maximum of three words to this list.
> Use *le changement climatique* for 'climate change'.
> Use the perfect tense to say that the weather has changed and the present tense to say what it is like now.
> Use French words only in your plan. They will help you with vocabulary as well as remind you of what to write next. See Exam technique W2.

6 What can we as individuals do about it?
- talk about cycling and walking
- talk about recycling
- talk about saving energy
- say what else you are going to do to protect the environment

> **Stratégie**
> Suggested words in your plan: *vélo*, *recyclage*.
> Add a maximum of four words to this list.
> As well as mentioning what can be done (*on peut …*), say what you actually do (or don't do), e.g. walking, cycling, recycling.
> Start the last sub-division with *À l'avenir, je vais …*
> See Exam technique W5.

7 Should we stop going on holiday by plane?
- say if you sometimes go on holiday by plane
- say what you think of the price of plane tickets
- say if you sometimes holiday in Britain, where and how you get to your destination
- say what you think of travelling by plane in terms of the environment

> **Stratégie**
> Add up to six words to your plan.
> Use *en avion* to say 'by plane'.
> Use different ways of expressing your opinion, e.g. *à mon avis … / je pense que … / je trouve que …*
> Remember to check the number of words you have used in your plan. It should be 40 or fewer.

 **Lien**
> Higher sample assessment tasks for this Context can be found in the Higher book.

Exam technique – Speaking

S7 Ideas for practising

Treat each bullet point as a mini-task. Practise your answer to one bullet point at a time. Look at one word on your plan and say aloud all the things that the word is reminding you to say. Repeat the process for each word on your plan. Next, try to account for two words, then for three words, etc. Time your answer for one whole bullet point. Repeat the process for each bullet point. Record yourself if possible.

You can also practise with a partner. Together, work out the questions that your teacher might ask you in the exam and practise your answers to these questions in turn.

S8 Info about Interaction and Fluency

Interaction is about your ability to contribute to the conversation. To gain good marks, you will need to show initiative (see Exam technique S10).

Fluency is your ability to speak without hesitation. Try to speak with fluency but not too fast. If you are likely to be nervous when performing the task, practise it and practise it again. Time your whole response. Make a point of slowing down if you feel that you are speaking too fast. Practise with your plan in front of you so that you know what you are going to say next and therefore do not hesitate in the exam itself.

S9 Info about Communication, Range of language and Accuracy

The marks that you get for Communication are for getting the message over to the teacher who is examining you. The marks for Range of language are awarded if you have a good variety of vocabulary and grammatical structures in your responses. The marks that you get for Accuracy will be linked to how well you know and use the rules of French grammar and pronunciation. These three are closely linked because if you get the grammar wrong, it can change the meaning of your message. If this happens, you lose both Communication / Range of language, and Accuracy marks.

Grade booster

To reach grade D, you need to …

- Give a reasonable amount of information that is sometimes developed, e.g. for bullet point 3 of the sample Controlled Assessment on page 124, (what your room is like). When you feel that the language you are using is relatively simple, add extra information, e.g. 'I have a desk and a computer. I play games on it.'

- Use sentences that are generally simple but occasionally more complex, e.g. for bullet point 5 you could say that your brother lays and clears the table daily but that your sister does not do very much. It is the kind of sentence that is quite long but manageable.

To reach grade C, you need to …

- Offer some evidence of an ability to sustain a conversation and occasionally show initiative, e.g. for bullet point 2, you could give relevant information that has not been requested, such as details about your pet: you have a dog, he's three years old, fun, you like taking him for a walk, etc.

- Express points of view and sometimes develop them, e.g. for bullet point 4, give your opinion using different phrases such as *à mon avis / je pense que / je crois que / j'aime / je n'aime pas / je trouve que*, etc. Develop some of your answers using *car / parce que*.

Aiming for Higher? You need to …

- Show a range of vocabulary and an ability to use some complex sentences, e.g. for bullet point 6, use a variety of vocabulary to say what one can do in town and also to state your intentions.

- Answer without hesitation and extend responses beyond the minimum, e.g. for bullet point 1 there is the potential for you to give a lot of information: what is in your house, what each room is like, the size of the garden, what is in it, etc.

Exam technique – Writing

W7 Marking of the tasks

AQA examiners will mark your work. A senior examiner will check the work of the examiner. This is to ensure that candidates are given the correct mark for their work.

The pair of Writing tasks count for 30% of the whole GCSE French exam, so each of the Writing tasks is worth 15%. Your work will be marked in terms of Content, Range of language, and Accuracy. Each task will be marked out of 30 marks. Fifteen of these marks are for Content, 10 are for Range of language and 5 are for Accuracy.

W8 Info about Range of language

If you are aiming at grade C, you can't get away with just simple, short sentences. You need to join sentences together using connectives such as *et, mais, car* and *parce que*. You also need to vary your vocabulary and use different grammatical structures.

W9 Info about Content

You will be awarded marks under the heading 'Content' for:

- the amount of relevant information you give
- expressing and explaining ideas and points of view
- developing the points you make
- producing a well-structured piece of work.

Refer to Exam technique W6 for the number of words you should aim to write.

Grade booster

To reach grade D, you need to …

- Express points of view and sometimes develop them, e.g. for bullet point 7 of the sample Controlled Assessment on page 127, write about what you think of travelling by plane and explain how it harms the environment. Offer alternatives that are less harmful, e.g. travelling by train.
- Show evidence of some variety of vocabulary and structures, e.g. for bullet point 3, state what can / should be done, using a variety of phrases: *il faut / on doit / on peut / il est possible de*.

To reach grade C, you need to …

- Write longer sentences using appropriate linking words fairly accurately, e.g. for bullet point 4 you can list what you do for the environment, linking clauses with *et*. You can also introduce what you don't do by using *mais / par contre*.
- Communicate clearly quite a lot of relevant information, e.g. for bullet point 1, where the instruction is open-ended, give a lot of information. While describing your town, you can also say what facilities there are, whether you like your town and give reasons for your opinion.

Aiming for Higher? You need to …

- Show that you can use a variety of structures, including verb tenses, with reasonable accuracy, e.g. for bullet point 6, mention what you do for the environment and what you intend to do in the future. If you can introduce a reference to the past, all the better, e.g. 'Last year, I joined the environment club at my school'.
- Write simple French accurately, as errors are likely to occur in more complex sentences, e.g. for bullet point 1 write simple sentences using phrases such as *elle est située, il y a, c'est, j'aime, je préfère*. Focus on accuracy.

7.1 G Mon collège

Objectifs

Places and activities at school

Using *de* after a negative

Learning key phrases by heart

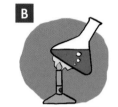

1 📖🎧 Match each description (1–7) with the correct picture (A–G).

Dans mon collège …

1 il y a une cantine.
2 il y a une cour de récréation.
3 il y a une salle des professeurs.
4 il y a deux laboratoires de chimie.
5 il y a trois salles d'informatique.
6 il n'y a pas de salle de musique.
7 il n'y a pas de gymnase.

2 **G** Transform these positive sentences into negative ones.

1 Il y a une bibliothèque.
2 Il y a un stade de foot.
3 Il y a un laboratoire de langues.
4 Il y a des tableaux interactifs.
5 Il y a un professeur de mandarin.

3 🖊 Copy the sentences from Activities 1 and 2 that apply to your school. Adapt the others so they can also describe your school.

Exemple: *Dans mon collège, il y a … Il n'y a pas de …*

> **Using *de* after a negative**
>
> Remember to use *de* (or *d'* before a vowel or an 'h') after a negative.
>
> *Il n'y a pas de tableau interactif.* – There is no interactive whiteboard.
>
> *Il n'y a pas d'ordinateur.* – There is no computer.
>
> Also practise how to say that you can or can't do something.
>
> See page 142 ➡
>
> **Grammaire** *page 188*

4 **V** Match the places in a school (1–8) with the correct descriptions (a–h).

1	la salle des professeurs	a	Là, on utilise des ordinateurs.
2	la cantine	b	On peut y pratiquer un instrument.
3	la cour de récréation	c	C'est réservé aux profs.
4	les salles de classe	d	On y fait du sport quand il pleut.
5	la salle d'informatique	e	On y parle avec ses amis et on s'amuse.
6	le gymnase	f	Là, on peut lire un livre.
7	la bibliothèque	g	C'est là où on mange à midi.
8	la salle de musique	h	C'est là où on a nos cours.

5a 🎧 Listen to eight students saying what they can do at school. Make notes in English. What can they do and where?

5b 🎧 Listen again. Which three statements below are true?

1 You can learn English in the language laboratory.
2 You can play rugby at the stadium.
3 You can use computers in the IT room.
4 You can eat your lunch in a classroom.
5 You can play the piano in the music room.
6 You can talk to your friends in the library.

6 ✏️ Your partner has sent you an email that includes the question: *Qu'est-ce qu'on peut faire à ton collège?* Write a reply, including at least five French sentences that explain what activities you can do and where. Use some of the words below.

Exemple: *On peut jouer du piano dans la salle de musique.*

stade	bibliothèque	laboratoire de sciences
	cantine	salle de musique
salle d'informatique		cour de récréation

Learning key phrases by heart

You will find it very useful in speaking and in writing to know certain key phrases. Learn the following by heart:

il y a	there is / there are
il n'y a pas de	there isn't / there aren't
on peut	one / we / you can
on ne peut pas	one / we / you cannot

Also learn how to write them with their correct spelling.

Stratégie 6

7.1 F   La vie au collège

1 🅥 Match the French with the English.

1	la rentrée	a	a study period (when one of your teachers is away)
2	une heure d'étude	b	a personal diary
3	un carnet de notes	c	a school book
4	une carte de sortie	d	a school diary (booklet with your marks / grades)
5	un journal intime	e	an exit pass (to leave the school premises)
6	un livre scolaire	f	the first day of the school year
7	le professeur principal	g	the form tutor

Manon, élève de sixième, écrit dans son journal intime

Mon journal intime

Lundi

Aujourd'hui, c'était la rentrée. Ma mère m'a accompagnée au collège et je n'ai pas aimé ça. Je ne suis plus un bébé! À huit heures, j'ai rencontré mon professeur principal et il est plutôt sévère. Puis, on a eu cours jusqu'à midi. Je suis allée à la cantine. Ce qu'on mange à la cantine, ce n'est jamais bon.

Mardi

Aujourd'hui, j'ai eu dessin, anglais et informatique. J'adore ces matières. J'ai aussi retrouvé trois de mes copines de l'école primaire qui sont aussi en sixième mais dans des classes différentes. On a beaucoup parlé à la récréation. Hier, elles n'étaient pas contentes non plus, mais aujourd'hui, ça va mieux.

Mercredi

Il n'y a pas de cours cet après-midi. Ça, c'est bien. Je dois sortir avec ma mère pour aller acheter mes livres scolaires et mes cahiers. Plus tard, Hélène va venir chez moi. C'est une nouvelle copine qui est dans ma classe. On va faire nos devoirs ensemble.

Jeudi

On n'a commencé les cours qu'à dix heures. C'est bien parce que je suis restée au lit jusqu'à neuf heures. Cet après-midi, entre trois heures et quatre heures, on a eu une heure d'étude parce qu'il n'y avait pas de professeur de sciences. Il était absent. L'étude, c'est une salle de classe où on fait ses devoirs si un professeur est absent.

Vendredi

J'ai trouvé la semaine plutôt longue. Je suis assez fatiguée parce qu'aujourd'hui, j'ai eu cours de huit heures à midi et de deux heures à cinq heures. Heureusement, c'est le week-end maintenant.

2a 📖 🎧 Read Manon's diary and decide whether these statements are true (**T**), false (**F**) or not mentioned in the text (**?**).

1 Manon did not enjoy her first day in secondary school.

2 She is in the same class as three of her primary school friends.

3 She only had one lesson on Wednesday afternoon.

4 She has to buy her own school books.

5 Hélène likes the same subjects as Manon.

6 On Thursday, Manon did her homework at lunch time.

7 She likes French and geography.

8 She was tired on Friday as she had a lot of homework to complete during the week.

2b 📖 🎧 Read Manon's diary again. Which three of these aspects of school life does Manon <u>not</u> like?

1 the canteen

2 being taken to school by her mother

3 English lessons

4 starting lessons at 10 a.m.

5 Wednesday afternoons

6 her Friday timetable

3a 🎧 Zoë has just come back from her exchange visit to a school in the UK. Listen to her talking to her friend Hélène about her day at the comprehensive school. Decide whether the statements below are true (**T**), false (**F**) or not mentioned (**?**).

1 Zoë and Hélène would happily wear a school uniform.

2 There is no morning registration in French schools.

3 Zoë did not like the assembly she attended.

4 In the UK school, students have five lessons a day.

5 French students have to buy their own school equipment.

6 French students have more homework than British students.

3b 🎧 Listen again and answer these questions in English.

1 What school uniform do students in the UK school wear?

2 What happens before lessons in the UK school?

3 How many lessons do students have every afternoon?

4 At what time do lessons start and finish?

5 What equipment is not given to students in French schools?

6 What is likely to cause French students to have to repeat a school year?

4 🅖 Transform these positive sentences into negative ones as indicated in brackets. The ones marked * have an extra factor to think about, as you will need to use *de / d'*.

Exemple: Elle achète des livres scolaires. (**never**)*
          Elle <u>n'achète jamais de</u> livres scolaires.

1 Je prends un repas à la cantine. (**never**)*

2 Manon a trois amis dans sa classe. (**only**)

3 Je suis contente de mes notes. (**not**)

4 Hélène a des devoirs à faire. (**no more**)*

5 Elle a une carte de sortie. (**not**)*

6 Elle a une heure d'étude. (**never**)*

> **Using different negatives** 🅖 *Grammaire*
>
> When you change a sentence from positive to negative, you must change *un, une* or *des* to *de* or *d'*. You must remember to do this with all of the negative forms, e.g. *ne … plus, ne … jamais* as well as *ne … pas*.
>
> *J'ai des devoirs.* → *Je n'ai plus de devoirs.* (I haven't got any more homework.)
>
> Also learn about linking phrases with *qui*.   *See page 143* ➡
>
> *page 188*

5 🗨 Work with a partner to compare life in your school to life in a typical French school. Partner A plays the part of an interviewer from a French school. Partner B talks about life in a British school and makes comparisons. Below are some suggested questions.

■ Tu vas au collège quels jours de la semaine?

■ À quelle heure est-ce que tu es arrivé(e) au collège ce matin?

■ La pause-déjeuner dure combien de temps?

■ À quelle heure est-ce que tu vas quitter le collège cet après-midi?

■ Est-ce que tu as acheté tes livres scolaires?

■ Tu aimes ton uniforme?

■ Est-ce que tu aimes ton collège?

> **Making longer sentences** *Stratégie 5*
>
> When speaking, try to make your sentences longer by joining up simpler ones.
>
> Useful words are *et* (and), *mais* (but), *parce que* (because) and *qui* (who).
>
> Think of some simple sentences about your school and join them together.

> 🔗 **Lien**
>
> 7.1 Higher is available in the Higher book.

7.2 G Respectez les règles!

Le règlement

1 Il faut porter son uniforme scolaire.

2 Il faut écouter les professeurs et travailler dur en classe.

3 Il faut faire ses devoirs.

4 Il faut respecter les professeurs.

5 Il faut arriver à l'heure.

Il faut respecter le règlement.

6 Il ne faut pas fumer au collège.

7 Il ne faut pas parler avec ses amis en classe.

8 Il ne faut pas mâcher de chewing-gum.

9 Il ne faut pas porter de bijoux au collège.

10 Il ne faut pas se maquiller.

1a 📖 🎧 Read the first five rules. They all state what students have to do. Which rule (1–5) refers to …

a doing your homework?

b wearing your school uniform?

c punctuality?

d showing respect to teachers?

e working hard in lessons?

1b 📖 🎧 Read the next five rules. They state what students must not do. Which rule (6–10) refers to …

a chatting in lessons?

b chewing gum?

c wearing make-up?

d smoking in school?

e wearing jewellery?

2 **Ⓖ** Copy the sentences and fill in each gap with *il faut* or *il ne faut pas* as appropriate.

1 _____ travailler en classe.
2 _____ arriver en retard.
3 _____ respecter le règlement.
4 _____ se maquiller.
5 _____ réviser pour les examens.

3a 🎧 Listen to this French teacher addressing some students. Choose from the words below what the teacher is referring to in each statement (1–6).

> punctuality   homework   chewing gum
> exams   uniform   the class being noisy

3b 🎧 Listen again and complete these sentences with the correct information.

1 This student is not wearing a _____.
2 This student is _____ minutes late.
3 The _____ exam is on _____.
4 'Stop _____, please.'
5 'Put this _____ in the _____.'
6 'Where is your _____ homework?'

4 🗨 Work with a partner. Take turns to ask for and give your opinion of each of the ten rules in *Le règlement* (Activity 1) and any other rule you think is important.

Il faut faire ses devoirs. Tu es d'accord?

Oui, je trouve que c'est normal.

Tu es d'accord?		
C'est une bonne / mauvaise idée.		
Je trouve / je crois / je pense	que c'est	normal / logique / stupide / important, etc.

Grammaire — page 188

Il faut and il ne faut pas

Notice how *il faut* is used to mean 'you must' and *il ne faut pas* is used to mean 'you must not'.

Note that the word that follows is a verb in the infinitive, e.g. *porter, arriver, respecter,* etc.

Also revise how to give and understand commands.

See page 142 ➡

Stratégie 4

Cognates and near-cognates

Cognates and near-cognates are words which are either spelt the same way in French and in English, e.g. *important, excellent,* or are very similar, e.g. *uniforme, examens, réviser,* etc.

When you use such words in speaking, take great care with pronunciation. In most cases, they should not sound the same as they do in English, e.g. 'to revise' in French is *réviser* – but you should say the word as if it was written 'rayveezay'.

Check the pronunciation of words you don't know before using them.

7.2 F   Problèmes scolaires

1 ❶ Sort these sentences into three groups: school work, school rules or facilities.

Les examens sont difficiles.

Il faut arriver en cours à l'heure.

Il faut porter un uniforme.

Il y a trop de devoirs.

Il n'y a pas assez d'ordinateurs.

Les bâtiments sont vieux.

Problèmes scolaires – Tante Hélène répond

Problèmes

1 Quand je vois des garçons ou des filles de ma classe qui portent des vêtements très chics, je suis jalouse. Moi aussi, je voudrais porter des vêtements comme ça, mais ils sont trop chers! *Pascale, 14 ans*

2 Beaucoup de cours sont barbants et je ne les aime pas. Je n'aime pas beaucoup les profs non plus. Si on leur demande de faire des activités amusantes, ils se fâchent. Moi, je ne fais pas assez attention en classe, donc j'ai de mauvaises notes! *Laurence, 15 ans*

3 Comme il n'y a pas assez d'ordinateurs dans notre collège, une copine a demandé à notre prof principal s'il était possible d'utiliser son ordinateur portable. Il lui a dit que non. On n'a pas le droit de s'en servir en cours. *Sanja, 16 ans*

4 On n'a pas le droit de porter de bijoux au collège et je trouve ça vraiment bête. Si je porte mon bracelet ou ma boucle d'oreille, quel problème est-ce que ça pose? *Marc, 14 ans*

Réponses

A Je trouve que les profs devraient te permettre de l'utiliser. Mais tu peux quand même t'en servir pour faire tes devoirs et pour réviser.

B Je sais que c'est bien de porter des vêtements à la mode, mais la mode, ce n'est pas vraiment important. Il ne faut pas être jalouse, ça ne change rien.

C Aucun problème. Je ne comprends pas pourquoi ils interdisent d'en porter. Je te recommande cependant de respecter le règlement. Les bijoux, ce n'est pas très important.

D Je comprends, c'est difficile et quelquefois ennuyeux, mais il faut faire un effort. C'est ton avenir qui en dépend. Je suppose que plus tard, tu voudrais un travail intéressant? Penses-y, ça va te motiver.

2a 📖 🎧 Read the text and match the students' problems (1–4) with Tante Hélène's replies (A–D).

2b 📖 🎧 Read the text again. Which three sentences are correct?

1 Tante Hélène says that laptops are not as good as school computers.
2 Fashion is an issue for Pascale.
3 Tante Hélène suggests thinking of a future career as a way to get more motivated.
4 Not being allowed to wear jewellery bothers Marc.
5 There is excellent IT provision in Sanja's school.

3a 🎧 📹 Watch the video and / or listen to Section A of the conversation. The French Education minister is visiting a London comprehensive school, where he interviews a brother and sister. Their family moved from France a few years earlier and they are now fully integrated into British school life. Answer the questions in English.

1   What are the **two** advantages of wearing a school uniform, according to Justine?
2   What does she not like about her uniform?
3   Which three rules does she not agree with?

3b 🎧 📹 Watch the video and / or listen to Section B. Answer the questions in English.

1   How much homework does Romain get each week?
2   How long does he take to complete it?
3   What does he complain about?
4   How does the minister conclude the interview?

4 Ⓖ Match these questions with the correct answers.

1   Tu portes ton uniforme en voyage scolaire?
2   Tu fais tes devoirs au collège?
3   Tu aimes le chewing-gum?
4   Tu connais mon professeur principal?
5   Tu as acheté ton ordinateur récemment?

a   Non, je ne l'ai jamais rencontré.
b   Non, je le mets seulement au collège.
c   On me l'a donné pour mon anniversaire.
d   Non, je les fais chez moi.
e   Non, je ne l'aime pas.

5 🖊 Write an article about school pressures and problems, based on your school or an imaginary school. Don't forget to give your opinions and offer possible solutions wherever you can. Include your views on:

■ school uniform   ■ school rules   ■ homework.

Je pense que / qu'	certains cours sont barbants.
À mon avis,	il y a trop de devoirs.
Je trouve que / qu'	les examens sont (trop) difficiles.
On n'a pas le droit de / il est interdit de	porter des bijoux / fumer au collège.
Les bâtiments sont vieux / modernes.	
On n'a pas assez de / d'	ordinateurs
On a trop de / d'	tableaux interactifs.
Il faut / on doit	porter un uniforme scolaire.

Lien

7.2 Higher is available in the Higher book.

Grammaire *page 179*

How to say 'it' and 'them'

The French words *le, la, l', les* (meaning 'the') have a different meaning when you see them immediately before a verb. They are then called direct object pronouns.

him	*le, l'*	*Je le vois souvent.*
her	*la, l'*	*Je la connais.*
it	*le, la, l'*	*Le bus? Je le prends matin et soir.*
them	*les*	*Nos professeurs? Oui, je les aime bien.*

Also learn about indirect object pronouns.   *See page 143* ➡

Stratégie 5

Checking spelling and accents

Although infinitives and past participles often sound the same, they need different endings, e.g. *on doit utiliser* (you have to use) but *j'ai utilisé* (I used).

Make sure you know the difference between *ou* (or) and *où* (where) – they also sound the same.

Check that you have remembered circumflexes (e.g. *hôpital*) and cedillas (e.g. *français*).

7.3 G Mes matières

Objectifs

Talking about your present studies

Le, la, l', les + school subjects

Giving reasons for opinions

1 📖 🎧 Read what Marine says about what homework she gets each day. Note down the subjects in English for each day.

> Le lundi, on nous donne des devoirs de français et d'histoire.

> Le mardi, c'est des devoirs d'anglais et de géographie.

> On a des devoirs de biologie et de dessin le mercredi.

> Le jeudi, c'est les maths et l'espagnol.

> Les profs de musique et de chimie nous donnent des devoirs le vendredi.

> Le samedi, on nous donne des devoirs d'informatique et de physique.

2 📖 🎧 Choose a symbol (A–F) for each sentence. Then draw a smiley or grumpy face to indicate the opinion expressed.

1 J'aime l'EPS. C'est génial.
2 Je déteste l'anglais. C'est ennuyeux.
3 J'aime bien l'informatique. Je pense que c'est extra.
4 J'aime beaucoup la chimie. Je trouve que c'est bien.
5 Je n'aime pas la géographie. Ce n'est pas du tout intéressant.
6 Ma matière préférée, c'est l'histoire. À mon avis, c'est super.

3 🗨 Work with a partner to make up six dialogues following the instructions below.

Exemple: A Tu aimes le français?
  B Oui, j'aime bien le français.
  A Pourquoi?
  B Parce que c'est intéressant.

1 le français? ✓
2 les maths? ✗✗
3 l'EPS? ✓✓

4 le dessin? ✗
5 la biologie? ✓✓
6 l'anglais? ✓

✓	= j'aime (bien /assez)
✓✓	= j'adore / j'aime beaucoup / ma matière préférée, c'est …
✗	= je n'aime pas (beaucoup)
✗✗	= je déteste / je n'aime pas du tout

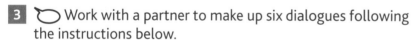

4a 🎧 Listen to these students commenting on their timetable. Which subject is each student (1–4) commenting on? What do they think of it and why?

4b 🎧 Listen again and correct these statements. Each statement contains one error.

1 Camille has three English lessons per week.
2 Marine has a maths lesson every day except Mondays.
3 Thomas finds physics really interesting.
4 Maxime has two hours of science a week.

4c 🎧 Listen once more. Who might have said …?

1 Moi, je vais choisir cette matière parce que j'adore passer mon temps à l'ordinateur.
2 Je vais continuer mes études de sciences parce que c'est ma matière préférée.

4d ✏️ Now, copy and complete the sentences that explain what you would like to study after your GCSEs and why.

1 Je vais choisir … parce que …
2 Je vais continuer … parce que …
3 Je vais étudier … parce que …

5 Ⓖ Give your opinion of your subjects by copying and completing these sentences.

1 Ma matière préférée, c'est …
2 J'aime aussi beaucoup … C'est intéressant.
3 J'aime assez …
4 … c'est pas mal.
5 Je n'aime pas …
6 Je n'aime pas du tout …
7 Je déteste …

6 ✏️ Write a French sentence for each subject you study. Include your opinion and give the reason for that opinion each time.

J'adore	le …	parce que	c'est …
J'aime (bien / assez / beaucoup)	la …	car	ce n'est pas …
Je n'aime pas (beaucoup / du tout)	l' …		
Je déteste …	les …		
Je vais continuer / choisir			

Le, la, l', les **+ school subjects** — *Grammaire* — page 174

The word 'the' (the definite article) is not used in English in front of school subjects, but in French it should be used: *la géographie, l'espagnol, les maths.*

J'aime l'EPS mais je déteste le dessin. – I like PE but I hate art.

Also practise different ways of expressing opinions. *See page 142* ➡

Giving reasons for opinions — *Stratégie 6*

When you want to give a reason in French, you can introduce it by using *parce que* or *car*:

Je n'aime pas l'espagnol parce que c'est difficile.

Giving reasons for your opinions allows you to extend your speech or written work beyond the bare minimum. By doing so, you show off knowledge that would otherwise have remained unnoticed and you are likely to gain better marks in your exam.

7.3 F Continuer ses études ou non?

1 Read the speech bubbles. Who …

1 will look for an apprenticeship?
2 will go to university?
3 is going to stay on at school?
4 will sit the bac (equivalent to A-levels)?
5 would like a work experience placement?
6 will not stay on at school?

a Je vais continuer mes études.

b Je chercherai un apprentissage.

c Je voudrais un placement en entreprise.

d Je passerai le bac.

e J'irai à l'université.

f Je ne continuerai pas mes études.

Forum Internet: Faut-il continuer ses études?

Je trouve que, si on veut faire une carrière intéressante, il est important de continuer ses études. Moi, je veux réussir mon bac, et après, on verra. **Claire**

Pourquoi continuer ses études? Avec ou sans bac, il est difficile de trouver un boulot de toutes façons. Moi, je chercherai tout de suite du travail. J'aimerais bien gagner de l'argent. **Florent**

Moi, j'ai un frère qui est plombier. Il a dix-neuf ans maintenant. Il a commencé son apprentissage quand il avait seize ans. C'est un bon métier. Pour moi, l'apprentissage, c'est la meilleure solution. **Alexis**

Tu as sûrement raison si tu veux faire un travail manuel. Si, comme moi, tu veux être prof, tu es bien obligé d'aller à l'université. Ça dépend de ce que tu veux faire. **Lucie**

Il y a des étudiants qui sont à l'université parce qu'ils n'ont pas envie de travailler. C'est un peu facile, non? Moi, je vais continuer mes études parce que je sais ce que je veux faire plus tard. J'ai absolument besoin de qualifications. **Justine**

Moi, je pense qu'on peut faire les deux en même temps, c'est-à-dire avoir un travail à temps partiel et donc gagner de l'argent et aussi étudier pour avoir les diplômes qu'on veut. **Cédric**

2 📖🎧 Read the contributions to the internet forum and decide whether these statements are true (**T**), false (**F**) or the information is not given in the text (**?**).

1 Claire is not sure what career she would like to have.
2 Florent wants to continue with his studies.
3 Alexis wants to be a plumber.
4 Lucie want to go to university.
5 Justine wants to start working as soon as possible.
6 Cédric will have a part-time job while continuing with his education.

Lien

7.3 Higher is available in the Higher book.

3a 🎧 Listen to two 16-year-old students talking about what they intend to do next year. Which three statements below are true?

1 Romain's parents would like him to study for a 'bac littéraire'.
2 Romain likes studying foreign languages.
3 Although Romain has not quite made up his mind what he intends to study next year, Guillaume has done so.

4 Guillaume wants to stay on at school in order to study for a 'bac professionnel'.
5 Guillaume would not like to become an electrician, like his dad.
6 Guillaume is keen to secure a job for which he has been trained.

3b 🎧 Listen again and decide what Romain and Guillaume would like to do next year. Select your answers from the options below.

A	BAC GÉNÉRAL		
	1	2	3
	économique et social	littéraire	scientifique

B BAC TECHNOLOGIQUE

C	BAC PROFESSIONNEL	
	1	2
	au lycée	par apprentissage

4 **G** These sentences are all written in the future tense. Rewrite each of them using the immediate future (*aller* + infinitive).

Exemple: Je gagnerai de l'argent → Je <u>vais gagner</u> de l'argent.

1 Je ferai un bac général.
2 Il passera un bac professionnel.
3 Il apprendra un travail.
4 Je déciderai de mon avenir moi-même.
5 Qu'est-ce que tu choisiras?

5 🗨 Work with a partner. Take turns to ask and answer questions about your partner's intentions regarding future studies. Answer fully, giving explanations and reasons whenever possible.

Qu'est-ce que tu vas étudier l'année prochaine?		
Tu voudrais aller à l'université?		
Pour étudier quoi?		
J'aimerais	étudier …	parce que …
Je voudrais	aller …	
Je veux	devenir …	
Je vais		

> **Grammaire** *page 185*
>
> **Talking about the future**
>
> The future can be referred to in different ways.
>
> ■ Using the **immediate future tense**: use the present tense of *aller* followed by an infinitive to say 'what is going' to happen, e.g. *Je vais faire un apprentissage* – I am going to do an apprenticeship.
>
> ■ Using the **future tense**. The endings of the future tense are: *-ai, -as, -a, -ons, -ez, -ont*. For the stem of the verb, use the infinitive for *-er* and *-ir* verbs and the infinitive without the final e for *-re* verbs:
>
> *je mangerai   je finirai   j'attendrai*
>
> Note that, at Foundation, you are expected to recognise the future tense but do not need to use it yourself.
>
> Also learn how to recognise some irregular future tense verbs.   *See page 143* ➡

Qu'est-ce que tu vas étudier l'année prochaine?

Je vais étudier le français et l'espagnol parce que j'adore les langues étrangères. Et toi?

> **Stratégie 5**
>
> **Using a range of structures**
>
> Show off your knowledge by using a wide range of ways of referring to future events.
>
> ■ the immediate future: *je vais étudier …*
>
> ■ phrases such as *j'aimerais / je voudrais* (I would like), *je veux* (I want) *étudier…*
>
> ■ the future tense: *j'étudierai …*

School, college and future plans

1 Copy and complete these sentences to state three things you <u>can</u> do at school and three things you <u>cannot</u> do.

1 On peut …
2 On …
3 On …
4 On ne peut pas …
5 On ne peut …
6 On …

Grammaire page 187

Saying you can or can't do something

As you saw on page 101 (Topic 5.2 F), if you want to say that you (or people in general) can do something, use *on peut*:

On peut jouer au foot.

To make the sentence negative (i.e. 'cannot' instead of 'can'), add *ne … pas*:

On ne peut pas jouer au foot.

Note that the word that follows *on / on ne peut pas* is a verb in the infinitive.

2 Copy these commands and fill in each gap with the appropriate verb chosen from the list below. Give each verb its correct ending.

1 _____ votre travail!
2 _____ le règlement!
3 _____ votre uniforme scolaire!
4 _____ en classe à l'heure!
5 _____ bien pour vos examens!

arriver   porter   faire

réviser   respecter

Grammaire page 185

Commands (revision)

Reminder: when a verb is used with its *vous* verb ending but without the word *vous* in front of it, it is used as a command or instruction:

Écoutez!   Listen!

Mettez votre cravate!   Put your tie on!

Note these irregular verbs:

Faites …   Do …

Dites…   Say …

3 Use different ways to give your opinion about the following.

1 your school
2 your timetable
3 your tutor
4 one of your subjects
5 homework
6 exams

Grammaire

Expressing opinions

You can do this in various ways. You can use *je trouve que* (I find that*)*, *je pense que* (I think that), *je crois que* (I believe that), and *c'est* + an adjective (*intéressant, ennuyeux, barbant, amusant, super, génial*):

Je trouve que c'est amusant.   I find it fun.

You can also use verbs like *aimer* (to like), *adorer* (to love), *détester* (to hate), to which you can add if you wish *assez* (quite), *beaucoup* (a lot), *pas du tout* (not at all):

Je n'aime pas du tout l'histoire.   I don't like history at all.

4 Use *qui* to turn each pair of sentences into one sentence.

Exemple: J'étudie une matière. Elle est intéressante.
J'étudie une matière <u>qui est</u> intéressante.

1 Il y a des élèves. Ils m'énervent.
2 Il y a des matières. Elles sont difficiles.
3 Elle a une prof de maths. Elle explique bien.
4 Il y a des professeurs. Ils encouragent beaucoup leurs élèves.
5 Nous avons une pause-déjeuner. Elle dure une heure et demie.
6 J'ai compris l'exemple. Il est au tableau.

> **Grammaire** · page 180
>
> ### Linking phrases with *qui*
>
> ■ *Qui* (meaning 'who' or 'that') can refer to either people or objects, and is used to link phrases together.
>
> *Tu as un prof. Il est gentil.*
>
> *Tu as un prof qui est gentil.*
>
> You have a teacher who is kind.
>
> *Il y a un livre. Il est intéressant.*
>
> *Il y a un livre qui est intéressant.*
>
> There is a book that is interesting.
>
> ■ Remember you will score higher marks in Speaking and Writing if you use longer sentences that have linking words like *qui*.

5 Choose the correct translation for each sentence, a or b.

1 Je ne lui réponds jamais.
   a I never answer him.
   b I never answer you.
2 Il te pose une question.
   a He is asking me a question.
   b He is asking you a question.
3 Est-ce que tu leur as demandé?
   a Did you ask them?
   b Did you ask her?
4 Mes parents m'ont acheté un dictionnaire.
   a My parents bought us a dictionary.
   b My parents bought me a dictionary.
5 Elle nous a dit qu'on ne travaillait pas assez.
   a She told them that we work enough.
   b She told us that we didn't work enough.
6 Le professeur vous donne de bonnes notes.
   a The teacher gives them good grades.
   b The teacher gives you good grades.

> **Grammaire** · page 179
>
> ### Indirect object pronouns
>
> These are used to say 'to me', 'to you', etc. Like direct object pronouns, they come before the verb in French.
>
> ■ Singular: *me* (to me), *te* (to you), *lui* (to him / her / it).
>
> *Elle me donne un stylo.* – She gives a pen to me. (She gives me a pen.)
>
> ■ Plural: *nous* (to us), *vous* (to you), *leur* (to them).
>
> *Elle leur donne un livre.* – She gives a book to them. (She gives them a book.)

6 What do these sentences mean? Translate them into English.

1 Demain, il fera beau.
2 En décembre, j'aurai seize ans.
3 On aura deux semaines de vacances à Noël.
4 Je serai dentiste à l'avenir.
5 Elle ira à l'université si c'est possible.

> **Grammaire** · page 185
>
> ### Irregular future tense verbs
>
> There are no irregular endings in the future tense. Only some verb stems are irregular. Learn to recognise these verbs in the future tense:
>
> | | |
> |---|---|
> | *je ferai* | I will do |
> | *j'irai* | I will go |
> | *j'aurai* | I will have |
> | *je serai* | I will be |

School, college and future plans

Topic 7.1 Comparing schools

7.1 G Mon collège ➡ pages 130–131

l'	ami(e)	friend
	apprendre	to learn
la	cantine	canteen
la	chimie	chemistry
le	copain	friend / pal (m)
la	copine	friend / pal (f)
la	cour	playground
le	gymnase	gym
	jouer	to play
le	laboratoire	lab
la	langue	language
	lire	to read
le	livre	book
	manger	to eat
	l'ordinateur (m)	computer
	pratiquer	to practise
la	récréation	break time
la	salle des professeurs	staffroom
la	salle d'informatique	IT room
la	salle de musique	music room
la	science	science
le	stade	stadium
le	tableau interactif	interactive whiteboard

7.1 F La vie au collège ➡ pages 132–133

	accompagner	to accompany
l'	appel (m)	registration
l'	assemblée (f)	assembly
la	cantine	canteen
le	carnet de notes	record booklet for grades
la	carte de sortie	exit pass
la	chemise	shirt
le	cours	lesson
la	cravate	tie
les	devoirs (m)	homework
l'	élève (m / f)	pupil

	ensemble	together
	expliquer	to explain
	fatigué(e)	tired
l'	heure d'étude (f)	study period
le	journal intime	personal diary
le	livre scolaire	school book
la	matière	subject
le	pantalon	trousers
la	pause-déjeuner	lunch break
	porter	to wear
le / la	professeur principal	form tutor
le	redoublement	repeating a school year
	rencontrer	to meet
la	rentrée	first day of the school year
en	sixième	in Year 7

Topic 7.2 Addressing school pressures and problems

7.2 G Respectez les règles! ➡ pages 134–135

	à l'heure	on time
le	bijou	jewel, jewellery
la	cravate	tie
	d'accord	OK, agreed
les	devoirs (m)	homework
	dur(e)	hard
	écouter	to listen
	en retard	late
l'	examen (m)	exam
	fumer	to smoke
	jeter	to throw
	logique	logical
	mâcher	to chew
se	maquiller	to wear make-up
	mettre	to put, to put on
	porter	to wear
la	poubelle	dustbin
le	règlement	rules
	respecter	to respect

	réviser	to revise
	travailleur(-euse)	hard-working
l'	uniforme scolaire (m)	school uniform

7.2 F Problèmes scolaires ➡ *pages 136–137*

	à la mode	in fashion
	avoir le droit de	to have the right to, to be allowed to
	barbant(e)	boring
	bête	stupid
la	boucle d'oreille	earring
	chic	smart
la	couleur	colour
	discipliné(e)	well-behaved
	faire attention à	to pay attention to
	interdit(e)	forbidden
	jaloux(-ouse)	jealous
	motiver	to motivate
l'	ordinateur portable (m)	laptop
	pauvre	poor
le	point de vue	viewpoint
la	règle	rule
	riche	rich
les	vêtements (m)	clothes
le	voyage scolaire	school trip

Topic 7.3 Present and future studies

7.3 G Mes matières ➡ *pages 138–139*

	amusant(e)	fun
l'	anglais (m)	English
	assez	quite, enough
	barbant(e)	boring
	beaucoup	a lot
la	biologie	biology
la	chimie	chemistry
le	cours	lesson
le	dessin	art
l'	emploi du temps (m)	timetable
	ennuyeux(-euse)	boring
l'	EPS (f)	PE
l'	espagnol (m)	Spanish
	fort(e) (en)	good (at)

le	français	French
	génial(e)	great
la	géographie	geography
l'	histoire (f)	history
l'	informatique (f)	IT
	intéressant(e)	interesting
les	maths (f)	maths
	pas du tout	not at all
	penser	to think
la	physique	physics
	trouver	to find

7.3 F Continuer ses études ou non?
➡ *pages 140–141*

à	l'avenir	in future
	apprendre	to learn
l'	apprentissage (m)	apprenticeship
	avoir envie de	to feel like, to want
le	bac	an exam equivalent to A-levels
le	bac général / professionnel / technologique	the three main options for le bac
le	bac économique et social / littéraire / scientifique	the three choices within le bac général
	chercher	to look for
au	chômage	unemployed
le	diplôme	diploma
les	études (f)	studies
l'	entreprise (f)	company
	gagner	to earn
le	lycée	secondary school (for 15 to 18 years old)
le	métier	job, profession
	passer un examen	to sit an exam
le	plombier	plumber
	réussir un examen	to pass an exam
à	temps partiel	part time
le	travail	job, profession
l'	université (f)	university
la	voie	path

8.1 G Stages et petits jobs

On travaille

1 Le week-end, je travaille dans la ferme de mon père. C'est moi qui conduis le tracteur. C'est pas mal. **Maxime**

2 Moi, je fais partie d'un groupe qui s'appelle UFO. Je ne joue pas d'un instrument. C'est moi qui chante. Je trouve ça vraiment extra. **Clément**

3 Je suis cuisinière dans un petit restaurant à Calais et moi, j'aime ça. **Claire**

4 Après l'école, de quatre heures à six heures, je travaille dans un cabinet vétérinaire à Dijon. Je n'aime pas mon travail parce que c'est mal payé. **Floriane**

5 En ce moment, je fais un stage dans une école primaire à Caderousse. Comme j'adore les enfants, je pense que c'est super. **Sonia**

6 Pour mon stage en entreprise, je travaille dans un bureau. Je passe tout mon temps à l'ordinateur. Je déteste ça. C'est très ennuyeux. **Antoine**

1a 📖 🎧 Read what these teenagers say about their part-time jobs and work experience. Match the names (1–6) with the pictures (A–F).

1 Maxime	3 Claire	5 Sonia
2 Clément	4 Floriane	6 Antoine

1b 📖 🎧 Read the text again. Copy the opinion grid below and write the correct names in the boxes.

♥♥	♥	OK	X	XX

2a 🎧 Listen to five students reporting on their work experience. Was their experience positive (**P**), negative (**N**) or both positive and negative (**P + N**)?

2b 🎧 Listen again and choose each student's place of work from the list below.

in a sports centre   in a school   in a shop   in a hospital

in a hotel   in a factory   in an office

3 🅖 Copy and complete these sentences by adding an opinion to show what you thought about different aspects of your own work experience.

1 _____ mon stage en entreprise.
2 _____ le travail.
3 _____ les heures de travail.
4 _____ mes collègues.
5 _____ faire le café pour mes collègues.

4 ✏️ Write a few sentences about the last job you had, or about your work experience. You could include:

- when it was
- where you worked
- what work you did
- the working hours
- what you thought of your work.

J'ai travaillé du … au …	
J'ai travaillé à la caisse / …	
J'ai commencé à …. heures et j'ai fini à … heures.	
J'ai	aimé / adoré / …
Je n'ai pas	beaucoup aimé / …
C'était	intéressant / …

Giving opinions about something in the past

Grammaire page 184

To say what you thought of something, you can use the opinion phrases you already know in the perfect tense: *j'ai aimé* (I liked) is the perfect tense of *j'aime* (I like).

What do these mean?

J'ai adoré.

J'ai beaucoup aimé.

Je n'ai pas aimé.

Je n'ai pas du tout aimé.

J'ai détesté.

You can also use *c'était* (it was) followed by an adjective: *c'était intéressant.*

Also practise how to say 'in' a location or a country.   *See page 158* ➡️

Expressing your opinion

Stratégie 4

Opinion phrases are extremely useful as they can be used in different topics in writing as well as in speaking. Learn what they are in the present tense (so that you can say what you think) as well as in the perfect and imperfect tenses (so that you can say what you thought).

Use them also to give longer answers:

Où as-tu fait ton stage?

J'étais dans un bureau. J'ai beaucoup aimé le travail. C'était vraiment intéressant.

8.1 F — Les jeunes qui travaillent

1 **V** Choose a speech bubble (a–f) for each job (1–5).

1 checkout worker
2 worker in a school
3 waiter
4 postal worker
5 factory worker
6 office worker

a J'ai livré des paquets.

b J'ai travaillé à la caisse.

c J'ai travaillé dans une école primaire.

d Je sers les clients.

e Je fais des photocopies.

f J'ai travaillé dans une usine.

Quatre jeunes qui travaillent

Pendant les vacances scolaires, Juliette travaille toujours comme caissière dans un magasin. Elle travaille bien et elle est assez bien payée, mais elle dit que c'est un peu ennuyeux.

Comme Jérôme fait un stage, il n'est pas payé. Il est dans l'entreprise d'un électricien au centre-ville. Il voudrait être électricien un jour parce qu'il veut gagner un bon salaire.

Xavier voudrait travailler comme mécanicien à la fin de ses études. Mais pour son stage, il n'a pas trouvé de place de mécanicien, alors il a travaillé comme technicien dans une entreprise d'informatique. Il a bien travaillé parce qu'il adore les ordinateurs.

Zoé travaille tous les samedis comme vendeuse chez un boucher. C'est mal payé mais malheureusement elle n'a pas pu trouver autre chose. Elle espère bientôt trouver quelque chose de plus intéressant et surtout de mieux payé.

2a 📖 🎧 Read the article and match each picture (A–D) with the correct name.

2b 📖 🎧 Complete each of these sentences with the name of the person being referred to.

1 The job _____ wants is well paid.
2 _____ always has the same holiday job.
3 _____ worked for an IT company.
4 _____ has a Saturday job.
5 _____ is doing this job because it's the only one she could get.

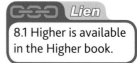

Lien

8.1 Higher is available in the Higher book.

3 🎧 Listen to these people talking about their jobs in Sections A and B, and about their work experience in Sections C and D. Choose the correct answer to complete each sentence.

Section A

1 Nicolas works in **a bakery / a butcher's / an office**.
2 He works **every Sunday / every Saturday / in the holidays**.

Section B

3 Émilie **works in a shop / works in an office / delivers the post**.
4 She **writes / sends / opens** letters.

Section C

5 Mehmet **has done / is doing / is going to do** his work experience.
6 He found the work **easy / hard / boring**.

Section D

7 Dominique worked **with horses / for a firm / on a farm**.
8 One day she wants to **go on the stage / work in agriculture / work with race horses**.

4 🄶 Complete these sentences with an adverb, as indicated in brackets.

1 J'ai travaillé _____. (**quickly**)
2 _____, je n'ai pas pu trouver de travail. (**unfortunately**)
3 _____, j'ai gagné beaucoup d'argent. (**luckily**)
4 _____, je reste chez moi le dimanche. (**normally**)
5 J'étais _____ payé. (**well**)
6 Et moi, j'étais _____ payé! (**badly**)

5 🗩 Work with a partner. Prepare answers to the following questions, then take turns to play the part of a teacher carrying out a debrief with a pupil after work experience.

- Où as-tu fait ton stage?
- Qu'est-ce que tu as fait?
- C'était comment?
- Est-ce que tu as aussi un petit job / un emploi le soir ou le week-end?
- Est-ce que tu voudrais un emploi permanent comme ça plus tard?

Pour mon stage, j'ai travaillé	dans un bureau / dans un magasin / dans une usine / dans une école.	
Le (samedi), je travaille		
Je fais / J'ai fait	des photocopies.	
Je sers / J'ai servi	les clients.	
C'est / C'était	barbant / dur / fatigant / pas mal / amusant	parce que …
J'ai trouvé le travail		
Un jour, je voudrais travailler	dans un bureau / …	

Stratégie 3

Listening for different tenses

Sometimes a listening passage has a section in the present tense and another in the perfect tense. Listen for auxiliaries (*avoir / être*) and past participles (*sorti, travaillé*). This tells you that the section is in the past tense.

Which section is in the present / past tense here?

Grammaire page 177

Adverbs

French adverbs are usually formed by adding -*ment* (which is the equivalent of the English ending '-ly') to the feminine form of the adjective.

Normalement, heureusement, malheureusement, facilement have been used in either the reading or the listening activities on these pages. What do you think they mean?

Many adverbs are irregular including: *vite* (quickly), *bien* (well), *mal* (badly).

Also learn to recognise and understand verbs in the passive form:

Il est bien payé.   He is well paid.
See page 159 ➡

Où as-tu fait ton stage?

Dans un bureau, près de chez moi.

C'était comment?

C'était barbant. J'ai fait des photocopies toute la journée!

8.2 G Je cherche un emploi

PETITES ANNONCES

CHERCHE EMPLOI

Cuisinier cherche emploi dans un café ou dans un restaurant. Ref. 1

Plombier qualifié cherche poste dans une entreprise. Ref. 2

Étudiant cherche travail saisonnier (juillet et août) Ref. 3

Mécanicien autos. 5 ans d'expérience. Cherche poste permanent dans garage. Ref. 4

Cherche travail le week-end. Expérience de vendeuse. Ref. 5

OFFRES D'EMPLOI

Réparations de voitures. Garage Robert. Expérience essentielle. Ref. 187

Caissier / caissière de supermarché pour l'été. Heures de travail négociables. Ref. 181

Magasin de vêtements cherche vendeur / vendeuse – samedis et dimanches de 8 heures à 18 heures. Ref. 211

Restaurant en ville cherche chef de cuisine – tous les jours de 9 heures à 16 heures. Expérience essentielle. Ref. 112

Plombier / plombière qualifié(e). Excellent salaire. Ref. 128

1a Read the adverts. Give the reference number of the job offered in column 2 that would suit each of the job seekers in column 1 (refs 1–5).

1b Read the adverts again. Answer each of the questions by giving the appropriate reference number.

1 Which job offer mentions a good salary?
2 Which job is for weekends only?
3 Which two jobs require the applicant to be experienced?
4 Which job applicant is a student?

Stratégie 2a–2b

2a 🎧 Listen to the job interview and write down the missing words for each of the following sentences.

1 Thomas applied for the position of _____ .
2 Thomas is _____ years old.
3 He has worked before in a _____ .
4 The working day starts at _____ o'clock and finishes at _____ o'clock.
5 The pay will be _____ euros an hour.
6 He can start work next _____ .

Using the context and the questions

Keep the context of the conversation in mind (i.e. a job interview) and also the questions you are asked to answer. It will help you work out the French words that you don't know.

2b 🎧 Listen to the interview again. Write these words / phrases in the order in which they are mentioned in the interview.

> hours of work   age   salary   experience
>
> name   when the job starts

3a Ⓖ In the questions below, 1–5 address the person as *tu*, while a–e ask the same questions but address someone else as *vous*. Match the two sets of questions.

1 Quel âge as-tu?
2 Comment tu t'appelles?
3 Tu as de l'expérience?
4 Quand peux-tu commencer?
5 Combien gagnes-tu?

a Vous avez de l'expérience?
b Quand pouvez-vous commencer?
c Quel âge avez-vous?
d Combien gagnez-vous?
e Comment vous appelez-vous?

Using *vous*

Remember that, while in English 'you' is the only form of address, the French use *tu* when talking to a friend, a child or a member of their family. For all other cases, *vous* is the appropriate form of address.

The verb forms used with *vous* are not the same as those used with *tu*:

Quel âge as-tu?

Quel âge avez-vous?

Turn to the verb tables on pages 193–197 to compare the *tu* and *vous* forms of *avoir*, *pouvoir* and other verbs.

Also practise asking questions with *est-ce que*. See page 158 ➡

Ⓖrammaire *page 178*

3b Ⓖ Transform these sentences, using *vous* instead of *tu*. Take care with the verb endings.

1 Tu fais un stage intéressant.
2 Tu travailles le samedi.
3 Tu gagnes dix euros de l'heure.
4 Tu répares les voitures.
5 Tu as un bon travail.

4 ✏ You have just found a job. Write to your French friend about it. Copy and complete the message, and add more information if you can.

> J'ai accepté un travail de _____ .
> Je commence _____ prochain.
> Je vais travailler de _____ heures à _____ heures, du lundi au _____ .
> Le salaire est de _____ euros de l'heure.
> Je trouve que c'est _____ .

8.2 F Au travail

Objectifs
- Job search and application
- Using *votre, vos*
- Masculine and feminine forms of job titles

1 Ⓥ Unjumble these French words for jobs and translate them into English. Add accents where they are needed.

1 fire in mire
2 nice musi
3 rut face
4 i erase trec
5 i reli cop
6 teach run
7 chore bu
8 i can mince e
9 dr venue
10 free rim

Offres d'emploi

Restaurant marocain
LE CASBAH
avenue de la Forêt,
Jard-sur-Mer,
tél. 02-44-63-91-45.
Nous cherchons quelqu'un pour travailler comme serveur / serveuse le week-end de 9 à 17 heures.
Formation: pas nécessaire.

Le supermarché du
CAMPING DE L'OCEAN
cherche
vendeur / vendeuse
pour travailler à la caisse tous les après-midi de 14 à 16 heures.
Salaire à discuter.
Expérience préférable.
Présentez-vous au chef du personnel.

Halte-garderie
ST-JACQUES
24, rue des Pins,
cherche
un(e) assistant(e) pour travailler pendant les grandes vacances avec des petits enfants du lundi au vendredi, tous les matins de 8h à 12h30.
Écrivez à l'adresse ci-dessus.

En ce moment, je travaille le samedi dans un petit magasin, mais ce que je voudrais, c'est un travail en semaine après l'école. Je ne veux pas finir trop tard parce que j'ai toujours beaucoup de devoirs à faire. Je vais y aller cet après-midi.

Yasmina

J'avais demandé à faire ce travail il y a deux ans, mais j'étais trop jeune à cette époque. Cette année, pas de problème, je pense. J'ai dix-sept ans maintenant. C'est bien comme travail saisonnier parce que je vais avoir mes après-midi de libre. Je vais leur envoyer une lettre.

Antoine

C'est exactement ce que je cherche. Je n'ai pas le temps de travailler en semaine, mais le samedi et le dimanche, c'est différent. Je n'ai jamais travaillé avant, mais ils disent que ce n'est pas essentiel. Je vais leur téléphoner ce soir.

Clara

2a Read the job adverts and also what each person is thinking in the thought clouds underneath. Which three sentences are true?

1 No experience is necessary if you want to work at Le Casbah.
2 The job at St-Jacques crèche is for afternoons only.
3 To work at the supermarket, they'd rather you had experience.
4 Antoine worked at St-Jacques crèche two years ago.
5 Yasmina wants to finish work early so as to have enough time to do her homework.
6 Clara needs to send a letter of application.

2b 📖 🎧 Read the adverts and thought clouds again. Who is best suited to each job?

1 Restaurant Le Casbah
2 Halte-garderie St-Jacques
3 Supermarché Océan

3a 🎧 Listen to Yasmina's interview (Section A) and choose the correct answers.

1 Yasmina's family name is **Farik / Fariq / Feriq**.
2 She is **15 / 16 / 17** years old.
3 She is offered a salary of **10 / 11 / 12** euros an hour.
4 She can start work next **Monday / Tuesday / Wednesday**.

3b 🎧 Listen to Antoine's interview (Section B) and choose the correct answers.

1 Antoine's age is **16 / a problem / no longer a problem**.
2 He has **two brothers and one sister / two brothers and two sisters / one brother and two sisters**.
3 He is offered a salary of **100 / 120 / 200** euros a week.
4 He can start work on **1 July / 1 June / 1 August**.

4 🄶 Transform these questions, using *vous* instead of *tu*.

1 Comment est ton travail?
2 Quel est ton salaire?
3 Tu habites chez tes parents?
4 Tu fais du baby-sitting pour tes parents?
5 Ta journée de travail commence à quelle heure?

5 🗨 Work with a partner to carry out an imaginary job interview. Partner A asks the questions and notes down Partner B's answers. Then swap roles, using different details. Ask and answer questions about the following:

- the type of job being applied for
- name and age, including spelling
- experience
- salary
- when you can start work.

C'est à propos du poste / de la place	d'assistant(e) / de vendeur(-euse).
J'ai de l'expérience. Je n'ai pas d'expérience.	
J'ai déjà travaillé	avec les enfants / dans un bureau.
Je gagne	dix / onze euros de l'heure / par semaine.
Je peux commencer	lundi / mardi, etc.

🔗 **Lien**

8.2 Higher is available in the Higher book.

Stratégie 2b

Masculine and feminine forms of job titles

Most words for jobs have a masculine and a feminine version:

employé / employée

caissier / caissière

vendeur / vendeuse

acteur / actrice

However, *professeur* (teacher), and *médecin* (doctor) don't change. For more on this, see page 173.

Make a list of jobs with their male and female versions. Use a dictionary if you like.

Grammaire page 176–177

Using *votre*, *vos*

When addressing someone politely with *vous*, the verb forms are different from those used for *tu*:

Tu fais tes devoirs le soir? but *Vous faites vos devoirs le soir?*

Note that *tes devoirs* has become *vos devoirs*.

To say 'your' in French, *ton* (masculine singular), *ta* (feminine singular), *tes* (masculine and feminine plural) become *votre* (masculine <u>and</u> feminine singular) or *vos* (masculine and feminine plural) when used with the *vous* form of the verb.

Also learn to recognise the pluperfect tense. *See page 159* ➡

C'est à propos de quel poste?

C'est à propos du poste de vendeuse.

Vous avez de l'expérience?

Oui, j'ai déjà travaillé dans un petit magasin.

8.3 G Les métiers

Objectifs
- Talking about jobs
- Leaving out *un / une* before job titles
- Using all the information you are given

Qu'est-ce que tu voudrais faire comme travail?

1 Je voudrais travailler dans une école. J'aime les enfants.

2 Moi, je voudrais travailler dans un restaurant. J'adore faire la cuisine.

3 Je voudrais un travail dans un café. J'aime bien servir les clients.

4 Moi, je voudrais travailler dans un bureau. Les ordinateurs, c'est super!

5 Je veux travailler dans un magasin de vêtements. J'aime beaucoup la mode.

1a 📖 🎧 Read the speech bubbles and choose a suitable job for each person from the list.

secrétaire	chef de cuisine	électricien	vendeur
médecin	professeur	garçon de café	

1b 📖 🎧 Read the speech bubbles again. What reason does each person give for their choice of job? Write the answers in English.

Using all the information you are given

Extra information will often help you get the correct answer, e.g. knowing that someone works in a restaurant is not enough for you to identify this person's job. The answer could be waiter, cook, manager, cleaner, etc. Focus on all the information you are given before you try to answer.

Stratégie 1a

2 **G** Copy the sentences and fill in each gap with an appropriate job title. (Remember that in English you would need two words to finish the sentence, but in French you only need one!) You will find the words for jobs on page 161. Alternative answers may be possible.

1 Il aime réparer les voitures. Il voudrait être _____.
2 Elle adore la musique. Elle aimerait être _____.
3 Elle voudrait travailler dans un hôpital. Elle veut être _____
4 Elle aimerait travailler dans un supermarché. Elle voudrait être _____.
5 Il aime bien la campagne. Il veut être _____.
6 Il aime beaucoup le théâtre. Il aimerait être _____.

Leaving out *un / une* before job titles

In English, if you talk about your possible future job, you might say 'I would like to be a train driver' or 'I intend to become an actor'. You have to include 'a' or 'an'.

In French, you just say *je voudrais être chauffeur de train* or *j'ai l'intention de devenir acteur / actrice*. You can see that the word for 'a' or 'an', which is *un* or *une*, is missing.

Also practise different ways of saying what you want or would like to do.

See page 158 ➡

Grammaire page 174

3a 🎧 Listen to six people talking about the jobs they would like to do. Match each of them with one of the pictures (A–F).

1	Luc	3	Robert	5	Rachel
2	Maeva	4	Adèle	6	Rémi

3b 🎧 Listen again. Who is the other person that each speaker refers to? What do they do for a living?

4 💬 Work with a partner. Take turns to talk about the work you would like to do and what the members of your family do now. Tell your partner:

- ■ what you want to do for a living
- ■ why you want to do this job
- ■ what each member of your family does
- ■ the reasons for their choice.

Je voudrais être mécanicien parce que j'aime bien réparer les voitures. Et toi?

Moi, j'aimerais être chauffeur de train parce que j'aime bien voyager.

Je voudrais / J'aimerais / Je veux	être	artiste / facteur (factrice) / ... parce que ...
J'aime (bien / beaucoup) / J'adore travailler avec les enfants / parler aux clients / ...		
Mon frère / Ma sœur / ...	voudrait / aimerait / veut	être	caissier(-ière) / ...
Il / Elle aime (bien / beaucoup) / adore ...		

8.3 F La vie professionnelle

Objectifs

Jobs, careers and post-16 choices

The future tense

Checking your written work

1 **V** Choose the correct ending for each of the following sentences.

1 Je voudrais devenir acteur. Je travaillerai ...
2 Je veux être professeur. Je travaillerai ...
3 Je serai hôtesse de l'air. Je travaillerai ...
4 Je deviendrai secrétaire. Je travaillerai ...
5 Je veux être fermier. Je travaillerai ...
6 J'ai décidé que je serai policier. Je travaillerai ...

a   avec des adolescents
b   dans un théâtre
c   en plein air
d   dans le tourisme
e   dans un bureau
f   avec le public

Qu'est-ce que tu feras dans la vie?

A Fabrice ira passer une année aux États-Unis. Il travaillera peut-être dans le tourisme, comme guide. Comme ça, il apprendra l'anglais. À son avis, c'est essentiel pour la carrière qu'il veut faire.

Catherine a déjà commencé son boulot. Elle travaille comme hôtesse de l'air. C'est un travail très dur. Elle ne peut pas rentrer chez elle tous les soirs et doit très souvent dormir dans un hôtel à l'étranger.

B Tina ira à l'université l'année prochaine. Pour le moment, elle est toujours au lycée et elle espère réussir son bac au mois de juin. Après ça, elle dit qu'elle a l'intention de devenir ingénieur, parce qu'elle pense que c'est un travail plus varié que d'autres professions. Elle a déjà fait un stage chez un ingénieur et elle a bien aimé ça.

Roger a décidé de devenir plombier. Il a choisi ça parce qu'il trouve que c'est un métier très pratique. «Tout le monde a besoin d'un plombier de temps en temps» dit-il. «En plus, on peut gagner beaucoup d'argent si on travaille bien. J'ai passé six mois en Irlande, où j'ai fait un stage de plombier. C'était vraiment intéressant.»

2a 📖 🎧 Read Section A and decide whether Fabrice (**F**) or Catherine (**C**) is being referred to.

1 _____ va aller en Amérique.
2 _____ passe beaucoup de temps en avion.
3 _____ n'est pas souvent à la maison.
4 _____ pense que les langues sont importantes.

2b 📖 🎧 Read Section B and decide whether Tina (**T**) or Roger (**R**) is being referred to.

1 _____ veut être étudiante.
2 _____ a travaillé à l'étranger.
3 _____ aimerait avoir un travail pratique.
4 _____ n'a pas de travail en ce moment.
5 _____ sera ingénieur un jour.

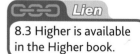

Lien

8.3 Higher is available in the Higher book.

3a 🎧 Listen to Section A and write down the letter of the job (A–D) each person would like.

 A  B  C  D

1 Nicolas
2 Mehmet
3 Olivier
4 Émilie

3b 🎧 Listen to Section B and match the beginnings and endings of the sentences.

1 Jérémy wants to be
2 He thinks it is
3 He likes the idea of working in
4 Charlotte wants to be
5 She thinks it is
6 She likes the idea of working in

a the open air.
b well paid.
c an office.
d a PE teacher.
e a programmer.
f not well paid.

4 **G** Copy the sentences and fill in each gap with the correct verb from the list.

1 Après les examens, Éric _____ dans un magasin.
2 Je _____ au bureau jusqu'à six heures.
3 Nicolas _____ au Canada.
4 Après le travail, je _____ le bus pour aller chez moi.
5 Mon père _____ à la maison à cinq heures.
6 Nous _____ nos devoirs avant le repas.
7 Vous _____ travailler du lundi au vendredi.
8 Tu _____ gagner beaucoup d'argent.

| arrivera | ira | prendrai | ferons | devrez |
| travaillera | resterai | pourras |

5 🖊 Write an email to your French penfriend, explaining your future plans:

- say what you will do as soon as you leave school
- say what career you hope to follow later and why
- mention advantages and disadvantages of this career.

Je travaillerai / je vais travailler	à l'étranger / en plein air. avec les enfants / adolescents. dans le tourisme / un bureau / l'informatique.
Je voudrais travailler comme / être / devenir	professeur / infirmier(-ière) / chauffeur / caissier(-ière) / …
J'ai choisi ce métier	parce que c'est	intéressant / bien payé / varié / …
Je ne veux pas être …		dur / ennuyeux / mal payé / …

Grammaire page 185

The future tense

You have already worked on aspects of the future tense in Topic 7. Here is a summary of what you should be able to do.

At Foundation level you don't need to use the future tense itself, but you have to be able to recognise it when someone uses it. Its endings are: *-ai*, *-as*, *-a*, *-ons*, *-ez*, *-ont*. There are no exceptions to this.

At Higher level you need to show that you can use the future tense.

To form the future tense of a regular *-er* or *-ir* verb, you need the infinitive form of the verb and then add the future tense endings, e.g. *je commencerai* (I will start), *ils finiront* (they will finish).

For regular *-re* verbs, delete the final e is from the infinitive before adding the endings, e.g. *il répondra* (he will reply),

Make sure you learn the verbs that are irregular in the future tense, e.g. *j'aurai* (I will have), *ils seront* (they will be).

Also practise expressing your hopes and intentions. *See page 159* ➡

Checking your written work

Stratégie 5

Before handing in written work, always make sure you have checked it carefully. Think about accents (for example é on a past participle), plural endings on nouns (*les parents*) and correct verb endings (*ils regardent*).

Jobs and employment

1 Copy the sentences and fill in each gap with the correct French word for 'in'.

1. J'ai travaillé _____ une école.
2. J'ai fait mon stage _____ Manchester.
3. J'étais _____ ville, _____ un magasin.
4. Mon stage était _____ une école primaire.
5. J'ai fait mon stage _____ Londres, _____ un supermarché.

> **Grammaire** *pages 189–190*
>
> ### How to say 'in' a location or a country
>
> - Before a town: *à*, e.g. *à Paris*.
> - Before a place you can go into: *dans*, e.g. *dans un bureau*.
> - Before most countries: *en*, e.g. *en France*.
>
> Note these two phrases: *en ville* (in town), *à la campagne* (in the countryside).

2 Transform these statements into questions by adding *est-ce que*. Then write what they mean in English.

1. C'est bien payé.
2. Vous pouvez commencer lundi.
3. Vous avez travaillé dans un magasin de vêtements.
4. Le travail est difficile.
5. Ça va.

> **Grammaire** *page 188*
>
> ### Asking questions with *est-ce que*
>
> Using *est-ce que* as a question word changes a statement into a question, e.g. *Vous avez de l'expérience* means 'You have experience'. *Est-ce que vous avez de l'expérience* means 'Do you have experience?'
>
> Note that *est-ce que* can often be omitted and instead, the speaker simply raises his / her voice at the end of the question. *Vous avez de l'expérience?* is perfectly acceptable as a way of asking the question.

3 How would each of these people (1–6) say what they want / would like to do for a living? Write six French sentences that start with *je*.

Exemple: Je veux (je voudrais / j'aimerais) être artiste.

1. baker
2. doctor
3. policeman
4. postman
5. air hostess
6. singer

> **Grammaire** *page 181*
>
> ### Saying what you want or would like to do
>
> You can start your sentence with *je voudrais*, followed by a verb in the infinitive: *Je voudrais travailler dans un collège* – I would like to work in a school / college
>
> You can also start with *j'aimerais* (which has a similar meaning to *je voudrais*) or *je veux* (I want):
>
> *Je veux être musicien* – I want to be a musician

4 In the paragraph below, find phrases that mean the following:

1 are bought
2 are sent
3 are done
4 are served
5 is forgotten
6 are delivered
7 is prepared

> Je suis bien payée et mon assistante est super. Quand j'arrive au bureau, le café est préparé et les croissants sont achetés. Ensuite les clients sont servis rapidement, les photocopies sont faites et les paquets sont envoyés et sont livrés sans problème. Rien n'est oublié. C'est fantastique!

Understanding the passive

The passive is used to say what is done to someone or something. It is formed from *être* followed by a past participle.

active form	passive form
Elle écrit la lettre.	*La lettre est écrite.*
She writes the letter.	The letter is written.
Il prépare le thé.	*Le thé est préparé.*
He prepares tea.	Tea is prepared.

Grammaire — page 186

---

5 Each of sentences 1–6 contains an example of the pluperfect tense. Each verb in the pluperfect is made up of two words – copy them. Then match four of these sentences with the pictures below.

1 Il savait que j'avais oublié le paquet.
2 Je pensais que tu n'avais pas trouvé de travail.
3 Elle était arrivée au bureau à huit heures ce matin-là.
4 Elle était très contente parce que j'avais préparé du bon café.
5 On m'a dit que tu n'avais pas aimé ton stage l'année dernière.
6 Elle m'a dit qu'elle avait travaillé dans un hôtel pendant trois ans.

The pluperfect tense

The pluperfect tense is used to refer to something further back in the past than the perfect or the imperfect. It is used to say what someone **had** done or **had been** doing. It is formed using the imperfect of *avoir* or *être* followed by a past participle:

*Je savais **qu'il avait travaillé** chez un boulanger.*

I knew he **had worked** in a bakery.

Grammaire — page 184

6 What would these people say about their ambitions? Write a sentence in French that starts with *je* for each of them.

1 Arnaud hopes to work in an office.
2 Élodie intends to be an air hostess.
3 Thomas hopes to work as a postman.
4 Marine intends to be a musician.
5 Maxime does not intend to work in a restaurant.

Expressing hopes and intentions

To say what you hope / intend to do as a job, use *j'espère* (I hope) or *j'ai l'intention de* (I intend), followed by a verb in the infinitive:

J'espère être médecin. – I hope to be a doctor.

You can also make these two verbs negative if you wish:

je n'espère pas être …

je n'ai pas l'intention d'être …

Grammaire — page 181

Jobs and employment

Topic 8.1 Part-time and casual work

8.1 G Stages et petits jobs ➡ *pages 146–147*

le	*bureau*	office
le	*cabinet vétérinaire*	vet's
	chanter	to sing
le / la	*collègue*	colleague
	conduire	to drive
l'	*école primaire (f)*	primary school
	ennuyeux(-euse)	boring
	extra!	great!
	faire partie de	to belong to
la	*ferme*	farm
les	*heures de travail (f)*	working hours
	intéressant(e)	interesting
la	*journée*	day
le	*magasin*	shop
	mal payé(e)	badly paid
	pas du tout	not at all
	pas mal	not bad
le	*stage*	placement
le	*stage en entreprise*	work experience
	sympa	nice
	travailler	to work

8.1 F Les jeunes qui travaillent ➡ *pages 148–149*

	autre chose	something else
en	*bois*	made of wood
	barbant(e)	boring
	bientôt	soon
le / la	*client(e)*	customer
	dur(e)	hard, difficult
l'	*entreprise (f)*	company
	faire un stage (en entreprise)	to do work experience
les	*grandes vacances (f)*	summer holidays
l'	*informatique (f)*	IT
	livrer	to deliver
le	*meuble*	piece of furniture

	mieux payé(e)	better paid
le	*paquet*	parcel
	pas tellement	not much
le	*patron*	boss
la	*place*	job, position
	quelque chose	something
	servir	to serve
	un peu	a little
la	*vache*	cow
	vite	quickly / fast

Topic 8.2 The world of work

8.2 G Je cherche un emploi ➡ *pages 150–151*

	bien payé(e)	well paid
	chercher	to look for
	combien	how much
	commencer	to start
	de l'heure	per hour
	difficile	difficult
l'	*emploi (m)*	job
l'	*entreprise (f)*	company
l'	*étudiant(e)*	student
l'	*expérience (f)*	experience
	gagner	to earn
les	*heures de travail (f)*	working hours
la	*journée*	day
l'	*offre (f)*	offer
le	*poste*	position
	quand	when
	saisonnier(-ière)	seasonal
le	*salaire*	salary
le	*travail*	work, job
	trouver	to find
la	*voiture*	car

8.2 F Au travail ➡ *pages 152–153*

	à lundi	see you (on) Monday
la	*caisse*	cash desk, till

le	*chef du personnel*	personnel manager
	chez le boulanger	at the baker's
	comme	as
	demander	to ask
	discuter	to discuss
	écrire	to write
	envoyer	to send
la	*formation*	training
	jeune	young
	libre	free
	maintenant	now
	oublier	to forget
	parfait(e)	perfect
	quelqu'un	someone
	par semaine	per week
en	*semaine*	during the week
	téléphoner	to phone
	trop	too

Topic 8.3 Looking to the future

8.3 G Les métiers ➡ *pages 154–155*

l'	*acteur*	actor
l'	*actrice*	actress
le	*caissier*	cashier (m)
la	*caissière*	cashier (f)
le	*chanteur*	singer (m)
la	*chanteuse*	singer (f)
le / la	*chauffeur de taxi*	taxi driver
le	*cuisinier*	cook (m)
la	*cuisinière*	cook (f)
l'	*école (f)*	school
l'	*électricien*	electrician (m)
l'	*électricienne*	electrician (f)
le	*facteur*	postman
la	*factrice*	postwoman
le	*fermier*	farmer (m)
la	*fermière*	farmer (f)
l'	*hôtesse de l'air (f)*	air hostess
l'	*infirmier*	nurse (m)
l'	*infirmière*	nurse (f)
le	*magasin (m)*	shop

le	*mécanicien*	mechanic (m)
la	*mécanicienne*	mechanic (f)
le	*médecin*	doctor
le	*musicien*	musician (m)
la	*musicienne*	musician (f)
le	*plombier*	plumber
le	*policier*	policeman
la	*policière*	policewoman
le / la	*professeur*	teacher
le / la	*secrétaire*	secretary
le	*serveur*	waiter
la	*serveuse*	waiter/ waitress
	travailler	to work
le	*vendeur*	sales assistant (m)
la	*vendeuse*	sales assistant (f)

8.3 F La vie professionnelle ➡ *pages 156–157*

	à l'étranger	abroad
	apprendre	to learn
	avoir l'intention de	to intend
	le bac	an exam equivalent to A-levels
le	*boulot*	job
la	*carrière*	career
	choisir	to choose
	devenir	to become
	devoir	to have to, must
	dur(e)	hard
	espérer	to hope
	en plein air	in the open air
	gagner	to earn, to win
l'	*hôpital (m)*	hospital
l'	*ingénieur (m / f)*	engineer
l'	*informatique (f)*	IT
le	*lycée*	secondary school (for 15 to 18 year olds)
le	*métier*	profession
la	*pratique*	practice
le	*programmeur*	programmer
le	*stage*	work experience, placement
	varié(e)	varied

Foundation – Exam practice

info

These pages give you the chance to try GCSE-style practice exam questions at grades D–C, based on the AQA Context of Work and education.

Lien

Higher practice exam questions (grades B–A*) are available at the end of this Context in the Higher book.

L'école des parents en République centrafricaine

A

Il est 7h20 du matin, et il fait déjà du soleil. Les 104 enfants (64 garçons et 40 filles) sont déjà tous dans la cour de l'école. Achille joue au foot avec ses copains. Il porte un tee-shirt et un short aux couleurs de son équipe de foot préférée. On ne peut pas avoir classe l'après-midi car il fait trop chaud. Achille a 12 ans et il va bientôt quitter l'école, son éducation est presque finie.

B

En janvier 2006, Achille habitait un autre village et allait dans une autre école. Un jour des soldats ont attaqué le village et ont brûlé les maisons. Toute la famille a dû partir et a passé quelques mois dans la forêt, dans des conditions affreuses. Maintenant, son père a construit une nouvelle maison.

C

L'école est à 800 mètres de la nouvelle maison d'Achille. Les parents ont construit l'école pour leurs enfants. Les parents font aussi la classe mais ils n'ont pas beaucoup d'équipement. Ils veulent une vie normale pour leurs enfants après cette période difficile. *«Cette école est très différente. Avant, il y avait des cahiers, des crayons, des professeurs. Ici, on n'a rien»* dit Achille.

D

À 12h30, après quatre heures de classe, Achille rentre chez lui. L'après-midi il fait trop chaud pour travailler aux champs, mais le soir il aide son père à cultiver des légumes. L'ambition d'Achille? Être fermier comme son père? Non, il veut être médecin.

1a 📖 Read the whole article and match the English headings (1–4) with the paragraphs (A–D).

1 An abandoned village
2 A boy with ambition
3 An early morning start
4 A return to normal life

(**Total** = 4 marks)

Reading for gist

You will not necessarily see an exact translation of the headings in the article. You need to work out which one best fits the gist of what each paragraph is about.

Stratégie 1a

1b 📖 Read the article in detail. Decide whether the following statements are true (**T**), false (**F**) or not mentioned (**?**).

1 School starts early to avoid working in the heat.
2 Achille spent several months in the forest.
3 His mother teaches at the school.
4 Achille has all the basic equipment he needs for school.
5 He works with his father in the school holidays.
6 He wants to train for a different career from his father.

(**Total** = 6 marks)

2a 🎧 Nadège is on the phone to the owner of a restaurant in Morocco, where she is soon to start a period of work experience. Listen to Section A and answer the questions in English.

1 When will she start work?
2 What hours will she work?
3 How far is the restaurant from her accommodation?
4 What clothes should she wear to work? (2)
5 When will she have days off? (2)

(**Total** = 7 marks)

Using the questions

It is always important to read the questions carefully before listening to the recording, as they will indicate the details that you need to listen for, e.g. question 5 asks about **days** off, so you know to listen for more than one day.

Stratégie 2a

2b 🎧 Listen to Section B. In what order (1–5) are the following topics (a–e) discussed?

a cooking fish
b eating with the owner
c working as a waitress
d visiting the market
e her experience of working in a café

(**Total** = 5 marks)

(**Total for Reading and Listening** = 22 marks)

Foundation – Speaking

Au travail

You are talking to your French friend about part-time jobs, work experience, future careers and your free time. Your teacher will play the part of your friend and will ask you:

1 what part-time job you do and when

2 further details about your part-time job

3 details about your work experience

4 what the possibilities are when you leave school

5 what career you envisage for yourself

6 what you do with your leisure time.

7 !

! Remember, you will have to respond to something that you have not yet prepared.

ⓘnfo

Important information:
This sample task is for practice purposes only and should not be used as an actual assessment task. Study it to find out how to plan your Controlled Assessment efficiently to gain maximum marks and / or work through it as a mock exam task before the actual Controlled Assessment.

---

1 What part-time job you do and when
  – say what job you do
  – say how long you have had your job for
  – mention your hours of work
  – say which days you work

> **Stratégie**
> Start your plan. Here are some suggested words for bullet point 1: *travailler, depuis, commencer, finir, jours.*
> If you don't have a job, feel free to make one up! Start with *je travaille* … or *je suis* …
> Use *le* + day to say you work on a particular day, e.g. *le samedi* (on Saturdays).

---

2 Further details about your part-time job
  – say where you work
  – say how you get to work
  – say how much you earn
  – say what you think of the job

> **Stratégie**
> Suggested words for your plan: *où, transport, salaire, opinion.*
> Use *est situé* to say where your place of work is.
> Use *livres de l'heure / par semaine / par mois* to say how much you earn an hour / a week / a month.
> When you say what you think of your job, try to give a reason as well.

---

3 Details about your work experience
  – say when it took place
  – say what work you did
  – say what you enjoyed about your work experience
  – compare a day at work with a day at school

> **Stratégie**
> Suggested words for your plan: *dates, travail, bien?, comparaison stage-collège.*
> Use *faire un stage* to say 'to go on work experience'. As this section is about something that has happened in the past, revise how to use the perfect tense. See the grammar section pages 183–184.
> Show some initiative by developing the last point, e.g. compare then give your opinion and justify it. See Exam technique S10.

4 What the possibilities are when you leave school
- say you can take up an apprenticeship
- say you can continue with your education then go to university
- say you can go straight into a job
- talk about your own intentions

Suggested words for your plan: *apprentissage, université, travailler, choix.*

Add a maximum of two words to this list.

Use *on peut* when you want to talk about possibilities for people in general.

To talk about your own intentions, you have to refer to the future. Use *je vais / je voudrais / j'aimerais / j'espère / j'ai l'intention de …* All of these are followed by a verb in the infinitive.

5 What career you envisage for yourself
- say what career you envisage for yourself
- explain one of the advantages of that job
- state one of the disadvantages
- say what you will do if that proves impossible

Suggested words for your plan: *pilote, avantage, désavantage.*

Add a maximum of three words to this list.

Use *je voudrais* (or another phrase that refers to a future event) + *devenir / être* + job title (without *un / une*) to say what you would like to be.

Start with *si ce n'est pas possible, je …* to introduce the last point.

In your plan, use words that suggest more than one sentence to you, e.g. *pilote* might suggest that it is your choice of career and that you love flying.

6 What you do with your leisure time
- say how much leisure time you have now
- say what you do when you stay at home
- say what you do when you go out
- say what you think you will do with your leisure time when you also have to work

Suggested words for your plan: *temps libre.*

Add a maximum of four words to this list.

Use *temps libre* for 'leisure time'.

Start with *quand je vais travailler …* to introduce the last sub-division suggested for this bullet point.

In your plan, use words that suggest more than one thing to you, e.g. *football* could refer to your playing with your friends or in a team, and watching it on TV or at a stadium. See Exam technique S2.

7 **!** At this point, you may be asked …
- if you are prepared to move to another area.
- what the members of your family do for a living.
- whether you have started your career, or whether you will settle down, get married and have children.
- whether you are planning to have a gap year.

Choose which **two** options you think are the most likely, and for each of these, note down **three** different ideas. In your plan, write three words that illustrate each of the two most likely options, e.g. for the third option suggested here you might choose: *s'installer, mariage, enfants.*

Learn these two options using your reminder words. See Exam technique S3.

Remember to check the total number of words you have used. It should be 40 or fewer.

 *Lien*

Higher sample assessment tasks for this Context can be found in the Higher book.

Foundation – Writing

Mon collège

Your French friend Jean-Luc has asked you to write an article in French for his school magazine. The article is entitled 'A day in the life of a pupil in Britain'. You could include:

1. the facilities in your school
2. your school routine
3. your subjects and teachers
4. your friends
5. extra-curricular activities
6. your school uniform
7. your ambitions for the future.

1 The facilities in your school

- introduce your school, giving its name and location
- mention the size of the school, giving numbers of students and teachers
- say a little about its organisation, e.g. mixed or single sex, age range
- mention the various buildings and say what the facilities are

Stratégie

Suggested words for your plan: *Woodshaw* (name + location of school), *où*, *grande*, *mixte*, *bâtiments*, *équipements*.

Start off by giving your name and giving the name of your school.

Use *il y a* (there is, there are), *nous avons / on a* (we have) and *c'est* (it is) to describe the school.

Don't be afraid to include relevant points that are not specifically mentioned, e.g. for the fourth sub-division suggested here you could include what you do in the various school buildings: *On a un grand gymnase où on joue au basket et un terrain de foot.* See Exam technique W6.

2 Your school routine

- say at what time you arrive, when lessons start and the number of lessons you have each day
- mention break and what you do then
- say what you do at lunchtime
- say at what time school finishes and how you get back home

Stratégie

Suggested words for your plan: *cours*, *récréation*, *heure déjeuner*, *retour maison*.

When referring to what you normally do, use the present tense, e.g. *normalement, j'arrive à …*

Use the past tense to refer to what you did yesterday, e.g. *hier, j'ai mangé …*

3 Your subjects and teachers

- mention compulsory subjects and options
- say which subject is your favourite and give a reason
- say which subject is your least favourite, again with a reason
- write about your favourite teacher, saying why you like him / her

Stratégie

Suggested words for your plan: *obligatoires*, *options*, *préférée*, *détestée*, *prof préféré*.

Use *il faut* + infinitive to say that you have to do something.

You could also use *j'ai choisi* followed by your options.

Use various ways of expressing your opinion and developing the point, e.g. *je pense que / je trouve que / ce que je préfère, c'est … / j'aime … parce que / car …*

Take care with spellings and verb endings. See Exam technique W10.

4 Your friends
- give some information about your friends at school
- choose one and describe him / her (physically and also character)
- say when and where you meet
- say what you did with him / her yesterday

Stratégie

Suggested words for your plan: *Martin* (name of friend), *physiquement, personnalité, activités*.
Add a maximum of two words to this list.
Use *on* for 'we', e.g. *on se retrouve* (we meet). The verb that follows *on* has the same ending as it would if you were using *il* or *elle*. See the grammar section pages 178–179.
Include a grammatical marker to your plan to help you remember that you want to mention yesterday's activities, e.g. *hier*.

5 Extra-curricular activities
- mention which extra-curricular activities are on offer at your school
- say which activity you are involved in
- say what you think of it and give a reason for your opinion
- say where and when the activity takes place

Stratégie

Suggested words for your plan: *liste, mon choix*.
Add a maximum of three words to this list.
Use *on peut* + verb to list what is on offer. See the grammar section on useful verbs, page 187. You could use *ça se passe* to introduce where and when the activity takes place.
If you are not involved in extra-curricular activities, be creative and make up some information!

6 Your school uniform
- say what you wear at school
- say what you think of it and give a reason
- say when the next non-uniform day will be and what you will wear
- say what you think of the fact that French students do not wear a school uniform

Stratégie

Suggested words for your plan: *description, opinion*.
Add a maximum of four words to this list.
Vary the ways in which you express your opinion, e.g. *je pense que / je trouve que*.
When you talk about your non-uniform day (*une journée sans uniforme*), you can say whether it is for a trip (*une excursion*) or for charity (*une bonne cause*).
Use the immediate future (*je vais* + infinitive) to explain this.

7 Your ambitions for the future
- say what you are intending to do next September
- mention the subjects you would like to study and give reasons for your choices
- say what career you hope to have in the future
- say whether you would like to stay in your area or live elsewhere / abroad and give a reason

Stratégie

Add up to six words to your plan.
Show that you know different ways of referring to things that you hope or intend to do. Use *je voudrais / j'aimerais / j'espère / j'ai l'intention de* … Remember that all of these are followed by an infinitive.
Use the future tense if you are sure about what you are going to do: *je vais* + infinitive or *j'irai* (I will go), *je ferai* (I will do).

 **Lien**

Higher sample assessment tasks for this Context can be found in the Higher book.

Exam technique – Speaking

S10 Showing Initiative

'Showing Initiative' does not mean that you suddenly ask your teacher 'What about you, where did you go on holiday?' (although you could do that!). You are generally expected to answer questions. For instance, if you are asked the question *Tu aimes le foot?*, you should first answer it directly and then try to develop your answer, e.g. *Oui, j'aime le foot. J'y joue trois fois par semaine avec mes copains.*

'Showing Initiative' means that you take the conversation elsewhere in a way that is connected to your answer and still relevant to the original question, e.g. *J'aime aussi jouer au basket. En fait, c'est mon sport préféré.* You were not asked about basketball, but you decided to add it to your response. It is relevant, linked to what you were asked and follows your developed answer quite naturally. That is 'Showing Initiative'. Use it to extend your answers and therefore show off extra knowledge of French.

S11 Using different tenses

In order to obtain grade C, you need to demonstrate that you can use more than one tense. You might refer to the present and the past, or you might refer to the present and the immediate future e.g. *je vais* + infinitive. As you don't know exactly which combination will be best for the task that you will be given, it is a good idea to make sure that you know how to talk about present, past and future events.

S12 Checklist for Speaking success

You will score well in the Speaking task if:

- you say a lot that is relevant to the question
- you have a good range of vocabulary
- you can include complex structures
- you can refer to present, past and future events
- your French accent is good
- you can speak fluently
- you can show initiative
- you can speak with grammatical accuracy.

Grade booster

To reach grade D, you need to …

- Express opinions when the occasion arises, e.g. for bullet point 2 of the sample Controlled Assessment on page 164, say what you like and don't like about your job: *J'aime bien les autres employés parce que ce sont des copains mais je n'aime pas les heures de travail.*
- Sometimes develop your answers, e.g. for the fourth sub-division of bullet point 3 (compare a day at work with a day at school), mention hours of work, friends, being paid, etc.

To reach grade C, you need to …

- Show a reasonable range of vocabulary and avoid repeating the same words, e.g. for bullet point 6, mention several different activities, using a different verb each time: *je regarde, j'écoute, je fais, je vais, je joue*, etc.
- Include the three time frames, e.g. for bullet point 4, use the present tense for the first three sub-divisions suggested and refer to the future for the last one. You can also include an imperfect tense if you wish: *Quand j'avais dix ans, je voulais être professeur mais maintenant, j'aimerais être …*

Aiming for Higher? You need to …

- Develop about half of your answers. Make a point of explaining what you are saying, e.g. for bullet point 1, don't give minimum answers. Say what job you do and whether you found it yourself. Say how long you have had your job and how long you intend to keep it. Mention your hours of work and say whether you find the job tiring, etc.
- Show some initiative. Aim to do so several times, e.g. for bullet point 5, develop the idea of your second choice of career. Say what appeals to you about it and what does not.

Exam technique – Writing

W10 Info about Accuracy

If you are aiming at grade C, you should spell French words and put French sentences together well enough for the examiner to understand them without any difficulty, though not necessarily completely correctly.

W11 Ideas for practising

Treat each bullet point as a mini-task. Write your answer to one bullet point at a time with the help of your plan. Ask your partner to take a critical look at your work. Take his / her suggestions on board and redraft your work. Study Exam technique W12, which lists what you should do in order to get the best possible mark, and try to improve your work using these hints.

Practise your writing using sample tasks from the AQA website or given to you by your teacher. Write a plan and attempt the task. As you are only allowed 60 minutes to complete the task in your exam, practise using approximately seven minutes for each bullet point, leaving you 10 minutes or so at the end for a final check. Use that time to check that what you have written makes sense and that it is as accurate as you can make it.

W12 Checklist for Writing success

You will score well if:

- you communicate a lot of relevant information clearly
- you can explain ideas and points of view
- you have a good range of vocabulary
- you can include complex structures
- you can write long sentences
- you can refer to past, present and future events
- you can write with grammatical accuracy
- you organise your ideas well.

Grade booster

To reach grade D, you need to …

- Use longer sentences linked by *et / mais / car / parce que*, e.g. for bullet point 6 of the sample Controlled Assessment on page 167: *je n'aime pas porter … car … mais j'aime bien … parce que …* (I don't like wearing … because …but I like … because …).
- Try and give a fair amount of information. Give yourself a target number of words for each bullet point, e.g. 25 to 30 words. If the answer appears to you to be quite easy, write a little more.

To reach grade C, you need to …

- Work out where you are going to use tenses other than the present, e.g. bullet point 7 encourages you to write about your future. Try not to be repetitive. Use different ways of referring to future events.
- Try and vary your vocabulary. For bullet point 5, think of different words for 'activity', e.g. *une activité, le club de …* You can also refer to activities using pronouns: *il* (it) for *le club, elle* (it) for *l'activité*.

Aiming for Higher? You need to …

- Give your point of view and explain it, e.g. for bullet point 3, when writing about your subjects and your teachers you have several opportunities to give your opinion and justify it. Make sure you do so in different ways.
- Write a response to the title of the task that gives relevant and detailed information, e.g. for bullet point 4, give a lot of details about your friends: who they are, what you do with them, if you have a best friend, what makes him / her special, how often you meet, what you did last time you met, etc.

French pronunciation

🎧 It is not hard to produce the correct sounds for a good French accent.

Remember that vowel sounds in French are not all exactly like English, and can change if they have an accent. You also need to know how some combinations of vowels sound. Vowels may have more than one sound depending on the word. Where this occurs below we have given examples.

a	chat, grand
e	sept, le, entrer
é	café
è	crème
ê	fête
i	dix
î	gîte
ie	géographie
o	dommage, poser
ô	drôle
oi	toi
u	tu
au or eau	beau
eu	deux
ou	rouge
œu	sœur
ui	puis

Vowels followed by n have a nasal sound, e.g. sans, gens, fin, bon, train, bien.

🎧 Then there are some patterns of letters which make these sounds:

ç or ce or ci (soft c)	garçon, morceau, cinéma
ch (like English 'sh')	chaussure
ge or gi (the g is soft)	géographie, gîte
gn (sounds like 'nyuh')	espagnol
h (silent)	hôtel, huit, thé
ill (sounds like 'y')	billet, bouteille
qu (sounds like 'k')	quel

r / rr	growled slightly in the back of your throat, e.g. Robert, marron
s or t	at the end of a word these are usually silent, e.g. gris, petit, mais
ail (at the end of a word)	travail
ain (at the end of a word)	demain
ais or ait (at the end of a word)	mais, fait
an or am; en or em	grand, chambre; sens, temps
im or in	impossible, international

1 Now try saying these well known French-speaking places with the correct accent.

Paris   Bordeaux   Marseille   Belgique   Avignon

🎧 **The alphabet sounds**

A	ah	B	beh	C	seh
D	deh	E	euh	F	eff
G	zheh	H	ash	I	ee
J	zhee	K	kah	L	ell
M	emm	N	enn	O	oh
P	peh	Q	koo*	R	err
S	ess	T	teh	U	oo*
V	veh	W	doobluh veh	X	eeks
Y	eegrek	Z	zed		

* oo pronounced with your lips pushed forward

Typing French accents and punctuation

One way to type letters with accents is to click on: Insert > symbol > then find the letter and accent you want.

Alternatively you can hold down the ALT key and type these numbers. Make sure that the Number Lock is on. It may be different for laptops.

131 = â	133 = à	135 = ç	130 = é	136 = ê	0156 = œ
138 = è	140 = î	147 = ô	150 = û	151 = ù	0128 = €

Dictionary use

Using a dictionary

French > English

- Make sure that you find the meaning that makes sense for the particular sentence you are translating. Many French words have more than one meaning, e.g. *le temps* = 'time' or 'weather'.

- If you are trying to work out the meaning of a verb, you will have to find the infinitive in the dictionary (ending in *-er, -re* or *-ir*) and then look at the verb ending to work out the person and tense of the verb, e.g. *mangez* > *manger* = 'to eat'.

English > French

- Make sure you know if the word you need is a noun (a person, place or thing), a verb (usually an action) or an adjective (describes a noun).

- Sometimes the word in English can be the same when written, even though you pronounce it differently.

Example of dictionary layout

Ignore the words in [ ]. They are there to show French speakers how to pronounce the English word.

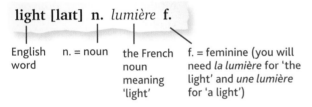

light [laɪt] n. *lumière* f.

| English word | n. = noun | the French noun meaning 'light' | f. = feminine (you will need *la lumière* for 'the light' and *une lumière* for 'a light') |

light [laɪt] adj. *léger* (not heavy); *clair* (colour)

adj. = adjective | the French adjectives for 'light' (two meanings)

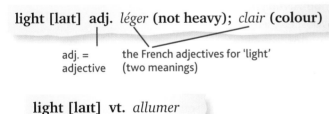

light [laɪt] vt. *allumer*

vt. / vi. = verb | the French verb 'to light' (i.e. 'to light a candle')

It is very important to understand that a dictionary will help you to find individual words, but you have to use your knowledge of how the French language works in order to put a sentence together. Very often the way a phrase is said is completely different from the English, e.g. *le chien de Paul* literally means 'the dog of Paul', but we would say 'Paul's dog'.

The most common mistake people make when using a dictionary is thinking that they can translate something literally word for word, without realising whether the French they have looked up is a noun, verb or adjective. The result can be quite funny for an English speaker who knows French, but a French speaker won't understand anything.

1 See if you can work out what this student wanted to say, then try to produce the correct version.

Je boîte une pièce de théâtre football.

Je ('I') – at least this word is correct!

boîte ('can') – noun, e.g. a can of drink

une pièce de théâtre ('play') – noun, e.g. a play at the theatre

football (football) – noun – this word is also correct.

Correct version: *Je peux jouer au football.*

Je peux ('I can') – irregular verb, present tense); *jouer* (infinitive of verb 'to play'); *au football* (*au* needed after *jouer* + sport).

2 Try to find the correct translations for these words.

1 a match (to light a candle)
2 a case (for clothes)
3 fair (as in fair hair)
4 move (as in move house)
5 fly (as in fly in a plane)
6 left (as in the past tense of leave)

(G) Grammaire

■ Contents

■ Glossary of terms

Adjectives   *les adjectifs*

Words that describe somebody or something:

petit   small   *timide*   shy

Adverbs   *les adverbes*

Words that complement (add meaning to) verbs, adjectives or other adverbs:

très   very   *lentement*   slowly

Articles   *les articles*

Short words used before nouns:

un / une   a, an   *des*   some, any
le / la / les   the

The infinitive   *l'infinitif*

The verb form given in the dictionary:

aller   to go   *avoir*   to have

Nouns   *les noms*

Words that identify a person, a place or a thing:

mère   mother   *maison*   house

Prepositions   *les prépositions*

Words used in front of nouns to give information about when, how, where, etc.:

à   at   *avec*   with
de   of, from   *en*   in

Pronouns   *les pronoms*

Short words used to replace nouns:

je   I   *tu*   you
il   he   *elle*   she
moi   me   *toi*   you

Verbs   *les verbes*

Words used to express an action or a state:

*je **parle***   I **speak**   *il **est***   he **is**

A   Nouns

Masculine and feminine nouns

All French nouns are either masculine or feminine.

In the singular, masculine nouns are introduced with *le, l'* or *un*:

le père   **the** father   *un livre*   **a** book
l'hôtel   **the** hotel

Feminine nouns are introduced with *la, l'* or *une*:

la mère   **the** mother   *une table*   **a** table
l'eau   **the** water

Some nouns have two different forms, masculine and feminine:

un copain   a male friend
une copine   a female friend
un coiffeur   a male hairdresser
une coiffeuse   a female hairdresser
un facteur   a postman
une factrice   a postwoman

Some nouns stay the same for masculine and feminine:

le prof   the male teacher
la prof   the female teacher
un enfant   a male child
une enfant   a female child

There are patterns to help you remember the correct gender of a noun.

■   All words ending in *-isme* are masculine:

l'alcoolisme, l'alpinisme, le racisme

■   Words ending in *-tion* are usually feminine:

la climatisation, la manifestation, la récréation, la station

There are many other patterns, e.g. nouns ending in *-age, -eau, -ment* (masculine); *-ie, -ière, -ité* (feminine). Look out for patterns when you are learning vocabulary, but make a note of exceptions.

Singular and plural forms

As in English, French nouns can be either singular (one) or plural (more than one).

Most plural nouns end in *-s*. Unlike English, the added *-s* is usually not pronounced.

un chat, deux chats   one cat, two cats

As in English, there are some exceptions.

■   With most nouns ending in *-al*, you change the ending to *-aux* in the plural:

un animal   an animal
des animaux   animals

■   With many nouns ending in *-au* or *-eu*, you add an *-x*:

un gâteau, des gâteaux   a cake, cakes
un jeu, des jeux   a game, games

■   Words already ending in *-s*, or in *-x* or *-z*, do not change:

le bras, les bras   arm, arms
le nez, les nez   nose, noses

■   A few nouns change completely:

un œil, des yeux   an eye, eyes

B Articles

Definite articles: *le, la, les* – the

The word for 'the' depends on whether the noun it goes with is masculine (m), feminine (f), singular or plural.

m singular	f singular	m + f plural
le	*la*	*les*

le grand-père	the grandfather
la grand-mère	the grandmother
les grands-parents	the grandparents

When a singular noun starts with a vowel or a silent *h*, *le* and *la* are shortened to *l'*:

l'ami	the friend
l'histoire	the story

In French, you often need to use *le, la* and *les* even when we wouldn't say 'the' in English:

- When talking about likes and dislikes:

J'adore le poulet.	I love chicken.
Elle déteste les maths.	She hates maths.

- When referring to abstract things:

La musique est très importante.	Music is very important.

Indefinite articles: *un, une, des, de* – a, an, some

Like the words for 'the' (*le / la / les*), the words for 'a / an' and 'some' depend on whether the noun they go with is masculine or feminine, singular or plural.

m singular	f singular	m + f plural
un	*une*	*des*

un vélo	a bike
une moto	a motorbike
une orange	an orange
des voitures	(some) cars

When talking about jobs, *un* and *une* are not used in French where 'a' or 'an' is used in English.

Il est professeur.	He is **a** teacher.

In negative constructions, *de* replaces *un, une* or *des* after *pas*:

*J'ai un frère. – Je n'ai **pas de** frère*.*	I don't have **any** brothers.
*Il y a une piscine. – Il n'y a **pas de** piscine.*	There is **no** swimming pool.

*J'ai des sœurs. – Je n'ai **pas de** sœur*.*	I don't have **any** sisters.

* Note that in French you use a singular noun after a negative construction, unlike English.

Change *de* to *d'* in front of a vowel or a silent *h*:

*Je n'ai pas **d'**animal.*	I don't have **any** pets.

Partitive articles: *du, de la, de l', des* – some, any

masculine	feminine	words beginning with a vowel or silent h	plural
de + le = du	*de + la = de la*	*de + l' = de l'*	*de + les = des*

du café	(some) coffee
de la limonade	(some) lemonade
de l'aspirine	(some) aspirin
des chocolats	(some) chocolates

- *du* always replaces *de + le*
- *des* always replaces *de + les*

Use *du, de la, de l', des* to mean 'some' or 'any':

*Je voudrais **du** poulet.*	I'd like **some** chicken.
*Elle prend **de la** limonade.*	She's having (**some**) lemonade.
*Elle boit **de l'**eau.*	She's drinking (**some**) water.
*Avez-vous **des** croissants?*	Do you have **any** croissants?

Also use *du, de la, de l', des* to talk about activities someone is doing or musical instruments someone is playing:

*Je fais **du** judo.*	I do judo.
*Elle joue **de la** guitare.*	She is playing the guitar.
*Il fait **de l'**équitation.*	He goes horse riding.
*Ils font **des** excursions.*	They go on trips.

After a negative, *de* or *d'* replaces these forms:

*Je ne fais pas **de** judo.*	I don't do judo.

C Adjectives

Feminine and masculine, singular and plural adjectives

In French, adjectives have different endings depending on whether they describe masculine, feminine, singular or plural nouns.

- The masculine singular form has no extra ending:

  Mon frère est petit. My brother is small.

- Add -*e* if the noun is feminine singular:

  Ma sœur est petite. My sister is small.

- Add -*s* to the masculine singular form if the noun is masculine plural:

  Mes frères sont petits. My brothers are small.

- Add -*s* to the feminine singular form if the noun is feminine plural:

  Mes sœurs sont petites. My sisters are small.

- When an adjective describes a group of masculine and feminine people or things, it has to be the masculine plural form:

  Mes parents sont grands. My parents are tall.

There are many exceptions in the feminine forms.

- With adjectives that already end in -*e*, don't add another -*e* in the feminine:

  un vélo rouge a red bike
  une moto rouge a red motorbike

- But with adjectives that end in -*é,* do add another -*e* in the feminine:

  mon film préféré my favourite film
  ma chanson préférée my favourite song

- With some adjectives, you double the final consonant before the -*e* in the feminine:

  Il est italien. He is Italian.
  Elle est italienne. She is Italian.

- Adjective endings -*eux* and -*eur* change to -*euse* in the feminine:

  un garçon paresseux ➡ *une fille paresseuse*
  a lazy boy a lazy girl
  un garçon travailleur ➡ *une fille travailleuse*
  a hard-working boy a hard-working girl

- The adjective ending -*eau* changes to -*elle* in the feminine:

  un nouveau vélo a new bike
  une nouvelle voiture a new car

- The adjective ending -*if* changes to -*ive* in the feminine:

  un copain sportif a sporty (boy)friend
  une copine sportive a sporty (girl)friend

- The feminine of *blanc* is *blanche*:

  Elle porte une robe blanche.
  She is wearing a white dress.

- The feminine of *frais* is *fraîche*:

  Je voudrais une boisson fraîche.
  I would like a cool drink.

- The feminine of *gentil* is *gentille*:

  Ma grand-mère est gentille.
  My grandmother is kind.

- The feminine of *sympa* is *sympa*:

  Ma mère est sympa. My mother is nice.

There are also some exceptions in the plural forms.

- Adjective endings -*al* and -*eau* change to -*aux* or -*eaux* in the masculine plural:

  J'ai des poissons tropicaux.
  I have got some tropical fish.
  J'ai de nouveaux livres.
  I have got some new books.

- With adjectives that end in -*s* or -*x*, don't add an -*s* in the masculine plural:

  Mes frères sont paresseux. My brothers are lazy.
  Les nuages sont gris. The clouds are grey.

Some adjectives, such as *marron* and *super*, do not change at all in the feminine or plural:

  Elle porte des bottes marron.
  She's wearing brown boots.

The position of adjectives

Most adjectives follow the noun they describe:

  un prof sympa a nice teacher
  une copine intelligente an intelligent friend
  des idées intéressantes interesting ideas

However, a few adjectives, such as *petit, grand, bon, mauvais, joli, beau, jeune* and *vieux*, usually come in front of the noun:

  un petit garçon a small boy
  une jolie ville a pretty town

A few adjectives that come in front of the noun have a special masculine form before a vowel or a silent *h*:

  un bel endroit a beautiful place
  un vieil homme an old man
  un nouvel ami a new friend

Adjectives of nationality

Adjectives of nationality do not begin with a capital letter:

  Nicolas est français. Nicolas is French.
  Laura est galloise. Laura is Welsh.

Like other adjectives, feminine adjectives of nationality have an -e at the end, unless there is one there already:

Sophie est française.   Sophie is French.
Juliette est suisse.   Juliette is Swiss.

Comparative and superlative adjectives

To make comparisons, use:

- *plus ... que*   more ... than / ...er than
  *La Loire est **plus** longue **que** la Tamise.*
  The Loire is **longer than** the Thames.

- *moins ... que*   less ... than
  *Les vélos sont **moins** rapides **que** les trains.*
  Bicycles are **less** fast **than** trains.

- *aussi ... que*   as ... as
  *Les tomates sont **aussi** chères **que** les pêches.*
  Tomatoes are **as** expensive **as** peaches.

For superlatives (the most ...), use:

- *le / la / les plus ...*   the most ... / the ...est
  *C'est la chambre **la plus** chère.*
  It is **the most** expensive room.
  *C'est **le plus** petit vélo.*
  It is **the smallest** bicycle.

- *le / la / les moins ...*   the least ...
  *C'est le film **le moins** intéressant.*
  It is **the least** interesting film.

The adjectives *bon* and *mauvais* have irregular comparatives and superlatives:

*Ce CD est **meilleur** que l'autre.*
This CD is **better** than the other one.

*Elle est la **meilleure**!*   She's the **best**!

*Je suis **pire** que ma sœur.*
I am **worse** than my sister.

*Mon frère est **le pire**.*   My brother is **the worst**.

Demonstrative adjectives: *ce, cet, cette, ces* – this, that, these, those

The French for 'this' or 'that' is *ce, cet* or *cette* and for 'these' or 'those' is *ces*.

masculine	feminine	masculine and feminine plural
ce	cette	ces

ce magasin   **this** / **that** shop
cette chemise   **this** / **that** shirt
ces baskets   **these** / **those** trainers

But *ce* changes to *cet* when the noun after it begins with a vowel or a silent *h*:

cet ami   **this** / **that** friend
cet hôtel   **this** / **that** hotel

Indefinite adjectives

The most common indefinite adjectives are:

autre(s)	other
certain(e)(s)	certain / some
chaque	each
même(s)	same
plusieurs	several
quelque(s)	some
tout / toute / tous / toutes	all

Chaque is always singular and *plusieurs* is always plural:

*Il y a une télévision dans **chaque chambre**.*
There is a television in **each room**.

*Il a **plusieurs voitures**.*   He has **several cars**.

Possessive adjectives, one 'owner'

mon / ma / mes	my
ton / ta / tes	your
son / sa / ses	his / her / its

There are three different ways of saying 'my' in French, as it depends on whether the noun is masculine or feminine, singular or plural. It is the same for 'your' and 'his' / 'her' / 'its'.

masculine singular	feminine singular	masculine and feminine plural
mon, ton, son	ma, ta, sa	mes, tes, ces

mon père   **my** father
ma mère   **my** mother
ton* père   **your** father
ta* mère   **your** mother
son pied   **his** / **her** / **its** foot
sa porte   **his** / **her** / **its** door
mes parents   **my** parents
tes* parents   **your** parents
ses fenêtres   **his** / **her** / **its** windows

* to someone you normally say *tu* to

French doesn't have three different words for 'his', 'her' and 'its'. The word changes according to whether the noun it is used with is masculine, feminine, singular or plural.

Possessive adjectives, several 'owners'

notre / nos our
votre / vos your
leur / leurs their

masculine and feminine singular	masculine and feminine plural
notre, votre, leur	*nos, vos, leurs*

***notre** père*	**our** father
***notre** mère*	**our** mother
votre père*	**your** father
votre mère*	**your** mother
***leur** frère*	**their** brother
***leur** sœur*	**their** sister
***nos** parents*	**our** parents
vos copains*	**your** friends
***leurs** profs*	**their** teachers

* to several people **or** to someone you normally say *vous* to

Interrogative adjectives: *quel, quelle, quels, quelles*

Quel (meaning 'which' or 'what') agrees with the noun it refers to.

m singular	f singular	m plural	f plural
quel	*quelle*	*quels*	*quelles*

*C'est **quel** dessin?*	**Which** drawing is it?
***Quelle** heure est-il?*	**What** time is it?
***Quelles** sont tes matières préférées?*	
What are your favourite subjects?	

D Adverbs

Adverbs are used with a verb, an adjective or another adverb to express how, when, where or to what extent something happens.

Many French adverbs are formed by adding *-ment* (the equivalent of '-ly' in English) to the feminine form of the adjective.

m adjective	f adjective	adverb
doux	*douce*	*doucement* – gently
final	*finale*	*finalement* – finally
heureux	*heureuse*	*heureusement* – fortunately
probable	*probable*	*probablement* – probably

There are several exceptions, which are not formed from the feminine form of the adjective, including these:

m adjective		adverb
vrai	-	*vraiment* – really
évident	-	*évidemment* – obviously

Many common adverbs are completely irregular:

bien well	*Elle joue **bien**.*	She plays well.
mal badly	*Il mange **mal**.*	He eats badly.
vite fast	*Tu parles **vite**.*	You speak fast.

Comparative and superlative adverbs

As with adjectives, you can make comparisons using *plus, moins* and *aussi ... que*:

*Tu parles **plus** lentement **que** moi.*
You speak **more** slowly **than** me.

*Je mange **moins** vite **que** ma sœur.*
I eat **less** quickly **than** my sister.

*Elle joue **aussi** bien **que** Paul.*
She plays **as** well **as** Paul.

The comparative of the adverb *bien* is an exception:

*Elle joue **mieux** que Paul.*
She plays **better** than Paul.

You can also use adverbs as superlatives:

*Il joue **le mieux**.*   He plays **the best**.

*Il a fini son travail **le plus vite**.*
He finished his work **the fastest**.

Adverbs of time, frequency, place, etc.

Adverbs of time include:

aujourd'hui	today
demain	tomorrow
hier	yesterday
après-demain	the day after tomorrow
avant-hier	the day before yesterday
déjà	already

Adverbs of frequency include:

quelquefois	sometimes
souvent	often
toujours	always
une fois par semaine / mois	once a week / month
encore	again
généralement	generally / usually
rarement	rarely
régulièrement	regularly

Adverbs of place include:

dedans	inside
dehors	outside
ici	here
là-bas	(over) there
loin	far
partout	everywhere

Adverbs of intensity and quantity (qualifying words) include:

assez	enough	*un peu*	a little
trop	too (much)	*très*	very
beaucoup	a lot		

Adverbs of sequence include:

d'abord	firstly	*enfin*	finally
après	afterwards	*puis*	then
ensuite	next		

E Pronouns

Subject pronouns: *je, tu, il, elle, on, nous, vous, ils, elles*

Subject pronouns usually come before the verb and express who or what performs the action.

singular	plural
je – I	*nous* – we
tu – you	*vous* – you
il – he / it	*ils* – they (m)
elle – she / it	*elles* – they (f)
on – we / you / they	

Je parle français.	**I** speak French.
Tu as quel âge?	How old are **you**?
Il s'appelle Théo.	**He** is called Théo.
Elle s'appelle Aïcha.	**She** is called Aïcha.
On se retrouve où?	Where shall **we** meet?
Nous habitons en ville.	**We** live in town.
Vous avez une chambre?	Do **you** have a room?
Ils s'appellent Do et Mi.	**They** are called Do and Mi.
Elles sont marrantes.	**They** are fun.

Je is shortened to *j'* if the word that follows begins with a silent *h* or a vowel:

J'aime les pommes.	**I** like apples.
J'habite en Écosse.	**I** live in Scotland.

There are two French words for 'you': *tu* and *vous*.

- Use *tu* when talking to someone (one person) of your own age or someone in your family.

- Use *vous* when talking to an adult not in your family (e.g. your teacher). The following phrases are useful to remember:

Avez-vous ... ?	Have **you** got ... ?
Voulez-vous ... ?	Do **you** want ... ?
Voudriez-vous ... ?	Would **you** like ... ?

- Also use *vous* when talking to more than one person – whatever their age and whether you know them well or not.

Il and *elle* can both also mean 'it', depending on the gender of the noun they replace.

> *L'hôtel est bien? – Oui, **il** est très confortable.*
> Is the hotel good? – Yes, **it** is very comfortable.

> *Je déteste ma chambre: **elle** est trop petite.*
> I hate my bedroom: **it** is too small.

On can mean 'we', 'you' or 'they', depending on the context:

> ***On** s'entend bien.*
> **We** get on well.

> *Comment dit-**on** «pencil» en français?*
> How do **you** say 'pencil' in French?

> ***On** parle français au Canada.*
> **They** speak French in Canada.

There are two French words for 'they': *ils* and *elles*.

- Use *ils* when all the people / things you are talking about are male, or it is a mixed group of males and females:

> *J'ai un frère et une sœur, **ils** s'appellent Nicolas et Aurélie.*
> I have a brother and a sister; **they** are called Nicolas and Aurélie.

- Use *elles* when all the people / things you are talking about are female:

> *J'ai deux copines espagnoles, **elles** habitent à Madrid.*
> I have two Spanish friends; **they** live in Madrid.

Direct object pronouns: *me, te, le, la, nous, vous, les*

Direct object pronouns replace a noun that is not the subject of the verb.

singular	plural
me / m' – me	*nous* – us
te / t' – you	*vous* – you
le / l' – him / it (m)	*les* – them
la / l' – her / it (f)	

Direct object pronouns come in front of the verb, unlike in English:

*Je **le** prends.*	I'll take **it**.
*Je peux **vous** aider?*	Can I help **you**?

Le and *la* are shortened to *l'* in front of a vowel or a silent *h*:

*Mon petit frère a deux ans. Je **l'**adore!*
My little brother is two. I love **him**!

Indirect object pronouns: *me, te, lui, nous, vous, leur*

Indirect object pronouns are used to replace a noun that would be introduced with the preposition *à*.

singular	plural
me / m' – (to) me	*nous* – (to) us
te / t' – (to) you	*vous* – (to) you
lui – (to) him / her / it	*leur* – (to) them

Je donne du café à mon père.
➡ *Je **lui** donne du café.*
  I give **him** some coffee.
Je parle à ma mère.
➡ *Je **lui** parle.*   I speak to **her**.
J'écris à mes grands-parents.
➡ *Je **leur** écris.*   I write to **them**.

Beware! Some French verbs are followed by a preposition when their English equivalents are not:

*Je téléphone **à** mon père.*	I ring my father.
*Je **lui** téléphone.*	I ring **him**.

Indirect object pronouns: *en* – of it / them; *y* – there

Use *en* to avoid repeating a noun that is introduced with *du, de la, de l'* or *des*:

Tu as des chiens?	Have you got any dogs?
*Oui, j'**en** ai trois.*	Yes, I've got three (**of them**).
Tu manges de la viande?	Do you eat meat?
*Oui, j'**en** mange.*	Yes, I do.

Y usually means 'there'. You can use *y* to avoid repeating the name of a place:

Tu vas à Paris?	Are you going to Paris?
*Oui, j'**y** vais demain.*	Yes, I'm going **there** tomorrow.

Order of object pronouns

When two object pronouns are used together in the same sentence, follow this sequence:

me		le		leur		y
te	come	la	come		come	
nous	before	l'	before	lui	before	en
vous		les				

*Je **te les** donne maintenant.*
I'm giving **them** to **you** now.

*Il **nous en** a parlé.*
He has talked to **us** about **it**.

Emphatic pronouns: *moi, toi, lui, elle, nous, vous, eux, elles*

These are also called disjunctive pronouns.
Use them:

■ for emphasis:

***Moi**, j'adore les fraises.*	I love strawberries.
***Toi**, tu as quel âge?*	How old are **you**?

■ after *c'est*:

*C'est **moi**.*	It's **me**.

■ after a preposition:

*avec **moi***	with **me**
*avec **nous***	with **us**
*pour **toi***	for **you**
*pour **vous***	for **you**

chez **lui**	at **his** house
chez **eux**	at **their** house
à côté d'**elle**	next to **her**
à côté d'**elles**	next to **them**

■ after a comparative:

*Elle est plus sympa que **toi**.*
She is nicer than **you**.

■ with *à*, to express possession:

Possessive pronouns

m singular	f singular	m plural	f plural	
le mien	la mienne	les miens	les miennes	mine
le tien	la tienne	les tiens	les tiennes	yours
le sien	la sienne	les siens	les siennes	his / hers / its
le nôtre	la nôtre	les nôtres	les nôtres	ours
le vôtre	la vôtre	les vôtres	les vôtres	yours
le leur	la leur	les leurs	les leurs	theirs

*C'est **le mien** ou **le tien**?*   Is it **mine** or **yours**?

*Il est **à toi**, ce CD?*
Does this CD **belong to you**?

Relative pronouns: *qui, que, qu', dont*

Relative pronouns are used to link phrases together.

Use *qui* as the subject of the relative clause. It can refer to people and things, and means 'who', 'that' or 'which':

*le copain **qui** habite à Lyon*
the friend **who** lives in Lyon

*le livre **qui** est sur la chaise*
the book **that** is on the table

Use *que* (*qu'* before a vowel or a silent *h*) as the object of the relative clause. It means 'whom' or 'that':

*le copain **que** j'ai vu*
the friend (**that** / **whom**) I saw

*le livre **qu'**il a acheté*   the book (**that**) he bought

■ Remember that *que* is not optional. Although it is often not translated in English, you cannot leave it out in French.

■ If you cannot decide between *qui* and *que*, remember that *qui* is subject and *que* is object. If the relative clause already has a subject, then the pronoun you need must be *que*.

*J'ai trouvé un job **qui** me va.*
I have found a job **that** suits me.
– The subject of *va* is *qui*.

*C'est une couleur **que** je déteste.*
It's a colour (**that**) I hate.
– The subject of *déteste* is *je*, and *que* is object.

You will need to understand sentences containing the word *dont*. It is usually translated as 'whose' or 'of which'.

*J'ai un ami **dont** le père est espagnol.*
I have a friend **whose** father is Spanish.

*J'ai cinq robes **dont** trois sont rouges.*
I've got five dresses **of which** three are red.

Demonstrative pronouns: *ce, cela, ça, celui-ci*, etc.

Ce (shortened to *c'* before a vowel) means 'it', 'that' or 'those' and is usually followed with a form of *être*:

Ce sont mes parents.   **Those** are my parents.
C'est facile.   **It**'s easy.

Cela means 'that' and is often shortened to *ça*:

Cela m'étonne.   **That** surprises me.
*Tu aimes **ça**?*   Do you like **that**?

Ça is also used in various phrases:

Ça va?   Are you OK?
Ça ne fait rien.   It doesn't matter.
*C'est **ça**.*   That's right.

Celui (masculine), *celle* (feminine), *ceux* (masculine plural) and *celles* (feminine plural) are used with *-ci* or *-là* for emphasis or contrast, meaning 'this one', 'that one', 'these ones' or 'those ones':

*Tu veux **celui-ci** ou **celui-là**?*
Do you want **this one** or **that one**?

*J'hésite entre **celles-ci** et **celles-là**.*
I'm hesitating between **these** and **those**.

Indefinite pronouns: *quelqu'un, quelque chose, tout, tout le monde* and *personne*

The French for 'someone' is *quelqu'un*:

*Il y a **quelqu'un** à la maison.*
There's **someone** at home.

The French for 'something' is *quelque chose*:

*Vous avez perdu **quelque chose**?*
Have you lost **something**?

The French for 'all' is *tout / toute / tous / toutes*:

*C'est **tout**.*	That's **all**.
*Je les aime **tous**.*	I love them **all**.

The French for 'everybody' is *tout le monde*:

Tout le monde *aime le chocolat.*
Everybody likes chocolate.

The French for 'nobody' is *personne*. In a sentence, it is followed by *ne* in front a verb or *n'* before a vowel, and it doesn't need *pas*:

Personne ne *veut danser.*
Nobody wants to dance.

F Verbs

French verbs have different endings depending on who is doing the action and whether the action takes place in the past, the present or the future. The verb tables on pages 193–197 set out the patterns of endings for several useful verbs.

When using a name or a singular noun instead of a pronoun, use the same form of the verb as for *il / elle*:

*Martin **parle** espagnol.*   Martin **speaks** Spanish.

When using two names or a plural noun, use the same form of the verb as for *ils / elles*:

*Thomas et Lola **jouent** au basket.*
Thomas and Lola **are playing** basketball.

*Mes frères **écoutent** de la musique.*
My brothers **are listening** to music.

The infinitive

The infinitive is the form of the verb you find in a dictionary, e.g. *jouer, finir, être*. It never changes.

When two verbs follow each other, the second one is always in the infinitive.

■ All verbs of liking, disliking and preferring (such as *aimer, adorer, préférer, détester*) are followed by the infinitive:

*J'aime **jouer** de la guitare.*
I like **playing** the guitar.
*Je préfère **écouter** des CD.*
I prefer **listening** to CDs.

■ Modal verbs *vouloir, pouvoir* and *devoir* and the verb *savoir* are also followed by the infinitive:

*Tu veux **aller** au cinéma?*
Do you want **to go** to the cinema?

*On peut **faire** du shopping.*
You can **go** shopping.

*Je dois **faire** mes devoirs.*
I must **do** my homework.

*Je sais **conduire**.*
I know how **to drive**.

■ Verbs expressing a future wish or intention are followed by the infinitive:

*J'espère **partir** en vacances.*
I hope **to go** on holiday.
*Je voudrais **aller** en Italie.*
I'd like **to go** to Italy.

The infinitive is used after *avant de* to mean 'before doing something':

*Je me lave les mains avant de **manger**.*
I wash my hands before **eating**.

Some verbs always need *à* between them and the infinitive:

*aider quelqu'un **à***	to help someone **to**
*apprendre **à***	to learn **to**
*arriver **à***	to manage **to**
*commencer **à***	to start **to**
*continuer **à***	to continue **to**
*s'intéresser **à***	to be interested **in**
*inviter quelqu'un **à***	to invite someone **to**
*réussir **à***	to succeed **in**
*Il **apprend à** nager.*	He is **learning to** swim.

Some verbs always need *de* between them and the infinitive:

*arrêter **de***	to stop
*décider **de***	to decide **to**
*essayer **de***	to try **to**
*être obligé(e) **de***	to be forced **to**
*oublier **de***	to forget **to**
*refuser **de***	to refuse **to**

*J'ai **oublié de** fermer la porte.*
I **forgot to** close the door.

Faire + infinitive

Faire + infinitive is used to say that someone is having something done:

> *Je **fais réparer** ma voiture.*
> I **have** my car **repaired**.

> *Il **se fait couper** les cheveux.*
> He **is having** his hair **cut**.

> *Ils **font construire** une maison.*
> They **are having** a house **built**.

The perfect infinitive: *après avoir / être* + past participle

The perfect infinitive is the infinitive of *avoir* or *être* (depending on which one the verb normally uses to form the perfect tense), plus the past participle of the verb. It is used after *après* to mean 'after doing something':

> ***Après avoir regardé** l'heure, il est parti.*
> **After looking** at the time, he left.

> *Il a lu le livre **après être allé** là-bas.*
> He read the book **after going** there.

> *Elle a mangé **après s'être levée**.*
> She ate **after getting up**.

The present tense

Use the present tense to describe:

- something that is taking place now:
  > *J'**écoute** un CD.*
  > I **am listening** to a CD.

- something that happens regularly:
  > *J'**ai** maths le lundi.*
  > I **have** maths on Mondays.

Present tense verb endings change depending on who is doing the action:

> *Je **parle** à ma grand-mère.*
> I **speak** to my grandmother.

> ***Nous lavons** la voiture.*
> **We wash** the car.

Most verbs follow a regular pattern.

Regular -*er* verbs

To form the present tense of -*er* verbs, remove the -*er* from the infinitive to form the stem, e.g. *parl* from *parler*. Then add the endings shown below.

parler – to speak / to talk	
je parl**e**	nous parl**ons**
tu parl**es**	vous parl**ez**
il / elle / on parl**e**	ils / elles parl**ent**

Some other regular -*er* verbs:

adorer	to love	*habiter*	to live
aimer	to like	*jouer*	to play
détester	to hate	*regarder*	to watch
écouter	to listen	*rester*	to stay

Regular -*ir* verbs:

To form the present tense of -*ir* verbs, remove the -*ir* from the infinitive to form the stem, e.g. *fin* from *finir*. Then add the endings shown below.

finir – to finish	
je fin**is**	nous fin**issons**
tu fin**is**	vous fin**issez**
il / elle / on fin**it**	ils / elles fin**issent**

Other regular -*ir* verbs:

choisir	to choose
remplir	to fill

Regular -*re* verbs:

To form the present tense of -*re* verbs, remove the -*re* from the infinitive to form the stem, e.g. *attend* from *attendre*. Then add the endings shown below.

attendre – to wait	
j'attend**s**	nous attend**ons**
tu attend**s**	vous attend**ez**
il / elle / on attend	ils / elles attend**ent**

Other regular -*re* verbs:

descendre	to go down
répondre	to reply
vendre	to sell

Irregular verbs

Some verbs are irregular and do not follow these patterns. Turn to pages 194–197 for details of the most common ones.

Reflexive verbs

Reflexive verbs have an extra pronoun in front of the verb:

me	je **me** réveille	I wake up
te	tu **te** lèves	you get up
se	il / elle **s'**appelle	he / she is called
	on **se** lave	we have a wash
nous	nous **nous** amusons	we have fun
vous	vous **vous** couchez	you go to bed
se	ils / elles **s'**excusent	they apologise

Note that *me, te* and *se* are shortened to *m', t'* and *s'* in front of a vowel or a silent *h*.

Common reflexive verbs are:

s'amuser	to have fun
s'habiller	to get dressed
s'appeler	to be called
se laver	to have a wash
s'asseoir	to sit down
se lever	to get up
se coucher	to go to bed
se passer	to happen
s'ennuyer	to be bored
se promener	to go for a walk
s'excuser	to apologise
se réveiller	to wake up

The perfect tense

Use the perfect tense to talk about what somebody did or has done.

> *Il **a mangé** un sandwich.*
> He **ate** a sandwich. / He **has eaten** a sandwich.

To make the perfect tense of most verbs, use the present tense of *avoir* + past participle:

parler – to speak / to talk	
j'**ai parlé**	nous **avons parlé**
tu **as parlé**	vous **avez parlé**
il / elle / on **a parlé**	ils / elles **ont parlé**

Some verbs use the present tense of *être* instead of *avoir*:

aller – to go	
je **suis allé(e)**	nous **sommes allé(e)s**
tu **es allé(e)**	vous **êtes allé(e)(s)**
il **est allé**	ils **sont allés**
elle **est allée**	elles **sont allées**
on **est allé(e)(s)**	

Verbs that use *être* to form the perfect tense include:

aller	to go
arriver	to arrive
descendre	to go down
entrer	to enter
monter	to go up
mourir	to die
naître	to be born
partir	to leave
rentrer	to come back
rester	to stay
retourner	to return / to go back
sortir	to go out
tomber	to fall
venir	to come

All reflexive verbs use *être* to form the perfect tense. Don't forget the extra pronoun that comes before the part of *être*:

se lever – to get up	
je **me suis levé(e)**	nous **nous sommes levé(e)s**
tu **t'es levé(e)**	vous **vous êtes levé(e)(s)**
il **s'est levé**	ils **se sont levés**
elle **s'est levée**	elles **se sont levées**
on **s'est levé(e)(s)**	

When using *être*:

- add *-e* to the past participle if the subject is female:

  *Elle est parti**e** en Écosse.*
  She went off to Scotland.

- add *-s* to the past participle if the subject is masculine plural:

  *Ils sont arrivé**s** en retard.*   They arrived late.

- add *-es* to the past participle if the subject is feminine plural:

  *Elles sont arrivé**es** en retard.*   They arrived late.

When making a negative statement in the perfect tense, *ne* comes before *avoir / être* and *pas* comes after it:

Je n'ai pas mangé.	I **haven't** eaten.
Elle n'est pas sortie.	She **didn't** go out.

Past participles

The past participle of *-er* verbs ends in *-é*:

aller – allé	gone
donner – donné	given
parler – parlé	spoken

The past participle of regular *-ir* verbs ends in *-i*:

choisir – choisi	chosen
finir – fini	finished

The past participle of regular *-re* verbs ends in *-u*:

attendre – attendu	waited
vendre – vendu	sold

Many common verbs have an irregular past participle:

*avoir – **eu***	had
*boire – **bu***	drunk
*devoir – **dû***	had to
*dire – **dit***	said
*écrire – **écrit***	written
*être – **été***	been
*faire – **fait***	done / made
*lire – **lu***	read
*mettre – **mis***	put
*pouvoir – **pu***	been able to
*prendre – **pris***	taken
*venir – **venu***	come
*voir – **vu***	seen
*vouloir – **voulu***	wanted

The imperfect tense

Use the imperfect tense:

- to describe what something or someone was like in the past:

  *Il y **avait** une grande piscine.*
  There **was** a big pool.

C'était délicieux.	It **was** delicious.
J'étais triste.	I **was** sad.

- to say what was happening at a certain time in the past:

  *Je **regardais** la télé quand il a téléphoné.*
  I **was watching** TV when he rang.

- to describe something that used to happen regularly in the past:

  *Je **prenais** le bus tous les matins.*
  I **used to catch** the bus every morning.

- after *si* to make a suggestion:

  *Si on **allait** au cinéma?*
  Shall we **go** to the cinema?

To form the imperfect tense, take the *nous* form of the verb in the present tense, remove *-ons* to form the stem, then add the correct endings:

finir – to finish	
(present tense: nous **finissons**)	
je finiss**ais**	nous finiss**ions**
tu finiss**ais**	vous finiss**iez**
il / elle / on finiss**ait**	ils / elles finiss**aient**

The verb *être* is the only exception. The endings are as above, but they are added to the stem *ét-*:

être – to be	
j'**étais**	nous ét**ions**
tu ét**ais**	vous ét**iez**
il / elle / on ét**ait**	ils / elles ét**aient**

Perfect or imperfect?

To help you decide between the perfect and the imperfect, remember that:

- the perfect tense usually describes single events in the past:

  *Hier, je **me suis levée** à six heures.*
  Yesterday, I **got up** at six.

- the imperfect describes what used to happen:

  *Je **me levais** à huit heures.*
  I **used to get up** at eight.

The pluperfect tense

This tense is used to refer to something further back in the past than the perfect or the imperfect, to say what someone had done or had been doing. You use the imperfect of *avoir* or *être*, plus a past participle:

J'avais parlé.	I **had spoken**.
Il était parti.	He **had left**.

*Vous **vous étiez habillés**.*
You **had got dressed**.

*Je savais qu'il **était allé** en Égypte.*
I knew that he **had gone** to Egypt.

The immediate future

Use the present tense of *aller* followed by an infinitive to say what you are going to do or what is going to happen:

je **vais pleurer**	I am going to cry
nous **allons manger**	we are going to eat
tu **vas partir**	you are going to leave
vous **allez boire**	you are going to drink
elle **va chanter**	she is going to sing
ils **vont dormir**	they are going to sleep

Je **vais continuer** mes études.
I'm **going to continue** studying.

Il **va neiger**.　　　It's **going to snow**.

The future tense

The future tense expresses what will happen or will be happening in the future:

Qu'est-ce que vous **ferez** après l'école?
What **will you do** after school?

Vous **travaillerez** dans l'informatique?
Will you work in computing?

It is used for predictions such as weather forecasts:

Il **fera** beau / froid / chaud.
It **will be** fine / cold / hot.

Le temps **sera** pluvieux / nuageux.
The weather **will be** rainy / cloudy.

Il **neigera**.	It **will snow**.
Il **pleuvra**.	It **will rain**.
Il **gèlera**.	It **will freeze**.

To form the future tense, add the correct ending to the infinitive of the verb:

parler – to speak / to talk	
je parler**ai**	nous parler**ons**
tu parler**as**	vous parler**ez**
il / elle / on parler**a**	ils / elles parler**ont**

With some verbs, you add the same set of endings to an irregular stem instead of the infinitive:

aller – j'**ir**ai	pouvoir – je **pourr**ai
avoir – j'**aur**ai	savoir – je **saur**ai
être – je **ser**ai	venir – je **viendr**ai
faire – je **fer**ai	voir – je **verr**ai
falloir – il **faud**ra	vouloir – je **voudr**ai

The imperative

Use the imperative to give advice or instructions.

Use the *tu* form with a person your own age or a person you know very well:

Continue tout droit.	**Go** straight on.
Prends la première rue.	**Take** the first street.
Tourne à gauche.	**Turn** left.

Use the *vous* form with a person you don't know very well or to more than one person:

Continuez tout droit.	**Go** straight on.
Prenez la première rue.	**Take** the first street.
Tournez à gauche.	**Turn** left.

The imperative is the same as the *tu* or the *vous* form of the present tense, but without using a word for 'you' first. In the case of *-er* verbs, you miss off the *-s* of the *tu* form (unless the verb is followed by *y* or *en*):

Va au lit!	**Go** to bed!
Achète des pommes.	**Buy** some apples.
Vas-y!	**Go** on!
Achètes-en un kilo.	**Buy** a kilo (of them).

Note that all *vous* form imperatives end in *-ez* except for faire:

Faites vos devoirs!　　　**Do** your homework!

Reflexive verbs in the imperative are hyphenated with their reflexive pronouns:

Lève-toi.	Stand up.
Asseyez-vous.	Sit down.

The conditional

You use the conditional in French when 'would' is used in English:

Je **voudrais** te voir.
I **would like** to see you.

Si j'**étais** riche, j'**achèterais** un piano.
If I **were** rich, I **would buy** a piano.

The conditional has the same stem as the future tense and the same endings as the imperfect:

	future	imperfect	conditional
aimer	j'**aimerai**	j'**aimais**	j'**aimerais**
aller	j'**irai**	j'**allais**	j'**irais**

parler – to talk / to speak	
je parler**ais**	nous parler**ions**
tu parler**ais**	vous parler**iez**
il / elle / on parler**ait**	ils / elles parler**aient**

The subjunctive

The following expressions are followed by a form of the verb called the subjunctive:

avant que	before
bien que	although
à condition que	provided that
il faut que	we / you / one must / it is necessary that

The most commonly used of these phrases is *il faut que*.

The subjunctive form is usually the same as, or similar to, the present tense, so it is easy to recognise.

> *Il faut que vous **parliez** avec le patron.*
> You must **speak** to the owner.

Some exceptions are *faire, aller, avoir* and *être* – these are different, and you need to be able to recognise them.

> *Il faut qu'on **fasse** des économies d'eau.*
> We must **save** water.

> *Bien qu'il **ait** 25 ans, il habite toujours chez ses parents.*
> Although he **is** 25, he still lives with his parents.

> *Avant qu'elle **aille** à l'université, nous allons passer une semaine en Espagne.*
> Before she **goes** to university, we're going to spend a week in Spain.

> *Mon père m'a promis un nouveau vélo, à condition que mes résultats **soient** bons.*
> My father has promised me a new bicycle, provided that my results **are** good.

parler	faire	aller
(regular -er verb)		
que je parle	*que je fasse*	*que j'aille*
que tu parles	*que tu fasses*	*que tu ailles*
qu'il / elle / on parle	*qu'il / elle / on fasse*	*qu'il / elle / on aille*
que nous parlions	*que nous fassions*	*que nous allions*
que vous parliez	*que vous fassiez*	*que vous alliez*
que ils / elles parlent	*qu'ils / elles fassent*	*qu'ils / elles aillent*

avoir	être
que j'aie	*que je sois*
que tu aies	*que tu sois*
qu'il / elle / on ait	*qu'il / elle / on soit*
que nous ayons	*que nous soyons*
que vous ayez	*que vous soyez*
qu'ils / elles aient	*qu'ils / elles soient*

The passive

The passive is used to say what is done to someone or something. It is formed from a part of *être* and a past participle. The past participle must agree with the noun:

> active form: *Il lave la pomme.*
> He washes the apple.

> passive form: *La pomme **est lavée**.*
> The apple **is washed**.

The passive can be used in different tenses:

> present: *Les lits **sont faits**.*
> The beds **are made**.

> imperfect: *Les murs **étaient peints**.*
> The walls **were painted**.

> perfect: *J'ai **été invité**.*
> I've **been invited**.

> future: *La maison **sera vendue**.*
> The house **will be sold**.

The passive is used less often in French than in English, as most sentences can be turned round:

- either by using *on*:
  > ***On parle** français au Québec.*
  > French **is spoken** in Quebec.

- or by using a reflexive verb:
  > *Les tickets **se vendent** par carnets de 10.*
  > Tickets **are sold** in books of 10.

en + present participle

The English present participle ends in '-ing', and the French present participle ends in *-ant*. Take the *nous* form of the present tense, remove *-ons* and replace it with *–ant*: *arriver* ➡ *arrivons* ➡ *arrivant*

En + present participle can be used when two actions happen together:

> *Il fait ses devoirs **en chantant**.*
> He does his homework **while singing**.

> ***En travaillant** le soir, je gagne de l'argent.*
> **By working** in the evening, I earn money.

Useful verbs

avoir – to have

Use *avoir* to say how old someone is:

J'ai 15 ans.	I **am** 15 years old.

Use *avoir mal* to talk about a pain or an ache:

J'ai mal à la tête.	I **have** a head**ache**.

Use *avoir envie* to talk about feeling like or wanting to do something:

J'ai envie de courir.	I **feel like** running.

Use *en avoir marre* to talk about being fed up with something:

J'en ai marre des examens.
I'**m fed up** with the exams.

Some more useful expressions with *avoir*:

avoir chaud	to be hot
avoir faim	to be hungry
avoir froid	to be cold
avoir mal au cœur	to feel sick
avoir peur	to be afraid
avoir raison	to be right
avoir soif	to be thirsty
avoir tort	to be wrong

il y a – there is, there are

Il y a une banque.	**There is** a bank.
Il y a beaucoup de cafés.	**There are** lots of cafés.
Il n'y a pas de piscine.	**There isn't** a swimming pool.

faire – to do

This verb can mean 'to do', 'to make' or 'to go' (when talking about activities):

faire du judo	**to do** judo
faire la vaisselle	**to do** the washing up
faire le lit	**to make** the bed
faire de la natation	**to go** swimming

This verb is also used with *il* to talk about the weather:

Il fait beau.	The weather is nice.
Il fait mauvais.	The weather is bad.

jouer à and *jouer de* – to play

To talk about playing games and sports, use *jouer + au / à la / à l' / aux*:

Je joue au basket.	I play basketball.

To talk about playing a musical instrument, use *jouer + du / de la / de l' / des*:

Je joue des percussions.
I play percussion instruments.

se trouver – to be found, *être situé(e)* – to be situated

These verbs can be used in place of *être* to talk about where things are located:

La gare se trouve au centre-ville.
The station **can be found** in the town centre.

Make sure that *situé* agrees with the gender of the subject.

La ville est située au bord de la mer.
The town is **situated** by the sea.

Modal verbs: *devoir, pouvoir, vouloir*

Modal verbs are usually followed by an infinitive.

Use *devoir* (to have to) + infinitive to say what you must / mustn't do:

Je dois porter un uniforme.
I **have to wear** a uniform.

On ne doit pas jeter de papiers par terre.
You **mustn't drop** litter on the ground.

Use *pouvoir* (to be able to) + infinitive to say what you can / can't do:

On peut faire des randonnées.
You **can go** hiking.

Elle ne peut pas sortir pendant la semaine.
She **can't go out** during the week.

Use *vouloir* (to want to) + infinitive to say what you want and don't want to do. Adding *bien* changes the meaning:

Je veux partir.	I **want to leave**.
Je veux bien partir.	I **am quite happy to leave**.

The conditional of *vouloir*, *je voudrais*, means 'I would like':

Je voudrais partir en vacances.
I **would like** to go on holiday.

Note that *j'aimerais*, the conditional form of *aimer*, means the same as *je voudrais*:

J'aimerais faire de la planche à voile.
I **would like** to go windsurfing.

Impersonal verbs: *il neige, il pleut, il faut*

These verbs are only used with *il*:

Il neige.	**It**'s snowing.
Il pleut.	**It**'s raining.

Il faut can have different meanings depending on the context:

Il faut boire beaucoup d'eau.
You must drink a lot of water.

Il ne faut pas fumer.
You mustn't smoke.

Il me faut un kilo de tomates.
I need a kilo of tomatoes.

Il faut trois heures pour aller là-bas.
It takes three hours to get there.

G Negatives

To make a sentence negative, you normally put *ne* before the verb and *pas* after it:

Je parle espagnol. ➡ *Je **ne** parle **pas** espagnol.*
I don't speak Spanish.

Shorten *ne* to *n'* if the word that follows begins with *h* or a vowel:

C'est difficile. ➡ *Ce **n'**est **pas** difficile.*
It's **not** difficult.

In negative sentences, use *de* instead of *un, une* or *des*:

Il y a un cinéma. ➡ *Il **n'**y a **pas de** cinéma.*
There is **no** cinema.

J'ai des frères. ➡ *Je **n'**ai **pas de** frère.*
I don't have **any** brothers.

Other common negative phrases:

ne ... plus – no more	*Il n'y a **plus de** savon.* There is **no more** soap.
ne ... jamais – never	*Je **ne** fume **jamais**.* I **never** smoke.
ne ... rien – nothing / not anything	*Il **ne** fait **rien**.* He does**n't** do **anything**.
ne ... personne not anybody	*Je **ne** vois **personne**.* I don**'t** see **anybody**.
ne ... que – only	*Je n'ai **qu'**une sœur.* I **only** have one sister.
ne ... ni ... ni – neither ... nor	*Il **ne** parle **ni** français **ni** espagnol.* He speaks **neither** French **nor** Spanish.

Negatives in the perfect tense

In most negative phrases in the perfect tense, the phrase goes around the part of *avoir* or *être*.

*Je **n'**ai **pas** dormi.*   I **didn't** sleep.

But the negative phrases *ne ... que* and *ne ... ni ... ni* go around *avoir / être* and also the past participle:

*Je **n'**ai mangé **que** du pain.*
I **only** ate some bread.

Direct and indirect object pronouns are included within the negative phrase:

Je ne l'ai pas vu.   I didn't see **it**.

*Il ne **me** parle plus.*   He no longer speaks to **me**.

With reflexive verbs, the *ne* goes before the reflexive pronoun (*me, te*, etc.):

*Il **ne** s'est **pas** lavé.*   He **didn't** have a wash.

H Questions

You can turn statements into questions by adding a question mark and making your voice go up at the end:

Tu joues au tennis. ➡ *Tu joues au tennis**?***
Do you play tennis?

You can also add *est-ce que ...* at the beginning of the question:

Je peux vous aider. ➡ ***Est-ce que** je peux vous aider?*
Can I help you?

In more formal situations, you can change the word order so that the verb comes first:

Vous pouvez m'aider. ➡ ***Pouvez**-vous m'aider?*
Can you help me?

In the perfect tense, the auxiliary verb comes first:

Vous avez aidé la dame. ➡ ***Avez-vous** aidé la dame?*
Did you help the lady?

Many questions start with *qu'est-ce que ...*

***Qu'est-ce que** c'est?*   **What** is it?

***Qu'est-ce qu'**il y a à manger?*
What is there to eat?

***Qu'est-ce que** vous avez comme journaux?*
What kind of newspapers have you got?

Other question words

combien (de)	how much / how many	*Tu as **combien** de chats?* **How many** cats have you got?

comment	how	**Comment** vas-tu? **How** are you?
où	where	**Où** habites-tu? **Where** do you live?
pourquoi	why	**Pourquoi** est-ce que tu n'aimes pas ça? **Why** don't you like it?
quand	when	Il vient **quand**? **When** is he coming?
		Quand a-t-il commencé? **When** did he start?
quel / quelle / quels / quelles	which / what	Ça commence à **quelle** heure? **What** time does it start?
que / qu'	what	**Que** veux-tu? **What** do you want?
qui	who	C'est **qui**? **Who** is it?
quoi	what	Elle fait **quoi**? **What** is she doing?

▉ Prepositions

à, au, à la, à l', aux

À can mean:

in	J'habite **à** Nice.	I live **in** Nice.
at	Je me lève **à** sept heures.	I get up **at** seven.
to	Je vais **à** l'école.	I go **to** school.

Some special expressions with *à*:

à pied	on foot
à vélo	by bike
à gauche	on the left
à droite	on the right
aller à la pêche	to go fishing

masculine	feminine	nouns which start with a vowel or silent *h*	plural
à + le = au	à + la = à la	à + l' = à l'	à + les = aux

au théâtre	at / to the theatre
à la piscine	at / to the pool
à l'hôtel	at / to the hotel
aux États-Unis	in / to the USA

Use *au, à la, à l', aux* to talk about flavours and fillings:

un sandwich **au jambon**	a **ham** sandwich
une glace **à la vanille**	a **vanilla** ice cream
un gâteau **à l'orange**	an **orange** cake

Use with *avoir mal* to talk about a part of the body that hurts:

J'ai mal **à l'**oreille.	I've got ear ache.
Il **a mal aux** genoux.	His knees hurt.

de

De is shortened to *d'* before a vowel or a silent *h*.

De can mean 'of':

la mère **de** ma copine (the mother of my friend) my friend's mother

le prof **d'**histoire (the teacher of history) the history teacher

Note that the word order can be different from English:

un jus **d'orange**	an orange juice
un match **de** foot	a football match
la maison **de** mes grands-parents	my grandparents' house

De can also mean 'from':

Elle vient **d'**Écosse.

She comes **from** Scotland.

De is sometimes part of an expression:

près de	near
Il habite **près de** Lyon.	He lives **near** Lyon.
de ... à ...	from ... to ...
de neuf heures **à** cinq heures	**from** nine **to** five

De is used for expressing contents and quantities. Some examples are:

beaucoup de	a lot of
une boîte de	a jar / tin of
une bouteille de	a bottle of
cent grammes de	100 grammes of
un kilo de	a kilo of
un peu de	a little / a bit of

une **bouteille d'**eau	a **bottle of** water
un **kilo de** poires	a **kilo of** pears
un **peu de** sucre	a **little** sugar

In a different context, *venir de* can mean 'to have just …'

> Il **vient de** retourner de vacances.
> He **has just** returned from his holidays.

en, au / aux

En is used to introduce most names of countries. It means both 'to' and 'in':

> Je vais **en** Allemagne. I am going **to** Germany.
> Il habite **en** France. He lives **in** France.
> Elle part **en** Angleterre. She's going **to** England.

A few names of countries are masculine. These are introduced with *au* or *aux*:

> Il va **au** Portugal.
> He's going **to** Portugal.

> Elle habite **au** pays de Galles.
> She lives **in** Wales.

> Nous partons **aux** États-Unis.
> We're going **to** the USA.

More prepositions

à côté de	next to	**à côté de** la salle de bains **next to** the bathroom
avec	with	Je me dispute **avec** ma sœur. I argue **with** my sister.
chez	at / to someone's house	Je suis **chez** ma copine. I'm **at** my friend's house. Je vais **chez** mon copain. I'm going **to** my friend's house.
dans	in	Il est **dans** sa chambre. He is **in** his bedroom.
derrière	behind	**derrière** l'hôtel **behind** the hotel
devant	in front of	On se retrouve **devant** le théâtre? Shall we meet **in front of** the theatre?
en face de	opposite	**en face du** parking **opposite** the car park
entre	between	**entre** la salle à manger et l'ascenseur **between** the dining room and the lift

pendant	during	Qu'est-ce que tu fais **pendant** les vacances? What are you doing **during** the holidays?
près de	near	Mon chien est **près de** moi. My dog is **near** me.
pour	for	C'est super **pour** les jeunes. It's great **for** young people.
sous	under	Le chat est **sous** le lit. The cat is **under** the bed.
sur	on	Il y a des livres **sur** les étagères. There are books **on** the shelves.

Expressions of time

depuis – for / since

To say how long you've been doing something, use the present tense with *depuis*:

> J'apprends le français **depuis** quatre ans.
> I have been learning French **for** four years.

> J'ai mal à la gorge **depuis** hier.
> I have had a sore throat **since** yesterday.

To say how long you had been doing something, use the imperfect tense with *depuis*:

> J'attendais **depuis** une heure.
> I had been waiting **for** an hour.

pendant – for / during

To talk about a completed activity in the past and say how long it went on for, use the perfect tense and *pendant*:

> J'ai joué au squash **pendant** deux ans.
> I played squash **for** two years.

Il y a

You can use *il y a* with the perfect tense to mean 'ago'; not to be confused with *il y a* meaning 'there is' or 'there are'.

> Il a commencé à travailler **il y a** trois mois.
> He started working three months **ago**.

J Conjunctions

Conjunctions are words used to link parts of sentences together:

alors	so	*Je suis fatiguée, **alors** je me repose.* I am tired, **so** I'm having a rest.
car	because / as	*J'ai faim, **car** je n'ai pas mangé à midi.* I'm hungry **as** I didn't eat at lunchtime.
donc	therefore	*Je pense, **donc** je suis.* I think, **therefore** I am.
et	and	*J'ai 15 ans **et** j'habite en France.* I am 15 **and** I live in France.
et puis	and then	*Je me lève **et puis** je prends mon petit déjeuner.* I get up **and then** I have breakfast.
mais	but	*J'ai deux frères, **mais** je n'ai pas de sœur.* I've got two brothers, **but** I haven't got a sister.
ou	or	*Je joue au foot **ou** je vais à la patinoire.* I play football **or** I go to the ice-rink.
parce que	because	*J'aime la géographie **parce que** c'est intéressant.* I like geography **because** it's interesting.
quand	when	*Je prends le bus **quand** il pleut.* I take the bus **when** it rains.
si	if	*Samedi, je vais à la plage, **s'il** fait chaud.* On Saturday, I am going to go to the beach **if** it is hot.

Certain linking expressions are used with particular tenses:

- *au moment où*   just as

This expression is useful for linking a perfect tense phrase with an imperfect one:

> *Je suis arrivé **au moment où** mon père préparait le déjeuner.*
> I arrived **just as** my father was preparing lunch.

- *pendant que*   while

The expression is useful for linking an imperfect tense phrase with a perfect one:

> ***Pendant que** je nageais, ma copine a joué au volley.*
> **While** I was swimming, my friend played volleyball.

- *quand*   when

+ future: when talking about future intentions in English, the present tense is used after 'when', but in French the future is needed:

> ***Quand** j'irai à Boulogne, je mangerai du poisson.*
> **When** I go to Boulogne, I will eat fish.

+ imperfect: when talking about continuing or regular events in the past, the imperfect tense is used in both French and English:

> ***Quand** j'habitais à Paris, j'allais souvent au cinéma.*
> **When** I was living in Paris, I often used to go to the cinema.

- *tandis que*   while / whereas

This construction means 'whereas' when comparing an event in the past with an event in the future.

> *L'année dernière, j'ai fait de la voile, **tandis que** cette année je ferai du kayak.*
> Last year I went windsurfing, **whereas** this year I will go kayaking.

K Numbers

1	*un*	16	*seize*
2	*deux*	17	*dix-sept*
3	*trois*	18	*dix-huit*
4	*quatre*	19	*dix-neuf*
5	*cinq*	20	*vingt*
6	*six*	21	*vingt et un*
7	*sept*	22	*vingt-deux*
8	*huit*	23	*vingt-trois*
9	*neuf*	24	*vingt-quatre*
10	*dix*	25	*vingt-cinq*
11	*onze*	26	*vingt-six*
12	*douze*	27	*vingt-sept*
13	treize	28	*vingt-huit*
14	*quatorze*	29	*vingt-neuf*
15	*quinze*	30	*trente*

40	*quarante*	100	*cent*
41	*quarante et un*	101	*cent un*
42	*quarante-deux*	102	*cent deux*
50	*cinquante*	200	*deux cents*
51	*cinquante et un*	201	*deux cent un*
52	*cinquante-deux*	202	*deux cent deux*
60	*soixante*	300	*trois cents*
61	*soixante et un*	301	*trois cent un*
62	*soixante-deux*	302	*trois cent deux*
70	*soixante-dix*	1000	*mille*
71	*soixante et onze*	1001	*mille un*
72	*soixante-douze*	1002	*mille deux*
80	*quatre-vingts*	2000	*deux mille*
81	*quatre-vingt-un*	2001	*deux mille un*
82	*quatre-vingt-deux*	2002	*deux mille deux*
90	*quatre-vingt-dix*		
91	*quatre-vingt-onze*		
92	*quatre-vingt-douze*		

80, *quatre-vingts,* loses the final *s* before another digit or to give a page number or a date:

quatre-vingt-sept	eighty-seven
page quatre-vingt	page eighty
l'an mille neuf cent quatre-vingt	the year 1980

The same applies to 200, *deux cents,* and other multiples of *cent*:

deux cent dix	two hundred and ten
page trois cent	page three hundred

Ordinal numbers: *premier, deuxième,* etc.

The French for 'first' is *premier* in the masculine and *première* in the feminine:

mon **premier** cours	my **first** lesson
mes **premières** vacances	my **first** holiday

To say 'second', 'third', etc., simply add *-ième* to the original number:

deuxième	second
troisième	third

To say 'fifth', add a *u* before *-ième*:

cinquième	fifth

To say 'ninth', change the *f* of *neuf* to a *v*:

neuvième	ninth

If the original number ends with an *-e*, drop the *-e* before adding *-ième*:

quatrième	fourth
onzième	eleventh

To revise how numbers are used in dates and telling the time, see the reference section, pages 11 and 13.

Verb tables

L Verb tables

infinitive	present	perfect	imperfect	future
Regular -er verbs				
parler to speak	*je parle* *tu parles* *il / elle / on parle* *nous parlons* *vous parlez* *ils / elles parlent*	*j'ai parlé* *tu as parlé* *il / elle / on a parlé* *nous avons parlé* *vous avez parlé* *ils / elles ont parlé*	*je parlais* *tu parlais* *il / elle / on parlait* *nous parlions* *vous parliez* *ils / elles parlaient*	*je parlerai* *tu parleras* *il / elle / on parlera* *nous parlerons* *vous parlerez* *ils / elles parleront*
Regular -ir verbs				
finir to finish	*je finis* *tu finis* *il / elle / on finit* *nous finissons* *vous finissez* *ils / elles finissent*	*j'ai fini* *tu as fini* *il / elle / on a fini* *nous avons fini* *vous avez fini* *ils / elles ont fini*	*je finissais* *tu finissais* *il / elle / on finissait* *nous finissions* *vous finissiez* *ils / elles finissaient*	*je finirai* *tu finiras* *il / elle / on finira* *nous finirons* *vous finirez* *ils / elles finiront*
Regular -re verbs				
vendre to sell	*je vends* *tu vends* *il / elle / on vend* *nous vendons* *vous vendez* *ils / elles vendent*	*j'ai vendu* *tu as vendu* *il / elle / on a vendu* *nous avons vendu* *vous avez vendu* *ils / elles ont vendu*	*je vendais* *tu vendais* *il / elle / on vendait* *nous vendions* *vous vendiez* *ils / elles vendaient*	*je vendrai* *tu vendras* *il / elle / on vendra* *nous vendrons* *vous vendrez* *ils / elles vendront*
Reflexive verbs				
se laver to have a wash	*je me lave* *tu te laves* *il se lave* *elle se lave* *on se lave* *nous nous lavons* *vous vous lavez* *ils se lavent* *elles se lavent*	*je me suis lavé(e)* *tu t'es lavé(e)* *il s'est lavé* *elle s'est lavée* *on s'est lavé(e)(s)* *nous nous sommes lavé(e)s* *vous vous êtes lavé(e)(s)* *ils se sont lavés* *elles se sont lavées*	*je me lavais* *tu te lavais* *il se lavait* *elle se lavait* *on se lavait* *nous nous lavions* *vous vous laviez* *ils se lavaient* *elles se lavaient*	*je me laverai* *tu te laveras* *il se lavera* *elle se lavera* *on se lavera* *nous nous laverons* *vous vous laverez* *ils se laveront* *elles se laveront*

infinitive	present	perfect	imperfect	future
aller to go	je vais tu vas il va elle va on va nous allons vous allez ils vont elles vont	je suis allé(e) tu es allé(e) il est allé elle est allée on est allé(e)(s) nous sommes allé(e)s vous êtes allé(e)(s) ils sont allés elles sont allées	j'allais tu allais il allait elle allait on allait nous allions vous alliez ils allaient elles allaient	j'irai tu iras il ira elle ira on ira nous irons vous irez ils iront elles iront
avoir to have	j'ai tu as il / elle / on a nous avons vous avez ils / elles ont	j'ai eu tu as eu il / elle / on a eu nous avons eu vous avez eu ils / elles ont eu	j'avais tu avais il / elle / on avait nous avions vous aviez ils / elles avaient	j'aurai tu auras il / elle / on aura nous aurons vous aurez ils / elles auront
boire to drink	je bois tu bois il / elle / on boit nous buvons vous buvez ils / elles boivent	j'ai bu tu as bu il / elle / on a bu nous avons bu vous avez bu ils / elles ont bu	je buvais tu buvais il / elle / on buvait nous buvions vous buviez ils / elles buvaient	je boirai tu boiras il / elle / on boira nous boirons vous boirez ils / elles boiront
connaître to know	je connais tu connais il / elle / on connaît nous connaissons vous connaissez ils / elles connaissent	j'ai connu tu as connu il / elle / on a connu nous avons connu vous avez connu ils / elles ont connu	je connaissais tu connaissais il / elle / on connaissait nous connaissions vous connaissiez ils / elles connaissaient	je connaîtrai tu connaîtras il / elle / on connaîtra nous connaîtrons vous connaîtrez ils / elles connaîtront
croire to believe	je crois tu crois il / elle / on croit nous croyons vous croyez ils / elles croient	j'ai cru tu as cru il / elle / on a cru nous avons cru vous avez cru ils / elles ont cru	je croyais tu croyais il / elle / on croyait nous croyions vous croyiez ils / elles croyaient	je croirai tu croiras il / elle / on croira nous croirons vous croirez ils / elles croiront
devoir to have to	je dois tu dois il / elle / on doit nous devons vous devez ils / elles doivent	j'ai dû tu as dû il / elle / on a dû nous avons dû vous avez dû ils / elles ont dû	je devais tu devais il / elle / on devait nous devions vous deviez ils / elles devaient	je devrai tu devras il / elle / on devra nous devrons vous devrez ils / elles devront

infinitive	present	perfect	imperfect	future
dire to say	je dis tu dis il / elle / on dit nous disons vous dites ils / elles disent	j'ai dit tu as dit il / elle / on a dit nous avons dit vous avez dit ils / elles ont dit	je disais tu disais il / elle / on disait nous disions vous disiez ils / elles disaient	je dirai tu diras il / elle / on dira nous dirons vous direz ils / elles diront
dormir to sleep	je dors tu dors il / elle / on dort nous dormons vous dormez ils / elles dorment	j'ai dormi tu as dormi il / elle / on a dormi nous avons dormi vous avez dormi ils / elles ont dormi	je dormais tu dormais il / elle / on dormait nous dormions vous dormiez ils / elles dormaient	je dormirai tu dormiras il / elle / on dormira nous dormirons vous dormirez ils / elles dormiront
écrire to write	j'écris tu écris il / elle / on écrit nous écrivons vous écrivez ils / elles écrivent	j'ai écrit tu as écrit il / elle / on a écrit nous avons écrit vous avez écrit ils / elles ont écrit	j'écrivais tu écrivais il / elle / on écrivait nous écrivions vous écriviez ils / elles écrivaient	j'écrirai tu écriras il / elle / on écrira nous écrirons vous écrirez ils / elles écriront
être to be	je suis tu es il / elle / on est nous sommes vous êtes ils / elles sont	j'ai été tu as été il / elle / on a été nous avons été vous avez été ils / elles ont été	j'étais tu étais il / elle / on était nous étions vous étiez ils / elles étaient	je serai tu seras il / elle / on sera nous serons vous serez ils / elles seront
faire to do / to make	je fais tu fais il / elle / on fait nous faisons vous faites ils / elles font	j'ai fait tu as fait il / elle / on a fait nous avons fait vous avez fait ils / elles ont fait	je faisais tu faisais il / elle / on faisait nous faisions vous faisiez ils / elles faisaient	je ferai tu feras il / elle / on fera nous ferons vous ferez ils / elles feront
lire to read	je lis tu lis il / elle / on lit nous lisons vous lisez ils / elles lisent	j'ai lu tu as lu il / elle / on a lu nous avons lu vous avez lu ils / elles ont lu	je lisais tu lisais il / elle / on lisait nous lisions vous lisiez ils / elles lisaient	je lirai tu liras il / elle / on lira nous lirons vous lirez ils / elles liront

infinitive	present	perfect	imperfect	future
mettre to put	je mets tu mets il / elle / on met nous mettons vous mettez ils / elles mettent	j'ai mis tu as mis il / elle / on a mis nous avons mis vous avez mis ils / elles ont mis	je mettais tu mettais il / elle / on mettait nous mettions vous mettiez ils / elles mettaient	je mettrai tu mettras il / elle / on mettra nous mettrons vous mettrez ils / elles mettront
partir to leave	je pars tu pars il part elle part on part nous partons vous partez ils partent elles partent	je suis parti(e) tu es parti(e) il est parti elle est partie on est parti(e)(s) nous sommes parti(e)s vous êtes parti(e)(s) ils sont partis elles sont parties	je partais tu partais il partait elle partait on partait nous partions vous partiez ils partaient elles partaient	je partirai tu partiras il partira elle partira on partira nous partirons vous partirez ils partiront elles partiront
pouvoir to be able to	je peux tu peux il / elle / on peut nous pouvons vous pouvez ils / elles peuvent	j'ai pu tu as pu il / elle / on a pu nous avons pu vous avez pu ils / elles ont pu	je pouvais tu pouvais il / elle / on pouvait nous pouvions vous pouviez ils / elles pouvaient	je pourrai tu pourras il / elle / on pourra nous pourrons vous pourrez ils / elles pourront
prendre to take	je prends tu prends il / elle / on prend nous prenons vous prenez ils / elles prennent	j'ai pris tu as pris il / elle / on a pris nous avons pris vous avez pris ils / elles ont pris	je prenais tu prenais il / elle / on prenait nous prenions vous preniez ils / elles prenaient	je prendrai tu prendras il / elle / on prendra nous prendrons vous prendrez ils / elles prendront
recevoir to receive	je reçois tu reçois il / elle / on reçoit nous recevons vous recevez ils / elles reçoivent	j'ai reçu tu as reçu il / elle / on a reçu nous avons reçu vous avez reçu ils / elles ont reçu	je recevais tu recevais il / elle / on recevait nous recevions vous receviez ils / elles recevaient	je recevrai tu recevras il / elle / on recevra nous recevrons vous recevrez ils / elles recevront
savoir to know	je sais tu sais il / elle / on sait nous savons vous savez ils / elles savent	j'ai su tu as su il / elle / on a su nous avons su vous avez su ils / elles ont su	je savais tu savais il / elle / on savait nous savions vous saviez ils / elles savaient	je saurai tu sauras il / elle / on saura nous saurons vous saurez ils / elles sauront

infinitive	present	perfect	imperfect	future
sortir to go out	je sors tu sors il sort elle sort on sort nous sortons vous sortez ils sortent elles sortent	je suis sorti(e) tu es sorti(e) il est sorti elle est sortie on est sorti(e)(s) nous sommes sorti(e)s vous êtes sorti(e)(s) ils sont sortis elles sont sorties	je sortais tu sortais il sortait elle sortait on sortait nous sortions vous sortiez ils sortaient elles sortaient	je sortirai tu sortiras il sortira elle sortira on sortira nous sortirons vous sortirez ils sortiront elles sortiront
venir to come	je viens tu viens il vient elle vient on vient nous venons vous venez ils viennent elles viennent	je suis venu(e) tu es venu(e) il est venu elle est venue on est venu(e)(s) nous sommes venu(e)s vous êtes venu(e)(s) ils sont venus elles sont venues	je venais tu venais il venait elle venait on venait nous venions vous veniez ils venaient elles venaient	je viendrai tu viendras il viendra elle viendra on viendra nous viendrons vous viendrez ils viendront elles viendront
vivre to live	je vis tu vis il / elle / on vit nous vivons vous vivez ils / elles vivent	j'ai vécu tu as vécu il / elle / on a vécu nous avons vécu vous avez vécu ils / elles ont vécu	je vivais tu vivais il / elle / on vivait nous vivions vous viviez ils / elles vivaient	je vivrai tu vivras il / elle / on vivra nous vivrons vous vivrez ils / elles vivront
voir to see	je vois tu vois il / elle / on voit nous voyons vous voyez ils / elles voient	j'ai vu tu as vu il / elle / on a vu nous avons vu vous avez vu ils / elles ont vu	je voyais tu voyais il / elle / on voyait nous voyions vous voyiez ils / elles voyaient	je verrai tu verras il / elle / on verra nous verrons vous verrez ils / elles verront
vouloir to want	je veux tu veux il / elle / on veut nous voulons vous voulez ils / elles veulent	j'ai voulu tu as voulu il / elle / on a voulu nous avons voulu vous avez voulu ils / elles ont voulu	je voulais tu voulais il / elle / on voulait nous voulions vous vouliez ils / elles voulaient	je voudrai tu voudras il / elle / on voudra nous voudrons vous voudrez ils / elles voudront

Glossaire

A

à chaque fois   each time
à côté de   next to
à mon avis   in my opinion
à une époque   at one time
aboyer   to bark
l'abricot (m)   apricot
accompagner   to accompany
acheter   to buy
l'activité (f) physique   physical activity
les actualités (f)   the news
actuel(le)   present
admis   admitted
l'ado (m / f)   adolescent / young person
l'agneau (m)   lamb
agresser   to attack / to assault
l'agriculteur / agricultrice   farmer
aider   to help
ailleurs   elsewhere
aîné(e)   older
l'aire (f) de repos   stopping area (off the motorway, with basic facilities)
l'aire (f) de jeux   playground
l'alcool (m)   alcohol
alcoolisé(e)   alcoholic (drinks)
l'alcoolisme (m)   alcoholism
l'alimentation (f)   diet
aller   to go
aller à la pêche   to go fishing
aller chercher   to fetch
allergique   allergic
alors   so
l'alpinisme (m)   mountaineering
l'alto (m)   viola
améliorer   to improve
l'ampoule (f)   bulb
s'amuser   to enjoy yourself / to have fun
ancien(ne)   former
l'anglais (m)   English
animé(e)   lively
l'année (f) sabbatique   gap year
l'anniversaire (m)   birthday
l'annonce (f)   advert

annuler   to cancel
l'anorexie (f)   anorexia
août   August
l'appareil (m)   camera / machine
l'appareil numérique (m)   digital camera
l'appartement (m)   apartment / flat
apprécier   to appreciate
apprendre (appris)   to learn
l'apprentissage (m)   apprenticeship
après   after (that)
l'arbre (m)   tree
l'argent (m)   money
l'argent (m) de poche   pocket money
l'armoire (f)   wardrobe
l'arrêt (m) (d'autobus)   bus stop
arrêter   to stop
l'arrondissement (m)   administrative district of Paris
arroser   to water
l'aspirateur (m)   vacuum cleaner
assez   quite
assis(e)   sitting down / seated
assister à   to be present at / to take part in
l'association (f) caritative   charity / charitable organisation
l'athlétisme (m)   athletics
l'Atlantique (m)   the Atlantic
attaquer   to attack
attendre (attendu)   to wait
atterrir (atterri)   to land
attirer   to attract
au secours!   help!
l'auberge (f) de jeunesse   youth hostel
augmenter   to increase
autant que possible   as much as possible
l'automne (m)   autumn
l'automobiliste (m)   car driver
l'autoroute (f)   motorway
l'avenir (m)   the future
l'averse (f)   (rain) shower

avertir   to warn
en avion   by aeroplane
l'avis (m)   opinion
l'avocat / avocate   lawyer
avoir   to have
avoir … ans   to be … years old
avoir besoin de   to need
avoir chaud   to be hot
avoir du mal à   to have difficulty (doing something)
avoir envie de   to want to / to feel like
avoir faim   to be hungry
avoir froid   to be cold
avoir l'intention de   to intend
avoir l'occasion de   to have the chance to
avoir mal à la tête   to have a headache
avoir mal au cœur   to feel sick
avoir peur   to be afraid
avoir raison   to be right
avoir soif   to be thirsty
avoir tort   to be wrong
avril   April

B

le bac   an exam equivalent to A-levels
les bagages (m)   luggage
la bague   ring
se baigner   to bathe / to swim
baisser   to lower
la bande dessinée   comic book / cartoon strip
la banlieue   suburb
barbant(e)   boring
bas(se)   low
le basket   basketball
les baskets (f)   trainers
la bataille   battle
le bateau   ship / boat
en bateau   by boat
la batterie   drums
bavarder   to chat
le bazar   chaos
le beau-père   stepfather (also means father-in-law)

la Belgique Belgium
beaucoup (de) a lot (of)
la belle-mère stepmother (also means mother-in-law)
le / la bénévole volunteer
la bêtise something stupid
bien équipé(e) well equipped / with good facilities
bien payé(e) well paid
bien s'amuser to have a good time
bienvenue welcome
les bijoux (m) jewellery
la biologie biology
bio / biologique organic
la biscotte biscuit (like toast)
blanc(he) white
bleu(e) blue
le bloggeur blogger
le bœuf beef
boire (bu) to drink
la boisson drink
la boîte box / tin
la boîte aux lettres électronique (email) inbox
la boîte de nuit night club
bon anniversaire! happy birthday!
une bonne ambiance a good atmosphere
le bonnet hat
à bord on board
le bord de la mer seaside
la botte boot
la bouche mouth
le boucher / la bouchère butcher
la boucherie butcher's
bouger to move
le boulanger / la boulangère baker
la boulangerie (f) baker's (bread)
boulimique bulimic
le boulot work (informal)
la boum party
la bouteille bottle
la boutique shop
le bras arm
la Bretagne Brittany
briller to shine
bronzer to sunbathe / to get a tan

se brosser les dents to brush one's teeth
le brouillard fog
la brousse bush / bushes
le bruit noise
brûler to burn
bruyant(e) noisy
le bureau office / desk
en bus by bus
le but goal

C
la cabane shed / hut
le cabinet vétérinaire vet's
cacher to hide
le cadeau present
le cahier notebook
la caisse cash register / till
le caissier / la caissière cashier
le calcul (m) sums / arithmetic
calme quiet / placid
le camion lorry
la campagne countryside
le camping campsite
le canapé sofa
le candidat candidate
la canne à sucre sugar cane
le canoë-kayak canoeing
la cantine dining hall
la capuche hood
car because / as
en car by coach
le car de ramassage school bus
caresser to stroke
le carrefour crossroads
le carton cardboard
le casque helmet
casse-pieds infuriating / a pain
la cathédrale cathedral
la cave cellar
le CDI (centre de documentation et d'information) library
la ceinture belt
célèbre famous
célibataire single
le centre centre
le centre commercial shopping centre
le centre culturel cultural centre

le centre de recyclage recycling centre
le centre sportif sports centre
le centre-ville town centre
les céréales (f) cereal
le cerveau brain
la chaîne channel (TV)
la chaleur warmth, heat
la chambre bedroom
la chambre d'hôte bed & breakfast
le chameau camel
le champ field
le champignon mushroom
le changement climatique climate change
la chanson song
chanter to sing
le chanteur / la chanteuse singer
le chapeau hat
chaque each
la charcuterie pork butcher's / delicatessen
le chat cat
chaud hot
chauffer to heat
les chaussettes (f) socks
les chaussures (f) shoes
le chef du personnel personnel manager
la chemise shirt
le chemisier blouse
cher(-ère) dear / expensive
chercher to look for
les cheveux (m) hair
chic smart
le chien dog
la chimie chemistry
chimique chemical
chinois(e) Chinese
le choix choice
le chômage unemployment
choquant(e) shocking
chrétien(ne) Christian
le cidre cider
le ciel sky
le cimetière cemetery
le cinéma cinema
la circulation traffic
la cité housing estate

le citron lemon

le citron vert lime

le clavier keyboard

le / la client(e) customer

le climat climate

la climatisation air conditioning

le cœur heart

collecter (de l'argent) to collect / raise (money)

collecter des fonds to collect funds

le / la collègue colleague

combattre to combat / to fight

combien (de) how much / how many

la comédie comedy

comme d'habitude as usual

comment how

le / la commerçant(e) shopkeeper

la commode chest of drawers

compréhensif(-ve) tolerant / understanding

le comprimé tablet

compris(e) included

le / la comptable accountant

le compte bancaire bank account

compter to count

le concombre cucumber

le concubinage living together (without being married)

conduire (conduit) to drive

la confiance confidence

la confiance en soi self-confidence

se confier à to confide in

la confiserie sweet shop

le congélateur the freezer

la connaissance knowledge / consciousness

consacrer to devote (time)

le conseil council / advice

conseiller to advise

la console de jeu games console

la consommation consumption

consommer to consume

construire (construit) to build

contaminé(e) contaminated

le contrôle test

le corps body

la correspondance change (on train journey)

la Corse Corsica

la côte coast / rib

la côtelette chop / cutlet

la Côte d'Ivoire the Ivory Coast

le coton cotton

en coton (made of) cotton

se coucher to go to bed

la couleur vive bright colour

le coupable culprit

la cour de récréation playground

le cours lesson

le coût cost

coûter to cost

la couture high fashion

le couturier fashion designer

couvert overcast

le crayon pencil

créole creole

la crêpe pancake

la crevette prawn

la crise cardiaque heart attack

la croisière cruise (holiday)

en cuir (made of) leather

la cuisine kitchen / cooking / cuisine (national)

le cuisinier / la cuisinière cook / chef

cultiver to grow

D

dans in

le danseur / la danseuse dancer

le déboisement deforestation

au début at the beginning

décembre December

la décharge publique rubbish dump

les déchets (m) rubbish / waste

décider to decide

décoller to take off (plane)

décontracté(e) relaxed

découvrir (découvert) to discover

défavorisé(e) disadvantaged

le défilé (de mode) fashion show

dégoûtant(e) disgusting

le degré degree

dehors outside

le déjeuner lunch

délicieux(-ieuse) delicious

le deltaplane hang-gliding

déménager to move house

et demi(e) half past

le demi-frère half brother

le / la demi-pensionnaire day boarder (someone who has lunch at school)

démodé(e) out of date

les dents (f) teeth

dépendant(e) addicted

dépenser to spend (money)

se déplacer to get around

déprimé(e) depressed

derrière behind

désagréable unpleasant

désespéré(e) desperate

le dessin art

dessiner to draw

le dessin animé cartoon (film)

se détendre (détendu) to relax / to calm down

la détente relaxation / chilling out

détruire (détruit) to destroy

la dette debt

deux fois par mois twice a month

la deuxième rue the second street

devant in front of

devenir to become

le déversement dumping

les devoirs (m) homework

le dictionnaire (bilingue) (bilingual) dictionary

difficile (à croire) difficult (to believe)

dimanche Sunday

le dîner dinner

le directeur / la directrice headteacher

diriger to direct / to manage

discipliné(e) disciplined / punished

disparaître (disparu) to disappear

se disputer to argue

divorcé(e) divorced

les données (f) personnelles personal details

donner sur to look out over

dormir   to sleep
le dortoir   dormitory
le dos   back
doucement   gently
se doucher   to have a shower
doué(e)   gifted / clever
la douleur   pain
doux / douce   mild / soft / gentle
se droguer   to take drugs
les drogues (f) douces   soft drugs
les drogues (f) dures   hard drugs
le droit   law
à droite   on / to the right
drôle   funny
dur(e)   hard
durer   to last

E

l'eau (f)   water
l'éboueur (m)   refuse collector
échapper   to escape
les échecs (m)   chess
échouer à   to fail
l'éclair (m)   lightning
l'éclaircie (f)   sunny spell
écologique   ecological, green
l'écran (m) tactile   touch screen
l'effet (m) de serre   the greenhouse effect
l'égalité (f)   equality
l'église (f)   church
l'électricien(ne) (m / f)   electrician
l'élève (m / f)   pupil
l'emballage (m)   packaging
embaucher   to recruit
l'embouteillage (m)   traffic jam
émettre (émis)   to emit
l'émission (f) de télévision   TV programme
empêcher   to prevent / to get in the way of / to stop
l'emplacement (m)   place / site
l'emploi (m)   emloyment
l'employé(e) (m / f)   employee
emporter   to take (with you)
emprunter   to borrow
en avoir marre de   to be fed up of
en bonne forme   in good shape
en ce moment   at the moment
en ligne   online

en version originale   in the original language (films)
l'endroit (m)   place
l'ennemi (m)   enemy
l'ennui (m)   worry / problem / boredom
s'ennuyer   to get bored / to be bored
l'enquête (f)   enquiry / investigation
enregistrer   to record
enrichissant(e)   rewarding
l'enseignement (m)   teaching / education
enseigner   to teach
ensemble   together
ensoleillé(e)   sunny
ensuite   then
s'entendre (avec quelqu'un) (entendu)   to get on (with someone)
entouré(e)   surrounded
s'entraîner   to train
l'entraîneur (m)   trainer
entre   between
entre … et …   between … and …
l'entreprise (f)   business / firm
l'entreprise (f) de logiciels   software business
l'entretien (m)   interview
environ   about
l'environnement (m)   the environment
envoyer   to send
épicé(e)   spicy
l'épicerie (f)   grocery shop
l'épouse (f)   wife (spouse)
épouser   to marry (someone)
l'époux (m)   husband (spouse)
l'EPS (f)   PE
épuiser   to exhaust
l'équilibre (m)   balance
équilibré(e)   balanced
l'équipe (f)   team
l'équitation (f)   horse riding
l'escalade (f)   rock climbing
l'espace (m) vert   park
l'espagnol (m)   Spanish
l'espoir (m)   hope
l'essence (f)   petrol
l'est (m)   east

et   and
l'étage (m)   floor
l'étagère (f)   shelf
l'été (m)   summer
éteindre (éteint)   to switch off / to turn off
l'étranger (m) / l'étrangère (f)   stranger / foreigner
à l'étranger (m)   abroad
étranger(-ère)   foreign
être accro   to have a habit (addiction)
être hors d'haleine   to be out of breath
être en train de   to be in the middle / process of
étroit(e)   tight / narrow
l'étude (f)   study
l'événement   event
éviter   to avoid
excessif(-ve)   excessive
s'excuser   to apologise
l'explication (f)   explanation
expliquer   to explain
exprimer   to express
à l'extérieur   outside
extraverti(e)   extrovert, outgoing

F

fabriquer   to manufacture
se fâcher   to get cross
la faculté   university
faire (fait)   to do / to make
faire attention   to pay attention
faire beau   to be nice weather
faire de la planche à voile   to go windsurfing
faire de la voile   to go sailing
faire des économies (f)   to save up
faire des randonnées   to go hiking
faire des recherches   to do research
faire du cyclisme   to go cycling
faire du jardinage   to do the gardening
faire du lèche-vitrine   to go window shopping
faire la cuisine   to cook
faire la grasse matinée   to have a lie in

faire la lessive   to do the washing
faire la vaisselle   to do the washing up
faire le ménage   to do the housework
faire les achats   to do the shopping
faire les courses   to do the shopping
faire les magasins   to go shopping
faire mauvais   to be bad weather
faire partie de   to belong to
faire une cure   to take a course of treatment
il fait beau   the weather's nice
il fait chaud   it's hot
il fait froid   it's cold
il fait mauvais   the weather's bad
la famille nombreuse   large family
le / la fana   fan / enthusiast
fatigué(e)   tired
le fauteuil   armchair
le fauteuil roulant   wheelchair
la femme   woman / wife
la femme au foyer   housewife
la femme de ménage   cleaning lady
la fenêtre   window
la ferme   farm
la fête   party / celebration
la fête de l'Aïd el Kebir   Eid Ul Fitr festival
fêter   to celebrate
le feu   fire
feuilleter   to flick through
le feuilleton   soap (TV series)
les feux (m)   traffic lights
les feux (m) rouges   red lights (traffic lights)
février   February
les fiançailles (f)   engagement (to be married)
fidèle   loyal / faithful
fier / fière   proud
la fièvre   fever
le fils   son
la flûte   flute
le foie   liver
fondre   to melt
la fontaine   fountain

la forêt   forest
la forêt tropicale   rainforest
la formation professionnelle   professional training
se former   to train (for a job)
fort(e)   strong
le foulard   scarf
les frais (m)   expenses
le français   French
frapper   to hit
le froid   cold
le fromage   cheese
la frontière   border (between countries)
la fumée   smoke
fumer   to smoke
le fumeur   smoker

G

gâcher   to waste / to spoil
gagner   to win / to earn
garder   to look after / to keep
garder la forme   to keep in shape
la gare   railway station
la gare routière   coach station / bus station
à gauche   on / to the left
les gaz (m) d'échappement   exhaust fumes
geler   to freeze
gênant(e)   inconvenient / annoying
gêné(e)   embarrassed
gêner   to be a nuisance
en général   generally
le genou   knee
le genre   type
la géographie   geography
le gigot d'agneau   leg of lamb
le gilet   cardigan
le gîte   self-catering accommodation / holiday cottage
la glace   ice
la gomme   eraser
la gorge   throat
le goût   taste
goûter   to taste
le grain de café   coffee bean
la graisse   fat
grand(e)   large
la grand-mère   grandmother

le grand-père   grandfather
la grasse matinée   lie-in
gratuit(e)   free (no cost)
gratuitement   free
le grenier   attic
la grippe   flu
gris(e)   grey
gros(se)   fat
la guerre   war
le guichet   ticket office
la guitare   guitar
le gymnase   gym

H

l'habillement (m)   clothes
s'habiller   to get dressed
l'habitant(e) (m / f)   inhabitant
habiter   to live
d'habitude   usually
l'habitude (f)   habit
la haie   hedge
les halles (f)   food hall
les haricots (m) verts   green beans
l'herbe (f)   grass
à l'heure   on time
le héros (m)   hero
heures   o'clock / hours
l'heure (f) d'affluence   rush hour
l'heure (f) d'étude   study period
historique   historical
l'hiver (m)   winter
le / la HLM   block of high-rise council flats
l'homme (m) au foyer   house husband
l'horaire (m)   timetable
l'hôtel (m) de ville   town hall
l'hôtesse (f) de l'air   air stewardess
humide   humid
humiliant(e)   humiliating

I

il y a   there is / there are / ago (time)
il y a des nuages   it's cloudy
il y a du brouillard   it's foggy
il y a du soleil   it's sunny
il y a du vent   it's windy
il y avait   there was / were

l'île (f) island

l'immeuble (m) building / block of flats

l'immigré(e) (m / f) immigrant

inciter à to stir up / to incite

l'incivilité (f) rude behaviour

des inconnus (m) strangers

l'infirmier (m) / infirmière (f) nurse

l'informatique (f) information technology / ICT

l'ingénieur (m) engineer

injuste unfair

l'inondation (f) flood

inondé(e) flooded

(s')inquiéter to worry

l'instruction (f) civique citizenship

l'instruction (f) religieuse RE

interdit(e) forbidden

l'interprète (m / f) interpreter

intitulé(e) entitled

introduire to introduce

islamique Islamic

isolé(e) isolated

ivre drunk

J

j'en ai marre! I'm fed up!

jaloux(-se) jealous / possessive

jamais never

la jambe leg

janvier January

le jardin garden

le jardin public park / public garden

le jardin zoologique zoo

le jardinier / la jardinière (paysagiste) (landscape) gardener

jaune yellow

le jean jeans

jeter to throw (away)

le jeu (les jeux) game / game show

le jeu vidéo computer game

jeudi Thursday

les jeunes délinquants (m) juvenile delinquants

joli(e) pretty

jouer to play

jouer à la pétanque to play (French) bowls

le jour de l'an New Year's Day

le jour férié public holiday

juif(-ve) Jewish

juillet July

juin June

la jupe skirt

le jus juice

L

le laboratoire laboratory

en laine woollen

le lait milk

la langue vivante modern language

large loose-fitting / broad

le lavabo washbasin

se laver to have a wash

le lecteur DVD DVD player

le lecteur mp3 mp3 player

léger(-ère) light

le légume vegetable

se lever to get up

la librairie bookshop

la licence degree

le / la licencié(e) university graduate

lier to link

le lieu place

le lieu de travail workplace

la ligne line / route

lire (lu) to read

le lit bed

les lits (m) superposés bunk beds

le livre book

le logement housing / accommodation

loger to live / to stay

logique logical

la loi law

les loisirs (m) leisure activities

louer to rent / to hire

loyal(e) loyal / faithful

le loyer rent

la lumière light

lundi Monday

lutter to struggle

le lycée high school (for students aged 16–18)

M

mâcher to chew

le magasin shop

le maçon builder

mai May

maigre thin

le maillot de bain swimming costume

la main hand

la mairie town hall

mais but

la maison house

la maison de couture fashion house

le mal de mer seasickness

la maladie illness

malgré in spite of

la manche sleeve

manger équilibré to eat a balanced diet

la manifestation (public) demonstration

le mannequin fashion model

le manque lack

manquer to miss / to be lacking

le maquillage make-up

se maquiller to put make-up on

le marché market

marcher to work (of a machine)

mardi Tuesday

le mari husband

le mariage marriage / wedding

se marier to get married

le Maroc Morocco

marquer un but to score a goal

marron brown

mars March

les maths / mathématiques (f) maths

la matinée morning

de mauvaise humeur in a bad mood

de mauvaises notes (f) bad marks

le / la mécanicien(ne) mechanic

méchant(e) nasty / naughty

la médaille medal

la Méditerranée the Mediterranean

la méduse jellyfish

même same

mener to lead
la menthe mint
mentir (menti) to lie
la mer sea
mercredi Wednesday
la mère mother
le métier job / profession
le métro the underground (in Paris)
en métro on the underground
la météo weather forecast
mettre (mis) to put (on)
mettre à jour to update
se mettre en colère to get angry
mettre la table to set / lay the table
midi midday
mignon(ne) cute
le milieu rural rural environment
mince slim
minuit midnight
la mode fashion
moins le quart quarter to
mondial(e) global
le moniteur / la monitrice sports trainer / instructor
la monogamie monogamy
monoparental(e) single-parent
la montagne mountain(s)
montrer to show
se moquer de to make fun of
la moquette carpet
mort(e) dead
le moteur de recherche search engine
motiver to motivate
à moto by motorbike
mouillé(e) wet
le moyen de transport means of transport
multinational(e) multinational (company)
la municipalité local council
musclé(e) muscular
la musculation weight training
le / la musicien(ne) musician
le / la musulman(e) Muslim

N

nager to swim
naïf(-ve) naive, unsuspecting

la naissance birth
naître (né) to be born
la natation swimming
ne ... aucun not any / none
neiger to snow
nettoyer to clean
le nez nose
le niveau level
Noël (m) Christmas
noir(e) black
la noix nut
le nord north
normalement usually / normally
la nourriture food
nouveau (nouvelle) new
le Nouvel An New Year
les nouvelles (f) news
novembre November
le nuage cloud
nuageux cloudy

O

l'obésité (f) obesity
obligatoire compulsory
s'occuper de to be busy with / to look after
octobre October
l'œil (m) / les yeux eye / eyes
l'oeuf (m) egg
l'offre (f) d'emploi job advert / job offer
offrir (offert) to give (e.g. a present)
l'oignon (m) onion
l'ombre (f) shade
l'oncle (m) uncle
l'orage (m) thunderstorm
orageux(-euse) stormy
l'ordinateur (m) computer
l'ordinateur (m) portable laptop
les ordures (f) rubbish
l'oreille (f) ear
l'organisation caritative (f) charity / charitable organisation
ou or
où where
oublier to forget
l'ouest (m) west
l'ouvrier (m) / ouvrière (f) worker

P

le pantalon trousers
Pâques (f) Easter
le paquet packet
par by
par contre on the other hand
par terre on the ground
le parc à vélos bicycle park
le parc d'attractions theme park
parfois sometimes
le parking relais park-and-ride
partager to share
pas tellement not much
le passage à niveau level crossing
le passager / la passagère passenger
passer to spend (time)
se passer de to do without
passer l'aspirateur to do the vacuuming
passer un examen to take an exam
passif(-ve) passive
la pâte (à pain) (bread) dough
les pâtes (f) pasta
le patinage ice skating
la patinoire ice skating rink
la pâtisserie baker's (pastries, cakes)
le / la patron / patronne boss / manager
la pause-déjeuner lunch hour
pauvre poor
la pauvreté poverty
le pays étranger foreign country
le pays voisin neighbouring country
le paysage landscape / scenery
la pêche fishing
la peinture painting
la pelouse lawn
pendant during
pénible annoying / a nuisance
les percussions (f) percussion instruments
le père father
perfectionner to improve
permettre (permis) to allow
petit(e) small
le petit ami boyfriend

le petit déjeuner   breakfast
la petite amie   girlfriend
la petite annonce   small advert / classified advert
le pétrole   oil
un peu de   a bit of
peut-être   perhaps
la photocopieuse   photocopying machine
la physique   physics
la pièce   room
à pied   on foot
le pied   foot
la piscine   swimming pool
la piste cyclable   cycle path
pittoresque   picturesque
le placard   cupboard
la plage   beach
plaire (plu)   to please
le plaisir   pleasure / enjoyment
la planète   planet
le plat   dish
plein(e) de vie   lively
pleurer   to cry
pleuvoir (plu)   to rain
la pluie   rain
le plombier / la plombière   plumber
la plongée sous-marine   scuba diving
la plupart de   most of
pluvieux(-euse)   rainy
le point de vue   viewpoint
la poire   pear
le poisson rouge   goldfish
pollué(e)   polluted
la pompe   pump
la pom-pom girl   cheerleader
la porte   door
poser sa candidature   to apply
le poste   job / post
la poubelle   (dust)bin
le poumon   lung
le pourboire   tip
pourquoi   why
pourtant   however
pousser   to grow
pratique   practical
le premier / deuxième étage   first / second floor
la première rue   the first street

prendre (pris)   to take
prendre une douche   to have a shower
presque   almost
la pression   pressure
prêter   to lend
prévenir (prévenu)   to prevent / to inform / to warn
le printemps   spring
la prise électrique   electric socket
privé(e)   private
le prix   price
le problème   problem
produire (produit)   to produce
le produit de beauté   beauty product
des produits bio (m)   organic products
le / la professeur   teacher
le professeur principal   form tutor
le programmeur / la programmeuse   programmer
promener le chien   to walk the dog
promettre   to promise
la promotion   promotion / special offer
propre   clean
le / la propriétaire   owner
protéger   to protect
les provisions (f)   groceries
provoquer   to provoke
le pull à capuche   hoodie
punir (puni)   to punish

Q

le quai   platform
quand   when
quand même   all the same
et quart   quarter past
le quartier   area of a town
que   that / what
qu'est-ce que   what
qu'est-ce que c'est?   what is it?
quel(le)   which / what
quelquefois   sometimes
qui   who
quoi   what

R

le racisme   racism

raciste   racist
ramasser   to collect / to pick up
la randonnée   hike (on foot) / ride (bike or horseback)
ranger   to tidy / to put away
ranger sa chambre   to tidy one's bedroom
se rappeler   to remember
rarement   rarely
rater   to fail
recevoir (reçu)   to receive
recyclable   recyclable
le réchauffement de la planète   global warming
la récréation   break (in school day)
redécouvrir   to rediscover
le redoublement   repeating a school year
redoubler   to repeat a school year
la réduction   reduction
réduire (réduit)   to reduce
le régime   diet
la règle   rule / ruler
le règlement   rules
rejeter   to discharge / to pour
remarquer   to notice
rembourser   to pay back
remercier   to thank
remplacer   to replace
rencontrer   to meet
rendre (rendu)   to give back
renoncer   to give up
renouveler   to renew / to update
rénover   to renovate
les renseignements (m)   information
renvoyer   to sack
repasser un examen   to resit an exam
répondre   to reply
réservé(e)   reserved / quiet
résister à   to resist
résoudre   to solve
respirer   to breathe
rester   to stay
le retard   delay
retenir (retenu)   to keep
la retenue   detention
se réunir (réuni)   to meet up
la réunion   meeting

réussir (réussi) to pass (an exam) / to succeed

le rêve dream

se réveiller to wake up

le réveillon Christmas Eve / New Year's Eve party

réveillonner to celebrate on Christmas Eve or New Year's Eve

révéler to reveal, disclose

le rez-de-chaussée ground floor

le rhum rum

le rhume cold

rien à voir avec nothing to do with

rigolo(-te) fun / funny

rire to laugh

le risque risk

le riz rice

la robe dress

le robinet tap

le roman novel

le rond-point roundabout

rose pink

rôti(e) roast

rouge red

la route road

la rue street

S

le sable sand

le sac bag

sain(e) healthy

la Saint-Sylvestre the festival on 31st December

la Saint-Valentin Valentine's Day

saisonnier(-ière) seasonal

le salaire salary

sale dirty

salé(e) salty

la salle à manger dining room

la salle d'attente waiting room

la salle d'informatique ICT room

la salle de bains bathroom

la salle de séjour living room / sitting room

la salle des profs staff room

le salon living room / sitting room

samedi Saturday

sans domicile fixe homeless

sans plomb unleaded

le / la sans-abri homeless person

sauf except

le saumon salmon

sauver to save

les sciences (f) science

scolaire school / to do with school

le / la SDF (sans domicile fixe) homeless person

sec (sèche) dry

le sèche-cheveux hair-dryer

le / la secrétaire secretary

le séjour stay (in a place)

le sel salt

selon according to

le sens de l'humour sense of humour

le sens interdit no entry

se sentir (senti) to feel

septembre September

la série series

le serveur / la serveuse waiter / waitress

seul(e) alone

le short shorts

le sida AIDS

le siècle century

le sirop (cough) syrup

le site site (internet)

le skate skateboarding

la société company / business

la sœur sister

le soir (in) the evening

le soldat soldier

les soldes (m) the sales

le soleil sun

la solitude solitude / being on one's own

le sommeil sleep

sonner to ring (phone, bell)

le souci worry / problem

souffrir (souffert) to suffer

souhaiter to wish

souriant(e) cheerful / smiley

sous under

le sous-sol basement

les sous-titres (m) subtitles

le souvenir memory

souvent often

spacieux(-euse) spacious

le sparadrap plaster

le sport d'hiver winter sport

le stade stadium

la station balnéaire seaside resort

la station de métro underground station

la station de ski ski resort

la station de taxi taxi rank

la station thermale spa resort

stationner to park

stressant(e) stressful

le stylo pen

les sucreries (f) sweets / sweet things

le sud south

la Suisse Switzerland

suivant(e) following

sur on

le sweat sweatshirt

sympa nice / kind

T

le tabac tobacco

le tabagisme addiction to smoking

le tableau blanc interactif interactive whiteboard

la tablette tablet computer

la tâche task

la taille size

la taille zéro size zero

les talons (m) heels

tard late

tardif(-ve) late

le taux rate / level

le / la technicien(ne) technician

la technologie D and T

tel(le) such

la télé connectée smart TV

télécharger to download

le (téléphone) portable mobile (phone)

la température temperature

la tempête storm

le temps weather

de temps en temps from time to time

à temps partiel part-time

à temps plein full-time

tenir to hold

le terrain de camping campsite

la Terre   (the) Earth
le terroir   local area
la tête   head
le texto   text (message)
en TGV (train à grande vitesse)   by high-speed train
le thé à la menthe   mint tea
le théâtre   theatre
le Tiers-Monde   developing world
les toilettes (f)   toilet
la tombe   grave
le tombeau   grave
tomber amoureux(-euse)   to fall in love
le tonnerre   thunder
le / la touriste   tourist
tous les jours   every day
la Toussaint   All Saints Day
tout droit   straight on
tout le temps   all the time
en train   by train
le traitement de texte   word processing
le trajet   journey / trip
en tram   by tram
tranquille   quiet / calm
les transports (m) en commun   public transport
le travail   work
le travail bénévole   voluntary work
travailler   to work
travailleur(-euse)   hardworking
la traversée   crossing (e.g. the Channel)
tremper   to soak
très   very
le tricheur   cheat
triste   sad

la troisième   French equivalent of Year 10
trop   too
trop de monde   too many people
le trottoir   pavement
le trouble alimentaire   eating disorder
la trousse   pencil case
le tuba   snorkel

U

une bonne ambiance   a good atmosphere
une fois par semaine   once a week
l'usine (f)   factory
utiliser   to use

V

la vague   wave (water)
varié(e)   varied
la vedette   star / celebrity (male or female)
végétarien(ne)   vegetarian
la veille   eve / the day before
en veille   on stand-by
à vélo   by bike
le vendeur / la vendeuse   sales assistant
vendre (vendu)   to sell
vendredi   Friday
le vent   wind
le ventre   stomach
vérifier le montant   to check the balance (of an account)
le verre   glass
vers   towards
vert(e)   green
les vêtements (m)   clothes
le / la vétérinaire   vet

le veuf   widower
la veuve   widow
la viande   meat
la victime   victim
la victime éventuelle   potential victim
vider la poubelle   to empty the bin
la vie   life
vieux (vieille)   old
la ville   town / city
violet(-te)   purple
le violon   violin
la visite guidée   guided tour
vivre (vécu)   to live
vivre en concubinage   to live together (without being married)
la voie   path
la voile   sailing
voir   to see
voisin(e)   neighbouring
le / la voisin(e)   neighbour
en voiture   by car
le vol   flight
voler   to fly / to steal
le volet   shutter
vomir   to vomit
le vomissement   vomiting
le voyage   journey
le voyage scolaire   school trip
voyager   to travel
la vue   view

Z

la zone piétonne   pedestrian zone

Acknowledgements

Kathy Baxendale pp60, 70, 74 (1b), 78, 79, 103 (3a), 106; Mark Draisey pp13, 14, 16, 34 (1a), 46, 101, 117 (reporter), 130, 157, 159; Robin Edmonds pp34 (2G 1-3), 35 (4-6), 116, 123, 138; Tony Forbes pp19, 22, 23, 31, 35 (3a), 36, 54 (2a), 59 (3a A-F), 77, 98, 103 (2G); Dylan Gibson, p102 (A-F); Celia Hart pp11, 12, 15, 21, 27, 31, 35, 47, 55, 59 (4a), 71, 73, 75 (talking heads), 97, 99, 102, 103 (talking heads), 110 (1a), 117 (5), 135, 141, 149, 153, 155 (4); Abel Ippolito pp38, 40, 54 (1a, 2b), 58, 94, 107, 117 (3a A-C), 134, 146, 148, 155 (2 A-F); Andy Keylock pp64, 65, 87; Dave Russell p75 (map); Martin Sanders pp74 (1a), 110 (La météo), 122

The author and the publisher would also like to thank the following for permission to reproduce material:
p7, Design Pics Inc./Alamy; p9, Shutterstock; p10, A: BigStockPhoto.com, B: iStockphoto, C: Shutterstock, D: BigStockPhoto.com, mobile phone screen: iStockphoto; p14, topic banner: iStockphoto; p16 - 17, Shutterstock; p18, A: National Gallery of Art, Washington DC, USA, B: The Gallery Collection/Corbis; p20, A and B: iStockphoto, C: 123rf.com; p24, banner: iStockphoto, girl: BigStockPhoto.com; p25, beer and cigarette: Shutterstock, tablets: Image Source/Alamy; p30, topic banner: iStockphoto, girl: iStockphoto; p32, Pierre: iStockphoto, Amélie: BigStockphoto.com, Julien: Fotolia, Estelle: 123rf.com; p54, topic banner: Fotolia; p56, girl with popcorn: 123rf.com, girl on horseback: BigStockPhoto.com; p62, A: Fotolia, B and C: iStockphoto, D: Fotolia, A: Shutterstock, B: Fotolia, C: iStockphoto, D: Fotolia; p70, topic banner: iStockphoto, girl: iStockphoto, boy: Shutterstock; p72, A: Fotolia, B: BigStockPhoto.com, C: iStockphoto, D: Fotolia, E: iStockphoto; p76, boy with rucksack: Alan Dawson Photography/Alamy, girl on beach: Fotolia; p80, A: Stock Connection Blue/Alamy, B: Shutterstock, C: Chris Howes/Wild Place Photography/Alamy, D: Vespian/Alamy; p86, Shutterstock; p94, topic banner: Fotolia.com; p96, A: 123rf.com, B: iStockphoto, C: BigStockPhoto.com, D: 123rf.com; p100, A: Peter Phipp/Getty Images, B: Natureworld/Alamy, C: Bloomberg/Getty Images, D: Blickwinkel/Alamy; p104, Sally & Richard Greenhill/Alamy; p110, topic banner: iStockphoto; p112, Martin Jenkinson/Alamy; p113, whale and forest: 123rf.com; p114, A: Paul Thompson Images/Alamy, B: Becky Nixon/Alamy, C: Shutterstock, D: The Purple Door/Getty Images; p118, A: iStockphoto, B: Shutterstock, C: Fotolia; p122, boy on laptop: iStockphoto, Corsica harbour: Fotolia; p130, topic banner and boy on computer: iStockphoto; p132, BigStockphoto.com; p136, iStockphoto.com; p140, Photo Alto/Getty Images; p146, topic banner: Shutterstock; p156, iStockphoto, Fotolia, BigStockPhoto.com, iStockphoto; p158, Shutterstock; p162, Buena Vista Images/Getty Images; p163, Lonely Planet/Getty Images.